Historic Or

Treatise on decorativ
architectural ornar ...

James Ward

Alpha Editions

This edition published in 2020

ISBN : 9789354012358

Design and Setting By
Alpha Editions
email - alphaedis@gmail.com

HISTORIC ORNAMENT

Treatise on

DECORATIVE ART

AND

ARCHITECTURAL ORNAMENT

*TREATS OF PREHISTORIC ART; ANCIENT ART AND ARCHI-
TECTURE; EASTERN, EARLY CHRISTIAN, BYZANTINE,
SARACENIC, ROMANESQUE, GOTHIC, AND
RENAISSANCE ARCHITECTURE
AND ORNAMENT.*

BY

JAMES WARD

AUTHOR OF "THE PRINCIPLES OF ORNAMENT."

✳

With Four Hundred and Thirty-Six Illustrations

LONDON: CHAPMAN AND HALL, LIMITED

1909

PREFACE.

THE comprehensive nature of the subject of this work renders it impossible to deal with its various divisions and sub-divisions, except in a very condensed manner, within the limits of a handbook for students.

I have endeavoured to present to the reader, and to the student of ornamental and decorative art, some of the salient features which characterize the historic styles of ornament, and those that seem to me to show themselves as landmarks in the wide domain of Historic Ornament.

Realistic decoration was the earliest form of all art, as we find it in the etchings on the bones drawn by the pre-historic cave-dwellers ; but ornamental design or pattern drawing is a kind of invention which implies the orderly decoration of architectural forms and other objects, and is generally applied to such objects with the view of adding some enrichment that shall make them more pleasing to the sight.

The former belongs more to pictorial art, while the latter is purely decorative.

As the construction of ornament, in a great measure, ought to be based on the laws that govern the design of good architecture--this we gather from the design of the best ornament of the historic styles—it has been thought necessary to give a slight sketch of each of the principal orders and styles of architecture, placing them, as far as possible, in a chronological sequence in regard to the periods of their existence, and countries in which they flourished.

In some cases I have also thought it desirable to give a brief account of the religion of those nations that have created distinct styles of architecture and ornament; for in many cases, such as in the art of the ancient world and of the Middle Ages, we find that the art of a country was so bound up with the religion of its people, that to understand the former it is indispensable to have some knowledge of their religious ceremonies and beliefs.

I have here to express my indebtedness to various writers on ornamental art whom I have named in the pages of these volumes for some useful points of information, and to them and the publishers of this work for the use of the greater portion of the blocks of illustrations.

I have also to thank Mr. T. M. Lindsay for the use of his drawing of the monument of Lysikrates, and the Science and Art Department for permission to use many of the illustrations of their excellent handbooks on decorative art.

In a succeeding volume to this work, the various divisions of the Industrial Arts and Crafts will be treated in their historical developments of decoration and workmanship.

In conclusion, I trust that the contents of these pages will be helpful to students in art schools, and to others who may desire to have an introduction to the fascinating study of Historic Ornament.

J. WARD.

CONTENTS.

—

LIST OF ILLUSTRATIONS.

HISTORIC ORNAMENT.

INTRODUCTORY CHAPTER.

It can hardly be doubted that, for the education of the
student in ornamental design, or in architecture, a study
of the history of ornament and a knowledge of the principal historic styles of architecture is indispensable.

Historic styles of ornament remain for us, vast accu-
mulations of tried experiments, for the most part in the
character of conventional renderings of natural forms;
for however remote from nature some of these may be,
they can, as a general rule, be traced back without much
difficulty to their natural origin, where in most cases they
were used symbolically. Even the most arbitrary forms—
for instance, those found in Saracenic ornament—were only
developments from natural forms, and the innocent Greek
key pattern, that has earned the reputation of being the
ornament most unlike anything in nature, is supposed by
some to be but a rectilineal development of the rippling
waves; and, on the other hand, there is the hypothesis
that it is developed from the *fylfot*, a sacred sign that is
supposed to symbolize the rotary motion of the planets.

There is no ornament more common or so universal in
prehistoric, savage, Egyptian, Assyrian and Mediæval
decoration than the ubiquitous zigzag, or chevron, and
though extremely simple in itself, at least two-thirds of all
conventional ornament is based or constructed on its lines:
yet this simple ornament has been used as a symbol of
totally opposite and different things, by nearly all the

various tribes and nations that have used it in decoration.
With the Egyptians and Assyrians it has been a symbol
of water, with some savage tribes it denotes lightning,
with others it does duty for a serpent, with some others it
represents a series of bats, birds, and butterflies ; as with
the original tribes of Brazil, with the magic-loving Semang
tribes of East Malacca, it means a frog, and in some instances the branches of trees ; and lastly, with the natives
of the Hervey Islands, it symbolizes the human figure when
placed in duplicate parallel rows.

(For a fuller description, and illustrations of this and cog-
nate savage ornament, the reader is referred to Haddon's
"Evolution in Art," 1895.) We can hardly think of an
ornament more simple or more common than the zigzag,
and yet how varied in different countries are the sources
from which it springs.

This may be taken as a warning that it is not safe to
accept the same forms as always having the same origin,
when we find them in the art of different countries.

Apart from the symbolic origin of ornamental forms,
students of to-day may learn, from examples of the past,
how far they can go, in the converting of natural forms to
conventional ornament, without absolutely adapting such
examples to their present needs. The past styles in ornament have, in one sense, died out with the nations that
created them, and can never be satisfactorily revived,
although, as we have often seen, a new style may be built
on their foundations. The tendency of to-day is to under-
value the teachings of historic art, and, as a result, we see
much work in which both fitness and beauty are conspicuous by their absence.

In any notice of the historical development of ornamental art, the concurrent styles of architecture should, in
their general features at least, be illustrated, for it is not
always possible to divorce ornament from architecture,
and it is hardly possible to design or construct good ornament otherwise than according to the laws that govern

good architecture. Of course, we must admit that some very beautiful ornament, or rather decoration, has been designed otherwise than on architectural lines, but this kind of decoration has its beauty of technique and execution to recommend it, rather than its constructive qualities. Chinese and Japanese ornament will occur to the reader as examples of this kind of work, but the best ornament the world has ever seen has been constructed and is based on the laws that govern good architecture.

Some of these laws, such as stability, repose, variety, and proportion, are derived from nature. As all architectural styles, however, possess them more or less in common, we must look elsewhere for the sources from which the peculiar characteristics that distinguish the styles are developed and derived. The causes and forces are so subtle and the developments so gradual, that it is almost impossible to arrive at a satisfactory explanation, as religions, inventive faculty, and symbolism play an important *rôle* in style development. It is rather to the inventive faculties of man, than to hints supplied by nature, that we must look for the origin and development of what is called style in architecture or ornament. In every case this is arrived at by a slow process, and by the extensive and persistent use of distinguishing features selected according to the needs and requirements of the time, to satisfy the prevailing tastes. "Style" is then the something that man has invented or created; it may be called the soul of architecture, without which, a building, however pretentious, ceases to exist as an artistic conception.

Apart from the greatest or more striking features in the various divisions of historic architecture, such as the horizontal beam in Greek, the round arch in Roman and Romanesque, the pointed arch in Gothic and Mohammadan buildings, there are the mouldings that are so important in determining the period—they alone of themselves will often determine the style or date of a building

—and these features, above all others, are the least derived from nature. On the other hand, the decoration of mouldings, though suggested by their contours, is generally derived from natural forms.

The "best period" in the life of historic styles and its duration corresponds with that of the highest culture and religious thought of the people, at their settled and most flourishing epochs. When a change or revolution in the order of things sets in, we find generally the style of architecture changing also to adapt itself to the new laws and new thought. This illustrates, to a certain degree, the reason why the so-called Victorian Gothic has not developed to any great extent in England, although some of our best architects sought to revive the earlier Gothic some years ago.

The Mediæval mysticism, love for symbolism, and reverence are wanting in the mass of the people of this century, which characterized the people of Europe in the palmy days of Gothic architecture.

It has always been found that whatever the people ask for the artist is generally able to give, although he may not be always willing; but he must satisfy the popular demand if he is to live by his work, otherwise he must make way for others who are willing to produce work that will reflect the taste of the period.

We are handicapped in the development of anything new in the way of an architectural style by traditions of the past. Our knowledge of what has been done in the past, paradoxical as it may appear, has proved itself a great stumbling-block to the progress of new ideas. This partly accounts for the slowness of style-development in the present century. If fashion does not step in and disturb the march of events in the immediate future, we may hope for something distinct, if not exactly new, as an architectural style, in which a mixture of Gothic and Renaissance forms will be seen, the latter perhaps predominating. It may happen that later generations will look back and be able to discern something distinct in the way of style in buildings erected in the last quarter of this century, in the midst of much that is somewhat chaotic and confused.

In a book like this, which is intended chiefly as an introduction to the study of historic ornament, one cannot pretend to criticise the various styles of ornament, either from an artistic or scientific standpoint. It will be enough to attempt to point out the principal beauties or characteristics, to trace the history and overlapping of one style with another, and to trace, where possible, some units of ornamental forms to their symbolic ancestry. It is absurd to criticise the ornament of any period or country dogmatically, for we must remember, that although certain forms of art may not conform to the critics' idiosyncrasy, they may be quite orthodox and good art when judged by the artistic laws of their own country. The difference in race, religion, manners, and customs, must always be taken into account, before we begin to criticise the art of a nation to which we do not belong.

As already remarked, we are hampered by tradition in our attempts to produce originality in ornament, but there is very little tradition for the absolute copying of a particular style, except from nations who have had no decided art of their own. As far as we know of the history and practice in the whole field of ornamental design, from its remote beginnings it has been mostly all along a series of systems of developments, sometimes for good and sometimes for the opposite, but rarely, if ever, a system of copying. Some notable exceptions to this may be noticed, as when, for the expediencies known as "tricks of the trade," the Phœnicians made ivory carvings in exact imitation of Egyptian designs, and sold them to the Assyrians; and likewise bronze bowls and platters in both Assyrian and Egyptian imitations, and traded with them throughout the Ægean and Mediterranean, or when the Siculo-Arabian silks were made at Palermo in imitation

of Saracen designs, with mock-Saracenic inscriptions, and
sold for the real articles. Other instances might be cited,
but these were among the most successful.

As regards the purity of styles it may be safely said,
that, with rare exceptions, it is well-nigh impossible to
find a well-designed and complete scheme of decoration,
or a building that will stand the test of having perfect
unity in style; in fact, it may be more artistic on account
of its incompleteness in this respect, for any work of art
that is designed by receipt, like the Egyptian temples or
Mohammadan ornament, is rather wearisome. It is pleasant to see at times a little bit showing here and there of
the designer's individuality. When the monotonous repetition of the laws peculiar to any arbitrary style are
broken by a wilful and, perhaps, sinful artist, we often get
a refreshing and original rendering that is not by any
means displeasing.

In transitional design from one style to another, much
beautiful work may be seen. In connection with this the
Byzantine style may be mentioned, with its Classic and
Oriental forms, Elizabethan, Jacobean, Lombard Gothic,
and the French styles of Henri Deux and François 1er, in
most of which Gothic and Renaissance forms are happily
blended; and in the beautiful Siculo-Arabian textiles,
where Italian and Saracenic forms make an interesting
union. We learn from these examples that the successful
designer of ornament should have a thorough knowledge
of the historic styles, not for the purpose of reproducing
their forms, but in order to discover for himself the
methods by which the old artists arrived at the successful
treatment of nature and of former styles, so that by the
application of his knowledge, derived from the study of
nature and the works of former artists, he may be enabled
to give to the world some original and interesting work.

CHAPTER II.

THE first indications of the presence of man in Britain was brought to light in the shape of a flint flake found by the Rev. O. Fisher, in the presence of Professor W. Boyd Dawkins, in the lower brick earth of the Stoneham pit at Crayford, in Kent, in the year 1872. In the year 1876 a second flake was found in a similar situation at Erith, in Kent, considerably worn by use. This form of implement was used in the late Pleistocene age, and also in the Neolithic (Newer Stone age) and Bronze ages. It was employed in the historic ages by the Egyptians, and by the Romanized Britons of Sussex, in whose tombs it has been found. This implement is the latest survival of the Palæolithic age. Geologists have proved that Ireland, England and Europe were united in the Palæolithic age, and this accounts for the similarity of stone implements and other remains found in the river-drift deposits, in caves, and other situations in the river valley over this vast area. The roughly chipped flint implements are termed Palæo-lithic, or of the Old Stone age, in contradistinction to the smoother, finer chipped, or polished implements of the Neolithic or Newer Stone age.

It seems highly probable that the Asiatic Palæolithic man first swarmed off the great plateau of Central Asia, which in later times was the home of all those tribes that invaded Europe, India, and China, and certainly were of a race that is now as extinct as the prehistoric Mammoth

itself. The relation between the River-drift men of Asia
and Europe is doubtful. We may not be able to refer the
Palæolithic Cave-men to any present branch of the human
race, but as regards their artistic abilities, the only savage
people that bear any analogy to them in the present day

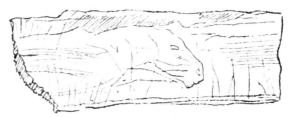

Fig. 1.   Horse, Upper Cave Earth, Robin Hood Cave.   ⅓.

is the South African tribe of Bushmen. These people,
however, are much inferior as artists to the early Cave-
men, which may be seen by comparing the work of both
(Figs. 7A and 7B.

From the drawings of animals which have been found

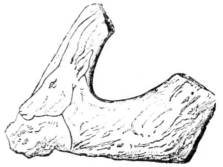

Fig 2.— Ibex Carved on Antler.

etched and carved on bone, horn, and stones, we can judge
of the high qualifications of the Cave-men as artists. Their
work in animal drawing ranks higher than that of any
historic savage race, and as artists they were infinitely of

a higher order than their more scientific successors, the
Neolithic men, or the men of the Bronze age.

It was owing to the discovery of these bone and ivory
etchings that geologists were able to definitely connect the
Cave-men of the Thames Valley with those of France,
Belgium, and Switzerland. At Cresswell Crags, in Derby-

Fig. 3.—Prehistoric Carving.

shire, in the caves, caverns, and fissures known as the Pin
Hole, Robin Hood's Cave, Mother Grundy's Parlour, a
great quantity of bones have been found, some of which
were broken by the hand of man, and amongst these some
flint implements in the lower cave earth. Above this in
the stalagmatic breccia more bones were found and imple-

Fig. 4.—Esquimaux Carving.

ments made of quartzite and flint, together with fragments
of charcoal. Lance heads, flint borers, a bone awl, and a
fragment of bone ornamented with a zigzag or chevron
pattern—probably the oldest bit of ornament known—were
found together with the most important find of all, namely,
a piece of rib bone with an etching of a horse's head and
neck with a hogged mane (Fig. 1), the first instance of an

animal form found in England. These objects may be
seen in the British Museum.

Evidences of the Palæolithic men have been found
in the Mendip Hill caves in Somerset, and at Kent's
Hole, near Torquay, Devon. Harpoons of deers' antlers,
barbed on one or both sides, also hammer stones, half
spherical in shape, have been brought to light from these
places.

The River-drift men preceded the Cave-men, as two

Fig. 5.—Etching of Reindeer on Bone, Kesslerloch Cavern.

different sets of implements found at different depths
testify. Those found at the greatest depths are rougher,
rounder, and more massive in character, with the outer
surface of flint or quartzite nodule still remaining, as seen
in some wedge-shaped hâches and hammer stones, they
consequently belong to the Older Drift period; while the
oval carefully chipped all round, and occasionally polished
implements, belong to a much later and higher cultured
state of the Palæolithic period. Both the River-drift men

and the Cave-men lived in caverns in this country and in France, as some savages do now. Implements of the

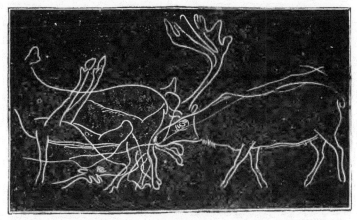

Fig. 6.—Etching of Reindeer on Slate.

Palæolithic age have been found in Europe, North Africa, Asia Minor and India. The earlier River-drift man was a

Fig. 7.—Etching of Mammoth on a piece of Mammoth Ivory.

savage and lived by hunting, as no evidence of culture has been found that can be ascribed to him. After unknown ages perhaps had elapsed the Cave-men appear with more

perfect instruments, and at least cultured in the knowledge
of drawing and carving, which they did, as can be judged
by the illustration given, with astonishing ability. The
accurate forms of animals, as horses, mammoths, bears,
aurochs, elks, reindeers, fish, seals, &c., and even attempts
at the human figure, are evidences of this.

Some authors see a certain analogy between the Cave-
men and the Esquimaux of the present day. In artistic
culture, however, the Cave-men are immeasurably supe-

Fig. 7A.— Human and Animal Form, drawn by Bushmen of South Africa.

rior to the latter, as may be seen by comparing their
respective efforts (Figs. 2, 3, 4, 5).

The Cave-men disappeared from Britain after it became
an island. Similar discoveries of implements and other
remains in Europe and Britain prove that the Cave-men of
both countries were in the same stage of culture. Pottery
has never been found in connection with the remains of
these people.

In France many important finds have been brought to
light illustrating the art work of the European Cave-men.
In the caves at Perigord, at Bruniquel on the Aveyron, at

Le Moustier, at La Madelaine in the Dordogne, and in the
Duruthy cave at Laugerie Basse, in the Western Pyrenees,
have been found many engravings of animals, and carvings on bone, smooth teeth, and antlers, also on sandstone,
slate, and schist. Evidences of the Cave-men using skins
for clothing is inferred from the engraving of skin-gloves
and other things found incised on the teeth of the great
cave-bear in the Duruthy caves. Hunting scenes were

Fig. 7B.—Animal Forms, drawn by Bushmen.

often engraved with great fidelity, and carved dagger-
handles made from the antlers of deer, with the animal
itself sometimes carved on them. One of the highest art
examples yet found is that of a reindeer grazing, and is
the only object on which an attempt is made to represent
herbage, and perhaps water (Fig. 5). This interesting
relic was found in the Kesslerloch Cavern.

CHAPTER III.

THIS period is divided from the Palæolithic Stone age by a great unknown gap. It is sometimes called the Later or Newer Stone age. In this period the flint implements were better shaped, many of them were ground and polished (Figs. 17, 18). Some of the flint and other stone implements were very like in form to those of the Bronze period, and as these implements were made, and continued to be used, in Northern Europe after the Bronze periods of the East had developed, it is quite possible that they were copied from the bronze objects (Figs. 10, 11, 17, 18).

A remarkable sickle or knife fourteen inches long is seen at Fig. 11; a flint saw (Fig. 12), semicircular knives or saws at Figs. 15, 16, and a bone and flint harpoon at Fig. 9. Some of the stone hammers or axes are of great beauty in shape and in workmanship (Figs. 17, 18); also pottery slightly burnt, but well decorated by incised straight lines and zigzags (Figs. 21 to 24).

The cultivation of land, the breeding and rearing of domestic animals, plaiting, and weaving was known and practised by these people. Amber, bone beads, and shells were used as personal adornments. Their burials were with or without cremation. The burial-places of these people are found all over the world, in Europe, Japan, India, and other parts of Asia, and in North America. They are named "Cromlechs" (stone circles), "Dolmen" (stone tables) (Fig. 25), "Menhir" (long stone). The burial-place, called a "Tumulus," is a great mound of

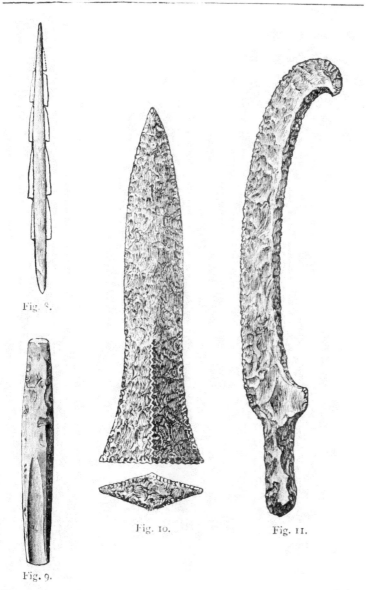

Fig. 8.

Fig. 9.

Fig. 10.

Fig. 11.

Figs. 8 to 11.—Flint Implements of the Neolithic Period (From *Danish Arts.*)

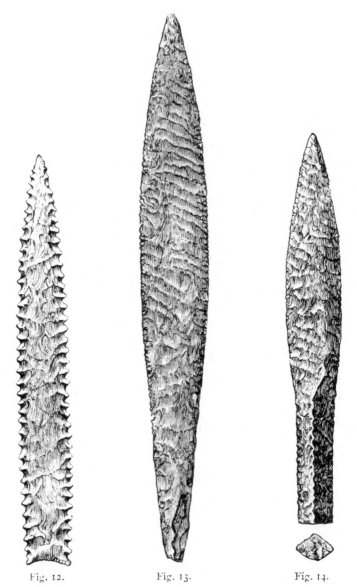

Fig. 12.   Fig. 13.   Fig. 14.

Figs. 12, 13, 14.—Flint Implements of the Neolithic Period. (From *Danish Arts.*)

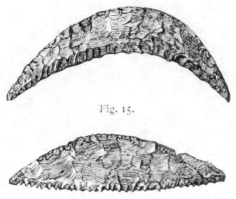

Fig. 15.

Fig. 16.

Figs. 15, 16.—Flint Implements of the Neolithic Period. (From *Danish Arts.*)

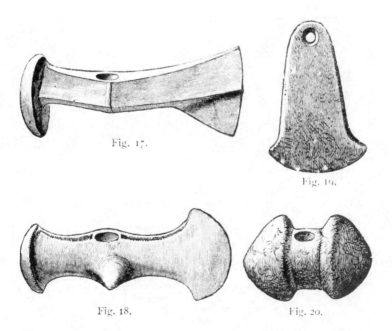

Fig. 17.

Fig. 19.

Fig. 18.

Fig. 20.

Figs. 17 to 20.—Polished Stone Hammers and Celts, Neolithic Period. (From *Danish Arts.*)

Fig. 23.

Fig. 21.

Fig. 24.

Fig. 22.

Figs. 21 to 24.—Pottery of the Neolithic Age. (From *Danish Arts*.)

earth, usually containing a burial chamber constructed in stone in the centre of the mound. The illustrations of the "Menhir" (long stones) (Fig. 26), and of the so-called

Fig. 26.— Menhir, Sardinia (P. & C.).

Giants' Tombs (Fig. 27) belong to the Stone age, and are found in the island of Sardinia.

We have seen that the Palæolithic men were hunters, and evidently had a lot of leisure time on their hands,

which they turned to good account by devoting some of it
to their artistic culture; while the Neolithic men were more

Fig. 25.—Dolmen at Hesbon (P. & C.).

of a race of mechanics and farmers, who had neither time
nor inclination for the cultivation of art, but were alto-

Fig. 27.—Giants' Tomb, Sardinia (P. & C.).

gether more scientific and mechanical than the men of the
Palæolithic period.

CHAPTER IV.

THE BRONZE AGE.

THE people of the Bronze age introduced a higher civilisation into the world than their predecessors of the Stone ages. There appears to be a great overlap between the Neolithic, Bronze, and Iron ages of Central and Northern Europe, and the historic periods of the Eastern countries bordering on the Mediterranean. We have evidence that great periods of time must have marked the epochs of the prehistoric ages, and that the Bronze age, like the Stone and Iron ages, began at different times in different countries. The tribes who brought with them the age of Bronze into Europe composed the Celtic van of the Aryan race. The earliest productions of this period were the simple wedges resembling flat stone axes, the sides of which are slightly thickened to form ridges or flanges; the centres are also raised, which produces a ridge to prevent the head from going in too far in the handle; in some the flanges are much developed, and have also a loop cast on the side for the purpose of tying it on to the haft. Some are made with a socket and loop; these have been called "Paalstabs," and have a flat chisel-like shape (Figs. 28, 30).

These earlier implements are often made of pure copper. Bronze is a mixture of copper and tin, generally from two to four per cent. of tin, and is consequently harder than copper. Knives, hammers, gouges, sickles, daggers, spears, swords, shields, many kinds of vessels, and articles of personal adornment made in bronze, belong to the earlier time of the Bronze period, and similar articles were made

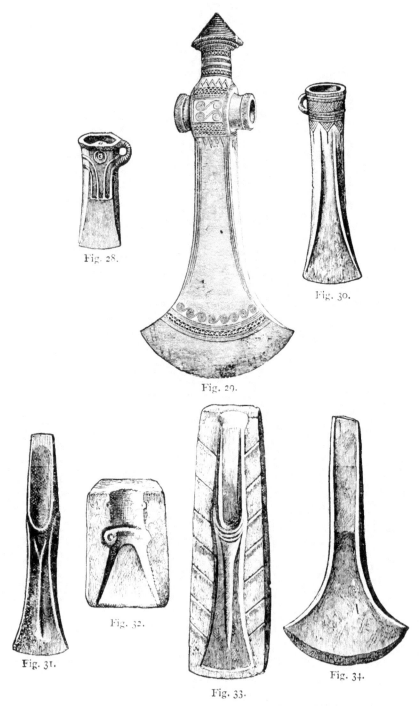

Fig. 28.

Fig. 30.

Fig. 29.

Fig. 31.

Fig. 32.

Fig. 33.

Fig. 34.

Figs. 28 to 30.—Bronze and Paalstabs. (From *Danish Arts.*)
Figs. 31 to 34.—Bronze Axes, Paalstabs, and Moulds. (From *Danish Arts.*)

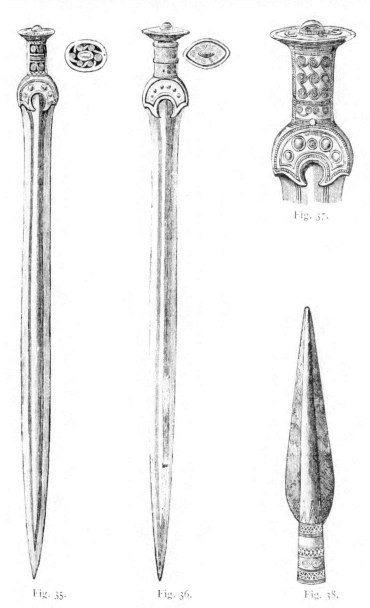

Fig. 37.

Fig. 35.   Fig. 36.   Fig. 38.

Figs. 35 to 38.—Bronze Swords and Spear-Head. (From *Danish Arts.*)

in this material in the prehistoric Bronze ages all over the known world (Figs. 35 to 40).

Figs. 39 and 40. — Bronze Button for Sword Belt. (From *Danish Arts*.)

An interesting object is a breast-plate, belonging to this early Bronze period; it is decorated with zigzags in bands, and a well-arranged scheme of spiral ornamentation (Fig. 41). Urns of earthenware, sometimes decorated with zigzags and sacred signs, have been found in graves. These urns contained ashes of the dead (Figs. 43, 44).

Many of the bronze implements and other articles have been found in tombs, in caves in great quantities, both finished and unfinished, in "Kitchen Middens," or refuse heaps, in river-beds, and in bogs.

Some of the objects found in North Germany, and par-

Fig. 41.—Breast-plate, with Spiral Ornaments. (From *Danish Arts*.)

ticularly in Denmark, Sweden, and Norway, are exceedingly beautiful in their shape and decoration. From nowhere else in the world come so many objects, and so much that is characteristic of the prehistoric Bronze age. This period has been ably treated, and at great length, by Mr. J.

Fig. 42.

Fig. 43.

Fig. 44.

Figs. 42, 43, and 44.—Urns of the Bronze Age (From *Danish Arts.*)

J. A. Worsaae, in his "Danish Arts," and by Mr. Hans Hildebrand, in his "Arts of Scandinavia," to which books we are indebted for the accompanying illustrations.

It may be noticed that much of the decoration on these objects consists of a few simple elements with much geometric repetition. The varied forms are chiefly spirals interlocking at regulated distances, concentric rings, tri-

Fig. 45 — Bronze Bowl found in Sweden. (*Scand. Arts.*)

angles, zigzag lines, and bands formed of lines which are reminiscences of the earlier withy lashings, with which

Fig. 46.—Urn of the Stone Age found in Swedish Dolmen. (*Scand. Arts.*)

the stone celts were fastened to their hafts. The raised, as well as the flat twisted-like bands, are derivatives from the twisted strings that would naturally be tied around the pottery of an early date to carry it by (Fig. 45).

The spirals, zigzags, ring-crosses, wheels, triskeles, reciprocal meanders, semicircles, &c., are geometrical developments of sun-snake, lightning, the sun itself, cloud-forms, moon-forms, star-forms, and the sacred fylfot or swastika, all of which had their

origin in Egypt, India, Central Asia, or Greece. At first
they were used as isolated signs, or pictographs, to

Fig. 47.—Bronze Hatchet found in Sweden. (*Scand. Arts.*)

represent physical phenomena, that were objects of

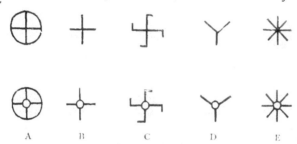

A   B   C   D   E

Fig. 48.—Sun Signs.

A, Wheel Cross or Wheel; B, Sun God Signs; C, Fylfot, or Swastika;
D, Triskele; E, Stars or Sun Signs.

Nature-worship with almost all the nations of the world

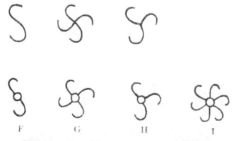

F   G   H   I

Fig. 49.—Sun Signs. (From *Danish Arts.*)

F, Sun-snakes; G, Swastika; H, Triskele; I, Star or Sun.
N.B.—The Swastika here is evidently a double Sun-snake.

after the dawn of civilisation, and when these signs
migrated into the art of other nations or later peoples,

who were either ignorant of their meaning or understood
them in an imperfect way, they ceased to be employed
as isolated signs of the various divinities they originally
represented, and were copied, and repeated, as required,
to fill in a geometrical way the space at hand to be ornamented.

A beautiful piece of workmanship is the bronze horn
(Fig. 50). Worsaae thinks that this horn was used in the
worship of the gods in the early Bronze age, owing to the
great number of sacred signs engraved on it. Sun-wheels,
sun-snakes, and sun-boats, developed into spiral ornament, may be seen on it.

There is one ornament that plays an important part in
the Bronze and Iron periods, of which much has been
written, the "fylfot" or "swastika." It has been found in
nearly every quarter of the ancient world, except Egypt
and Assyria, both in savage ornament and in the art
of cultured races. The "fylfot" or "many" or "full-
footed" cross in Anglo-Saxon, it is also known by the
names of "gammadion," "croix gammée," "croix cram-
ponée," "tetraskele," &c. The Indian name for it is the
"swastika" or "svastika," which means "good luck," or
"it is well." The fylfot, according to the opinion of many
archæologists, was originally the sign of the sun, and used
as a sacred symbol in the worship of the sun ; others think
it was a sign used to symbolize the rotatory motion of the
planets ; it is quite likely it has been used by different
early peoples for both. It has been associated with
other sun signs, as the circle, concentric circles, with the
S-shaped sun-snakes, as on the prehistoric whorls from
Hissarlik, and very frequently with the solar divinities, as
the horse, boar, ram, lion, ibex, and goose, &c. It is found
on Cyprian and Rhodian pottery and on the "geometric"
pottery of Greece. Its appearance on many objects of
early Christian art can be accounted for. In these cases
the Christian missionaries permitted the continued use of
it to their pagan converts, but they themselves attached a

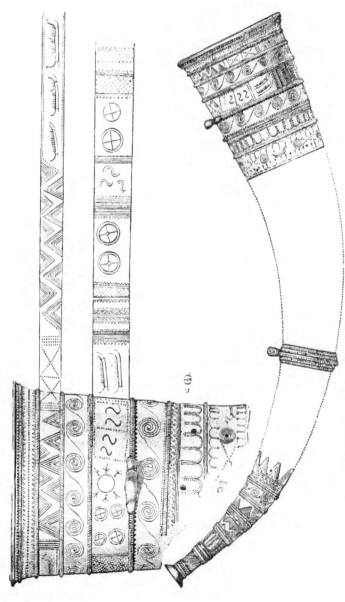

FIG. 50.—Bronze Horn or Trumpet, found at Wismar, in Mecklenburg. (From *Danish Arts*.)

new meaning to it, regarding it as merely a substitute for
the symbol of the cross.

Some writers have argued, with a good deal of plausi-
bility, that the Greek fret pattern, Chinese and Japanese
frets, were only developments from the fylfot. This is
purely conjectural, for as regards the Greek fret, it is
more likely that it had an Egyptian source, as so many of

Fig. 51.—Pinak or Plate, Archaic Period, from Camiros, Rhodes, showing
Fylfot, and Sun Signs, and Sacred Boar.   (British Museum.)

the Greek ornaments are but developments of Egyptian
and Assyrian forms. The fret used by the Greeks has
been found in Egypt in the ceiling ornament of tombs
more than a thousand years before it appeared in Greece.
The Chinese frets may have in some instances a fylfot
origin, but at present this is doubtful, as it has not yet been
proved. The drawing of the archaic Greek plate (*pinak*),
in the British Museum, given at Fig. 51, from the Greek
colony of Rhodes, is very interesting, as it shows a well-

developed fylfot between the legs of the boar, and an early
Greek fret band; the fret here may only be a water-sign,
or a river-edge representation. The spaces around the
boar (animal sacred to the sun) are filled up with sun-signs
and star-signs; even the large segment of radiating lines,
and the form over the animal's back may typify the sun.
The whole decoration has a high religious meaning in

Fig. 52.—Silver Brooch. Plated with Gold, in the form of a Double Sun-snake or
Swastika; found in Iceland. (*Danish Arts.*)

reference to sun-worship, and is evidently a copy by a
Greek artist of an oriental embroidery motive.

The fylfot has been found stamped on the pottery of the
lake dwellings of the Zuni, Yucatan, and other American
pottery, and on objects from Iceland, Ireland, and Scandinavia. A circular form of it is seen on the gold Scandinavian ornament (Fig. 52).

Whether it originally was a pure sun-sign, or whether it
signified the axial rotation of the earth round the North

Pole, it is full of remarkable interest, and enters more than any other symbolic sign into historic ornament generally. In India, China, and Japan, it has been much

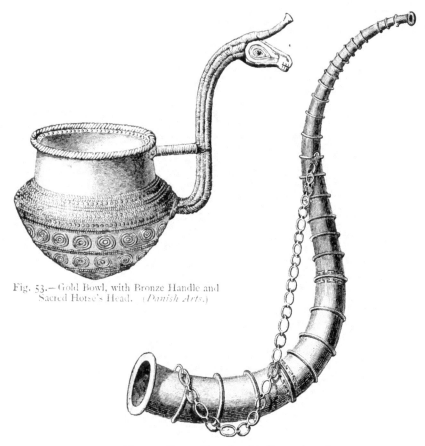

Fig. 53.— Gold Bowl, with Bronze Handle and Sacred Horse's Head. (*Danish Arts.*)

Fig. 54.—Bronze Horn found in Denmark. (*Danish Arts.*)

used; this was owing to the spread of the Buddhist religion in these countries. It is found on the toes of the "Foot-print" of Buddha, at the Amarávati Tope, India; and owing to its great religious significance in China, Japan,

Fig. 56.—Danish Bronze Knives, decorated with Sun-ships and other Sacred Figures. (Danish Arts.)

Fig. 57.

Fig. 58.

Fig. 55.—Collar of Bronze found in Sweden. Scand. Arts.)

Figs. 57 and 58.—Bronze and Gold Buttons found in Women's Graves, with the Tri-skele, Moon-Signs, and Sun Snakes. (Danish Arts.)

and Ceylon, we find it stamped on the account books, coins and dresses of both the living and the dead, as a universal sign of good luck.

The swastika, both straight and curved-armed variety, was used indiscriminately in the decoration of objects of the Iron age, whether in bronze, iron, gold, silver, wood, or stone. It was the sign among the Romans of Jupiter Tonans, who wielded the thunder and lightning; was the sign used for Thor, the god of thunder and lightning, with the early German peoples, and the curved variety of it was used as a symbol of their highest divinity by the northern nations of Scandinavia. From this widespread use of the swastika it is conjectured that it is an Aryan symbol, brought by the people of the Bronze age from their primitive home in the plateau of Central Asia.

CHAPTER V.

THE IRON AGE.

THE age of Iron, like the Bronze ages, varies very much in point of time in Europe as compared with Asia, and also there is a great overlapping between the times of the Iron age in the northern, middle, and southern parts of Europe. It is safe to say that the early part of this age belongs to prehistoric times as far as Central and Northern Europe is concerned, and although the Grecian Archipelago and Western Asia were in a high state of civilised culture five or six centuries before the Christian era, and were acquainted with the use of iron, it is clear that the extensive employment and decoration of iron implements and arms were chiefly in Switzerland, Northern Italy, and in the Valley of the Danube. This iron culture soon spread over to Gaul and Spain, and to the British Islands in the West, and Scandinavia in the North. The Romans, under their first emperors, imported their swords and other arms from Spain and the West on account of their good workmanship. From the many "finds" that have been brought to light in the above countries it is evident that, for five or six centuries before the commencement of the Christian era, there was a great activity going on in the manufacture of iron objects in these countries, principally swords and other warlike arms. The two most important "finds" are the "Halstaat" in Austria, and the La Tène "finds" near Marin, Lake Neuchâtel. The Halstaat find was composed of many gold and bronze articles, pottery, and a few iron weapons. The place where these things

were found was a Celtic tomb, and the iron articles found
in it are among the earliest known in Europe, which proves
them to have been made at the transition period from the
Bronze to the Iron ages. Besides the purely geometric
work the decoration on these articles consists of sun and
moon signs, wheel crosses, half moons, the sacred ship,
the swastika, triskele, &c.; crude representations of men
and animals, as horses, oxen, stags, he-goats, and geese,
all of which have a religious and symbolic meaning. All
these forms were used in the Bronze and Iron ages alike.
The find at La Tène, near Marin, Lake Neuchâtel, belongs
to a later period and is more important from an art point
of view, for besides the usual sacred decorations engraved
on the objects, some of the sword handles and sheaths are
beautifully sculptured or chiselled in iron, with well-
designed ornament and animal forms. (See Fig. 81, D, of
Gaulish or late Celtic workmanship.)

The shapes and materials of the weapons found at La
Tène, or of what is called the "La Tène Period," do not
bear much resemblance to the weapons of the Bronze age,
and the sheaths of the swords and daggers are sometimes
bronze and sometimes iron, but the blades are of iron.

Communication with the Etruscans and the Greeks by
the people of Central Europe is proved by the coins, vases,
and objects of personal ornament, and by the imitations of
Greek and Macedonian coins found in great quantities in
Middle and Western Europe and in Britain, that belong
to this late Celtic period. This accounts for the more
"advanced" nature of the decoration on the Marin swords
and daggers of the "La Tène Period," and this particular
culture-wave brought with it the beginnings of that ornament which, in later centuries, developed into the peculiar
Celtic and Runic twistings and interlacings that are so
common to Danish, Norwegian, Swedish, Anglo-Saxon
and Irish phases of decorative art, that was practised so
largely from the first to the twelfth centuries of our era.
This Celtic interlacing, though often more distressing than

a Chinese puzzle, and in some instances barbarous in the extreme, yet is often very interesting and beautiful in execution. Most of it can be traced to its origin in sacred signs and animal forms in classical ornament.

It will be interesting to trace briefly some of these developments of the Northern Runic and Celtic art of the Iron age. In the development of nearly all historic art, we find that the religious aspirations of man were the chief factors. In Egypt, Asia, Europe, or America, wherever art had an individuality, the greatest monuments were erected, and the finest works of art were created for the honour of the nation's gods. We have seen how the forms of ornament were generally derived from the figurative signs of sacred animals, plants, and other mystic symbols of a religious meaning, and were in the end converted in meaningless but æsthetic ornament. This is the history of nine-tenths of historic ornament that has survived the decay of nations. The ancient religion and beliefs of the pre-Christian peoples were those which they had brought with them when they first migrated from their Asiatic home, namely, the worship of the sun, moon, and lightning. Cæsar mentions in his " De Bello Gallico," VI., 21, that the " Germani people worshipped the visible helping gods, the sun, moon, and fire, and knew nothing whatever of other divinities." The symbolic signs and animal forms sacred to these phenomena, already mentioned, are found more or less on the utensils and weapons of the Gallic-German peoples of the Iron age, and in addition to these we see the representation of the Northern gods, the Trinity of the North, Thor, Odin and Frey, with and without the sacred animals peculiar to each. In the earlier times close intercourse with the Romans brought about a high degree of culture to the barbarian people of the Rhine Valley and more northern places; many statuettes of bronze inlaid with gold and silver, representing Roman gods, have been dug up in Denmark and other places in the north.

These statuettes were transformations of the Roman and

Etruscan gods that served for the Gallo-Germanic gods.
An illustration of the Roman influence is seen in a round
ornament of this period plated with gold, found at Thors-
berg, Slesvig. It is the decoration of an iron coat of mail.
The illustration of this (Fig. 59) is taken from Worsaae's
"Danish Arts," and is thus described by him :

Fig. 59.—Gold-plated Ornament found at Thorsberg.   (*Danish Arts.*)

" Five suns are placed crosswise, and between two of the
outer ones is seen a barbarised figure of Jupiter with horns
on his helmet; the sun in the centre is surrounded by a
circle of helmeted heads. Just as this recalls to our minds
the Germanic and Scandinavian god of thunder, Thor, who,
later, was often represented with a helmet on his head, so
the thin barbaric golden figures of horses, geese, and fish,

riveted on the ornament or brooch itself, remind us of the sun-god Frey." The Figs. 60 and 61 are metal mountings decorated with the triskele formed of sun-snakes, the swastika with straight arms, and the compound variety of the fylfot on the larger mounting. These illustrate a transition of the sacred sun form to more purely ornamental designs.

The imitation of Roman coins and medallions of the time of Constantine to ornaments that have been called "bracteates" was extensively carried on by the Germanic people. These bracteates have the design on one side only, with a loop or ring at the top to suspend them

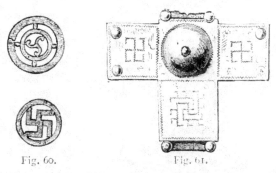

Fig. 60.   Fig. 61.

Figs. 60 and 61.—Metal Mountings from Thorsberg. (*Danish Art*.)

around the neck as an amulet. These golden bracteates have been found in great numbers in Scandinavia and Denmark, and scarcely anywhere else, which proves they were indigenous to these countries.

It is interesting to notice how they have been transformed from their Roman and Byzantine originals to purely sacred Celtic amulets of a new national type of ornament. Fig. 62, from Hildebrand's "Scandinavian Arts," is a barbaric copy of a Roman medallion. It is a poor attempt to copy the Imperial head, and the inscription is badly and meaninglessly copied. On the reverse is a figure of Victory, with signs of the cross, surrounded by a wreath and legend.

It appears that after the age of the Constantines, the
intercourse of the Germanic people with the Romans was

Fig. 62.—Barbarian Copy of a Roman Medallion found in Sweden.
(*Scand. Arts.*)

broken, owing to the invasion of the Huns, and for a long
time afterwards they were left to themselves without

Fig. 63.—Golden Bracteate from Scandinavia.   (*Danish Arts.*)

foreign influence, and were enabled to develop their
national art on the foundation of Roman culture, at the
same time substituting their own emblems of their national

gods in place of the classic ones in their decorative work. We can safely gather from this that the Hunnic invasion of the Roman Empire was the indirect means of giving to Northern Europe a distinct national style of art.

The illustrations of the golden bracteates here given (Figs. 63, 64) partly show how this development began. On Fig. 63 is Thor's head with his tiara or helmet, the he-

Fig. 64.—Golden Bracteate from Scandinavia. (*Danish Arts.*)

goat sacred to Thor, the triad three dots, and the swastika. On the border is the triskele (Odin's sign), Frey's cross, and the zigzag or lightning.

The larger bracteate (Fig. 64) has Thor with the he-goat surrounded by the swastika, triskele, and the cross (four suns forming the cross), the signs for Thor, Odin, and Frey. The inner border has the three dots, or triad; next border, Thor's head; and the outer border is composed of

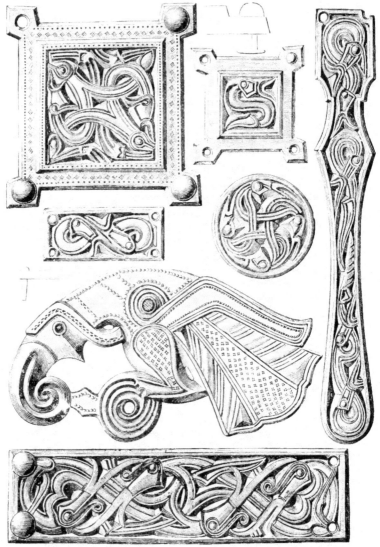

Fig. 65.—Parts of Harness in Gilt Bronze, Gotland. (*Scand. Arts.*)

he-goats. On the loop are signs of the sun and moon, and
under it sun-snakes (developed into spirals). The above

descriptions of the bracteates are chiefly taken from the
" Danish Arts."

Characteristic ornament of this period is shown at Fig. 65,
which are parts of a harness in gilt bronze from a tomb in

Fig. 66.—Fibula in Gilt Bronze,
Gotland. (*Scand. Arts.*)

Fig. 67.—Fibula in Gilt Bronze, Gotland.
(*Scand. Arts.*)

Gotland ; the patterns are composed of corrupted animal
and bird forms.

Figs. 66 to 68 are fibula decorations of the interlacing
animal forms, which are characteristic of the more attenuated and later development
of Scandinavian art.

The series of designs,
Figs. 69 to 73, are of great
interest in showing the development of patterns from
lion forms to the twisted

Fig. 68.—Part of Rim of Fig. 67.

snake ornament. The figures are taken from Hildebrand's " Scandinavian Arts." According to that author,
Fig. 69 is a Scandinavian copy or adaptation of a Roman
design, which consists of two lions *couchant.* The other
patterns (Figs. 70 to 73) are further developments of
corrupted lion forms. It is quite possible that the peculiar

interlacings of Scandinavian ornament may have been the result of imperfect copying of lion and bird forms. They

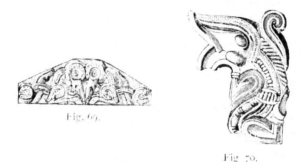

Fig. 69.

Fig 70.

Figs. 69 and 70.—Corrupted Figures of Lions. *(Scand. Arts.)*

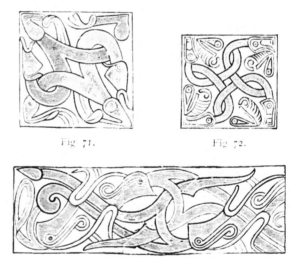

Fig. 71.

Fig. 72.

Fig. 73.

Figs. 71, 72, 73.—Animal Ornamental Patterns. Corrupted Figures of Lions. *(Scand. Arts.)*

were never intended for snake forms, as many of these have legs and feet, and serpents and snakes were unknown in the north. Many stranger derivatives of ornament have

Fig. 74.—Silver Goblet, with Gold-plated Decoration, found in Zeeland. (*Danish Arts.*)

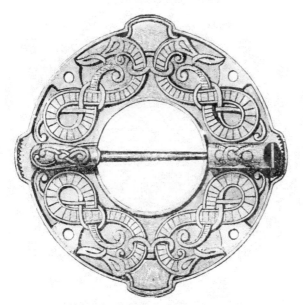

Fig. 75.—Under Side of a Fibula. (*Scand. Arts.*)

existed in the ornament of savage tribes.* When the
Gotlandic artist had reduced his lion forms to snakes he

Fig. 76.—Pottery of the Iron Age. (*Danish Arts.*)

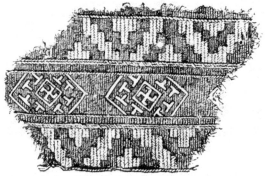

Fig. 77.—Piece of Woollen Cloth with Gold and Silver Threads, Viking Period.
(*Danish Arts.*)

carried his work to the verge of monotony with inter-
minable interlacings.

The decoration on the goblet (Fig. 74) is the sun-god

* See Haddon's "Evolution of Ornamental Art," 1895.

Frey, with his horse and geese; the masks are intended for those of Thor; his he-goat and sun signs are also seen. This goblet was evidently used in the sun-worship festivals.

A restrained and agreeable design is seen on the under side of a fibula (Fig. 75 ; a well-shaped earthen pot is decorated with zigzag work, and has the symbolical triad mark impressed on it (Fig. 76); and a remnant of woollen cloth, woven with silver and gold threads, has the swastika and the hammer of Thor as decoration. This was found in a grave at Randers of the tenth century. It belongs to the Viking period of the Iron age (Fig. 77.

CHAPTER VI.

THE LAKE DWELLINGS OF SWITZERLAND AND OTHER PARTS OF EUROPE.

IN Switzerland and in Upper Italy evidences have been found of numerous lake dwellings, and in Ireland and Scotland analogous dwellings on islands in lakes and morasses have been found, to which the name of "crannoges" ("wooden islands") has been given. The exact age of these dwellings has not been accurately defined, but an approximate date has been assigned to them. From the nature, kind, and decoration of the numerous articles that have been dug up from the foundation relic beds in the lakes of Switzerland, it appears that the duration of the "lake dwellings" period was from about the time of the later Stone age to the early Iron age; it therefore embraces portions of the Stone age, the Bronze age, and early Iron ages of Europe.

The lake dwellings were erected by certain tribes of the early inhabitants of Europe, for the better security of themselves and their property from the savage animals of the mainland, and from their enemies, the still more savage fellow-men. As far as can be made out from the remains found in the lakes, the lake dwellers were more civilised and less warlike than their neighbours that lived on land. The lake dwellings are the most ancient evidences of man's first constructive capabilities in the art of building. Herodotus tells us of a settlement on Lake Prasias (Tachyus), in Rumelia, where "men live on platforms supported by tall piles." Some tribes of the

Papuans of New Guinea still live on pile dwellings. The lacustrine habitation (Fig. 78), from "Les Races Sauvages," by M. Bertillon, is a representation of a pile dwelling on the Lake Mohrya, in Central Africa, of the present day.

The substructures, Fig. 79, A, B, and C, taken from

78.—Lacustrine Habitation in Lake Mohrya, Central Africa. (From *Les Races Sauvages*, by M. Bertillon.)

Keller's "Lake Dwellings," will give general ideas of the foundations of the dwellings in Switzerland and Upper Italy. At A is seen the earliest type, which reveals the section of the piles, upper flooring, water-line, and sloping bank of the lake. The piles were sometimes composed of split trees or stems, but more often of stems with the bark on, and were of various kinds of wood; they were

sharpened at the end by stone hatchets, and in later times
by bronze or iron axes, and were driven into the sand or
mud at a short distance from the shore.   The heads of the

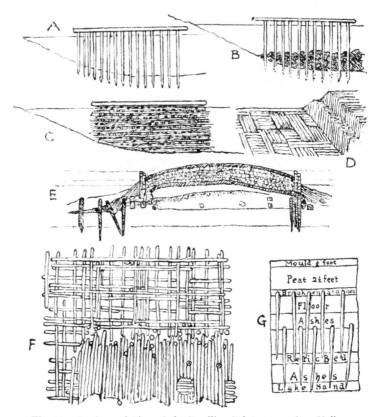

Fig. 79.—Section and Plans, Lake Dwelling Substructures from Keller.

A, General idea of arrangement of Piles ; B, shows the Piles driven into the mud, with stones
    thrown between them ; C, Section of Fascine Dwelling ; D, Diagram of Floor Fascine
    Construction from Niederwyl ; E, Section of Irish Crannoge in Ardakillin Lough ; F, Con-
    struction of Wooden Form (Niederwyl) ; G, Section of Lake Dwelling Beds at Roben-
    hausen.

piles were brought to a level, and planks or whole trees
were fastened on them as beams ; sometimes they were
fastened on by wooden pins, and sometimes were
"notched" into the heads of the piles.   Cross-beams

were often forced in between the uprights under the platform to steady the structure, and outside there was often fastened a clothing of wattle-work to act as a fender from various accidents. If it were found difficult to drive the piles into the bed of the lake to any great depth, artificial raising of the bottom was resorted to, by bringing cargoes of stones in boats and dropping them between the piles, thereby securing a perfectly secure substructure (Fig. 79, B). These artificial risings are called "stein-bergs."

Another and later variety of substructure is known as "fascine-work" (Fig. 79, C). Probably this fascine construction was the safest when the water of the lake rose in height. It consisted of layers of small trees or stems laid lengthwise, built from the bottom of the lake ; these sticks or trees were interwoven, and at intervals upright piles were driven in to keep them in position, and on the top of this structure, above high-water mark, the flooring platform was laid.

The "crannoges" or "wooden islands," of Ireland and Scotland, resemble very much the Swiss fascine dwellings. The Irish "crannoges" were often placed on natural islands, or on shallows or loughs, but sometimes were built up, like those in Switzerland, from the bottom of the lake. These "crannoges" were used as chieftains' fastnesses or places of retreat. They were built chiefly in the Stone age, and were used long after the age of Iron. At Fig. 79, E, may be seen a section of an Irish "crannoge" in Ardakillin Lough. At Fig. 79, F and D, are shown diagrams of platform and floor construction respectively of a lake dwelling at Niederwyl, Switzerland. On the top of this floor a plaster made of mud, loam, and gravel, was laid and beaten firmly down. As far as can be ascertained from the remains of upright corner posts that have been found in position, the houses were rectangular, though some may have been round like the huts of the contemporary people on the mainland. The walls of the houses are supposed to have been built of wattle-work plastered

over with mud and thatched, as evidences of this are seen in
the large pieces of burnt clay with wattle impression on it
that have been found ; this also points out the fact of the
houses or settlements being burnt down.   In some cases
the walls were of fascine construction.   Every hut was provided with its hearth, which consisted of three or four large
flat stones.   Clay weights used for the loom have been

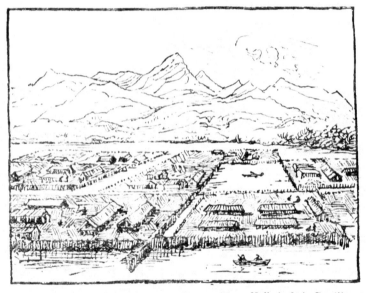

Fig. 80.—An Ideal Lake Settlement or Town.   (From Keller's *Lake Dwellings*.)

found in great quantities, which proves, together with
many fragments of flax cloth and woven " bast " which
have come to light, that weaving was known and practised
by the lake dwellers (Fig. 81, K).   Pottery has been found
in the relic beds, but is usually of a very coarse description.   Many broken bits of pottery have been found ornamented with lines, chevrons, or zigzags, and often with
the " rope " ornament, raised or impressed by a twisted
string or rope ; this kind of decoration is evidently sug-

gested by the band of string tied around the primitive
vessels of clay to keep them together, or for carrying purposes. See Fig. 81, B, F, G, H, I, and J.

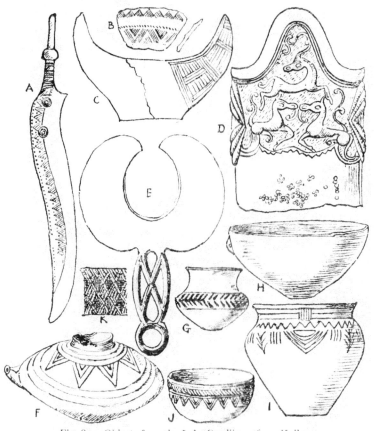

Fig. 81.—Objects from the Lake Dwellings (from Keller).

A, Bronze Knife (Lake of Bienne); B, Ornamented Pottery; C, Moon Image of earthenware;
D, Part of an Iron Sword (Gaulish work); E, Moon Image of bronze; F, G, H, I, J,
Earthenware Vessels; K, Embroidered Cloth.

The builders of the lake dwellings are supposed to have
been a branch of the Celtic population of Switzerland,
belonging to prehistoric times, and was in its last stage of
decadence before the Celts took their place in the history

of Europe. Although many remains of bronze and iron
implements have been brought to light from the relic
beds of the lake dwellings, this does not prove that the
inhabitants were acquainted with their manufacture, for
most of the articles were probably obtained by barter from
the people of the mainland.

A beautiful bronze knife is seen at Fig. 81, A, found in
the lake of Bienne, and part of a sword in iron, of Gaulish,
or "late Celtic" workmanship, from Marin, Lake Neuchâtel (Fig. 81, D).

Highly interesting are the "moon-stones" and "moon-
images" of this period, made in stone, earthenware, and
bronze. These crescent moon-images have a religious significance, and have doubtless been used to decorate the
tops of their entrance doors Keller) or other conspicuous
places in their dwellings, as emblematic images of their
worship of the moon.

The figure at C represents an earthenware moon-image
with a flat base for standing purposes. The decoration on
this is peculiarly interesting, as showing one of the earliest
fascine patterns, doubtless derived from the floor construction of the dwellings, or from the lashings of withy bands
used to fasten the stone axes and celts to their hafts. This
kind of ornament has been used very much in the Bronze
age weapons, implements, and other objects. The moon-
image at E is made of bronze, with a handle and a ring to
hang it by. It was probably worn as an amulet or decoration suspended from the neck of a Celtic priest. Remains
of many kinds of plants, seeds, corn, and fruit have been
found, usually in coarse earthen pots; also cakes and
loaves of bread, and mill-stone "crushers" for grinding
corn. Domestic animals, such as cows, goats, and dogs,
were kept by the lake dwellers. Fishing and fish-curing,
as may be easily inferred, was an important industry with
these interesting people.

CHAPTER VII.

ACCORDING to their most ancient traditions, the Egyptian race descended from a point high up on the Nile, or the land of Ethiopia, but modern science proves them to belong to a Caucasian race, and not of the Negro type. The name Egypt has been derived from "Het-ka-Ptah," one of the titles of the city of Memphis, which means "The Temple of the Genius of Ptah," and has been interpreted by the Greeks as "Aiguptos," the latter being the old name for the Nile.

On the south of Egypt dwelt the Nubians or Ethiopians; on the west the Libyans, a fair-skinned race, who, being a warlike people, were employed by the Egyptians as mercenary troops; and on the north-east the nomadic Semitic tribes of Edom and Southern Syria. The latter people often wandered west to feed their flocks in the Delta of Lower Egypt, and in course of time formed, with the Phœnician traders, a large proportion of the population of the lower kingdom of Egypt. It was on the north-east frontier, on the Isthmus of Suez, that Egypt had most to fear from her foreign enemies.

Nearly all the art of the various peoples and nations of the world was developed in relation to their religion, and most of it—as elsewhere stated—originated in symbolic signs that represented, under various forms, human or otherwise, the original objects or phenomena which they worshipped. This was the case especially so in Egypt;

Fig. 82.—Isis nursing her Son, Horus. (P. & C.) Height, 19 ins.

and this must be our plea to describe here briefly the principal outlines of the Egyptian religion.

The religion of the Egyptians had two developments, one tending towards Monotheism, and the other to Polytheism. They believed in one god, who was the king of all gods; and, on the other hand, they had their mythical gods, who personified whatever was permanent in natural phenomena, such as the sun, moon, sky, stars, earth, light, darkness, floods, the seasons, the year, and the hours. The goddess Nut represented the sky, and was known also under the names of Neith, Isis, Hathor, Sekhet, &c., which were the names of the sky at sunrise or sunset (Fig. 82). The sun had names without number, as Rā, Horus, Ptah, Tmu, Setek, Amen, &c. (Figs. 83, 84). Osiris and Sekru are names of the sun after he has set, or is "dead and buried" (Fig. 85). Osiris is king of the dead, and, in mythological language, he is slain by his brother Set, who personified night, who in his turn is slain by Horus (Fig. 82), who is the heir of Osiris. Horus signifies the "one above," and Amen-Rā, the great king of all the gods, signifies "the one who hides himself." The great Amen-Rā was the mightiest god in all the Egyptian pantheon. He was the great god of Thebes.

The gods were represented in human shape, and also in animal form. The animals, or animal combinations, were simply symbolical of the gods on account of certain attributes common to each, or in some cases because they bore the same name.

The Egyptians were intense believers in a future state, hence the great care bestowed on their dead, for they believed that the body should be preserved in order to insure a state of bliss for the soul in the future world. Every human being had its "double," or ghost "Ka," as well as its ghost "Ba," which we often find represented under the form of a human being with a hawk's head. Sometimes the image of a man was buried with him. This was to represent his "double," and is, therefore, called a

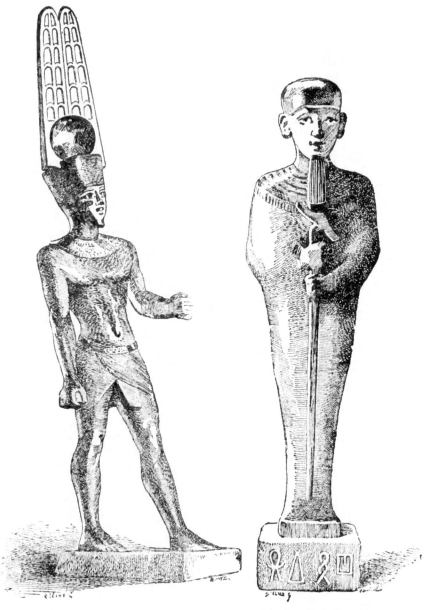

Fig. 83.—Amen, or Ammon, bronze.
(P. & C.)

Fig. 84.—Ptah, from a bronze
Actual Size.   (P. & C.)

"Ka" statue, or image. The "Ba," or soul, was supposed to be "luminous."

It is supposed that many of the animals and animal forms buried with and painted on the coffins of the Egyptian dead were, in remote times, the sacred animals or "Totems" belonging to the dead man's family. "Totem worship" may have been the most ancient form of the Egyptian religion. The Temple of Bubastis in the Delta was sacred to the goddess Bast, or Pasht, the cat-headed goddess (Fig. 86). The cat was, therefore, a sacred animal or a "Totem," in ancient Egypt, like the ibis, hawk, asp, beetle, &c., totems ; and so in the district or town of Bubastis the Cat Clan, or worshippers of the cat-headed goddess Pasht, built the rock-cut temple called Speos Artemidos, near Beni-Hasan, and dedicated it to her worship.

The writing of the Egyptians is classified under three heads : the "Hieroglyphic," or the form in which it appears on the monuments ; the "Hieratic," or priestly writing, as used on the papyrus documents ; and the "Demotic," a cursive or running kind of writing similar to the Hieratic, and a later development of it. In the year 1798 the famous "Rosetta Stone," now in the British Museum, was found near the Rosetta mouth of the Nile by a French officer. It passed into the hands of the British in 1802. On this stone is inscribed a decree of the priests of Memphis conferring divine honours on Ptolemy V., King of Egypt, B.C. 195. The inscription is in three forms, the Hieroglyphic, the Demotic, and in Greek characters. From this inscription was first obtained the key to the decipherment of the hieroglyphics, and interpretation of the ancient language of Egypt, and the names of the kings which in the hieroglyphics are enclosed in cartouches or oblong rings. Thus the clue was obtained to the identification of the letters of the Egyptian alphabet, which had hitherto baffled all the attempts of Egyptologists to find out. The credit of the identification is chiefly due to the French

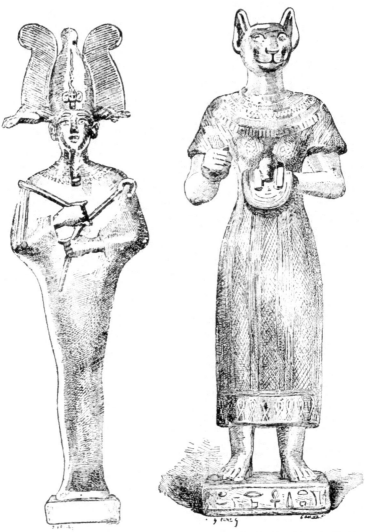

Fig. 85.—Osiris. (P. & C.)   Fig. 86.— The Goddess Bast, or Pasht.
                                        Actual Size. (P. & C.)

savant, Champollion, but a considerable share of the honour must be given to Thomas Young, who was the first to find out the correct value of many of the phonetic signs. The Egyptians, from the earliest period known, were acquainted with and skilled in medicine, in astronomy, in mathematics, philosophy, poetry, and fiction. The oldest literary papyrus at present known dates from the Third to the Fifth Dynasties (3966 to 3333 B.C.).

Egyptian art was at its best in the earliest Dynasties. The Fourth Dynasty was the great pyramid-building period, and the statues of this great epoch were more natural and artistic, and altogether were less conventional than those of later times.

It is notable that in the Eighteenth and Twenty-sixth Dynasties, after a long period of art depression, the artists went back for inspiration and better models to the work of the men of the Fourth and Twelfth Dynasties.

The history of Egypt can be traced back from 4,400 years before the Christian era, and is divided into thirty Dynasties, whose succession was the result of failure in any of the original lines of marriage, or marriage with a female of lower rank, or of a revolution. The thirty Dynasties are divided into three groups :—

Dynasties I.—XI. (B.C. 4400—2466) .. The Ancient Empire.
,, XII.—XIX. (B.C. 2466—1200) .. The Middle Empire.
,, XX.—XXX. (B.C. 1200— 340) .. The New Empire.

These dates and arrangements are formulated chiefly on the basis of a work written in Greek, and compiled by Manetho, an Egyptian priest who lived in the third century B.C.

The kings of Egypt have been named Pharaohs from the title " Peraa "—" great house." The seat or centre of the government shifted its position according to dynastic reasons, or from policy. During the ancient empire it was first at Memphis, and then moved to Abydos and other places in the south as the empire extended. When

Egypt was in the height of its glory the centre of government was chiefly at Thebes, but moving often according
to revolution or foreign oppression.   Rameses and his
near successors held their court at the northern city of
San, or Tanis.   The time of the New Empire was chiefly a
period of foreign rule and slow decadence, the seat of the

Fig. 87.—The Great Pyramid of Kheops, and Small Pyramids; from Perring.
(P. & C.)

empire shifted to nearly all the former places or capitals
and to Bubastis or Sais with each political change.

Menes was the first historical king of Egypt, and was
supposed to have founded Memphis, where the worship
of the god Ptah, "Creator of gods and men," was first
instituted, as well as that of Apis or Hapi, the sacred
bull—the Serapis of the Greeks.   For the next six hundred years we know scarcely anything of Egyptian
history except the names of the kings, until we come
to the great period of the Fourth Dynasty (B.C. 3766-3566).

Seneferu was the founder of this Dynasty. He conquered
the peninsula of Sinai, and worked the valuable mines
of copper and turquoise found in that country. His
son and successor, Khufu, better known as Kheops
(B.C. 3733-3700), was the builder of the Great Pyramid
at Gizeh (Fig. 87), which he erected for his tomb. The
king Kha-f-Rā (Kephren) (B.C. 3666-3600), built the
Second Pyramid, and his son, Men-kau-Rā (Mykerinos)
was the builder of the Third Pyramid. Men-kau-Rā was

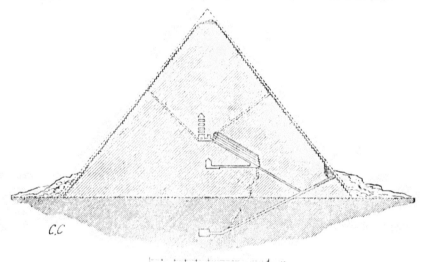

Fig. 88.—Section through the Great Pyramid of Kheops. (P. & C.)

a wise and humane sovereign, and it is recorded to his
honour, as an exceptional qualification, that "he did not
oppress his people." In this he was different to most of
the Pharaohs. His mummified remains are now in the
British Museum. The Sphinx, or man-headed lion, carved
out of the solid rock, is near the Great Pyramid, and is
supposed to be the work of a much earlier period (Fig. 91).

The Fifth Dynasty (B.C. 3566-3300) is not an important
one as far as art is concerned.

The Sixth (B.C. 3300-3100) was noted for the erection of

its pyramid tombs and for the religious texts that were inscribed on their interior walls.

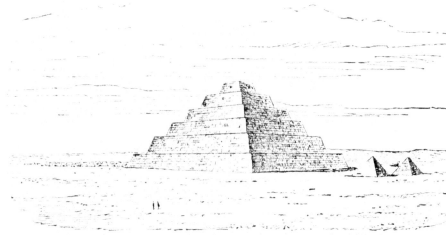

Fig. 89.—The Stepped Pyramid. (P. & C.) Supposed to be the most ancient building in Egypt.

From the Seventh to the Eleventh Dynasty (B.C. 3100-2466) is a period whose history is almost lost. It meant

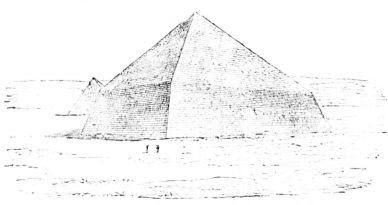

Fig. 90.—The Southern Pyramid of Dashour. (P. & C.)

to the Egyptians a period of more than six hundred years of tribal jealousies and fighting, at the end of which Egypt

was consolidated from north to south, and a powerful
Dynasty succeeded these internal struggles. The Twelfth
Dynasty was a brilliant one for the arts, and for great
works of engineering skill. The names of the Pharaohs
of this dynasty, Amenemhāt and Usertsen, are among the
most renowned in Egyptian history. Great temples were
restored or newly built at Thebes, Heliopolis, Tanis, and

Fig. 91.—The Great Sphinx. P. & C.)

Abydos. The great artificial lake, Mauur (Moeris of the
Greeks), or "great water," was constructed to receive the
surplus waters of the Nile, and to control its floods. The
Arabs call this lake "El-Fayyum," from another of its
Egyptian names "Phiom," the sea. It was completed in
the reign of Amenemhāt III. (B.C. 2300-2266). The same
king built the celebrated Labyrinth, the "Erpa-ro-hent,"
or "Temple at the entrance of the Lake," in which the
king himself was interred. His successor was the last
king of the Twelfth Dynasty. The Thirteenth and Four-

Fig. 92.—Colossi of Amenophis III. Statues of Memnon at Thebes. (P. & C.)

teenth Dynasties are dark periods in which the invasion of the Elamites and the Nomad tribes from Syria and Western Asia took place. The Fifteenth and Sixteenth Dynasties are the "Hyksos" dynasties. The Hyksos, or Shepherd Kings, were the chief of the above Nomad Asiatic tribes, and consequently usurpers of the native rule. A revolt took place in the reign of one of these kings of the Seventeenth Dynasty, and under Amāsis I., the founder of the Eighteenth Dynasty, the Shepherd Kings were finally driven out of Egypt.

About the end of the Hyksos rule the patriarch Joseph was sold into Egypt. King Nubti (B.C. 1750) is supposed to have been the Pharaoh of that time, and the Hyksos king, Apepa II., is supposed to have been the king that raised

Fig. 93.—Amenophis III. Presenting an Offering to Amen. (P. & C.)

Joseph to power. The explorer, M. Jacques de Morgan, expresses the opinion that the Shepherd Kings were the tomb-robbers, who, either from cupidity, or a wish to annihilate the last traces of a conquered race, pillaged every pyramid of its dead, and the treasures there concealed, for not a single pyramid has been found unviolated that was built before the Hyksos Dynasty. Thothmes III. (B.C. 1600) was a powerful and warlike king who compelled Assyria to pay him tribute. In the Eighteenth Dynasty, Egypt was more powerful than at any other period of her history. The great Temples of Thebes, Karnak, and Luxor were built during this dynasty.

A later monarch of this dynasty, Amenophis III., erected on the west of the Nile at Thebes two colossal statues of himself, that the Greeks have named the statues of Memnon, the fabled king of Egypt that was supposed to have been slain in the Trojan wars (Fig. 92).

Another king of this dynasty, Amenophis IV., made himself exceedingly notorious by trying to introduce a new religion, and for this he had his memory execrated, and was deeply cursed as a heretic by priests and people of the succeeding generations. It appears he had imbibed from his mother, Ti, who was an Assyrian princess, certain religious opinions which he determined to force on his own people. In order to do this he removed his capital from Thebes, where the national worship of the great god Amen was celebrated, to Khu-en-aten, the modern Tell-el-Amarna, which name he took for himself, and which means the " splendour of the sun-disk "; there he set up the sun-disk god, Aten (the radiant sun). The new religion, however, was obnoxious to the conservative Egyptians, and soon died out (Fig. 94).

The Nineteenth Dynasty (B.C. 1400-1200) was founded by Rameses I. He was a successful king, but his son Seti (Fig. 95) was a greater one, and had the reputation of being a great builder. It was he who built the great " Hall of Columns," at Karnak, which joins the pylon of Amenophis III. (Fig. 96).

He also built the temple at Kûrnah, and remains of his

work is seen at Abydos, Memphis, and Heliopolis. He
was succeeded by his famous son Rameses II., the Sesostris
of the Greeks, the supposed oppressor of the Israelites.
He was a very powerful monarch, and, from all accounts,

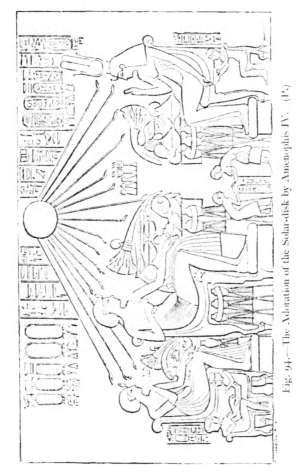

Fig. 94.—The Adoration of the Solar-disk by Amenophis IV. (P.)

in order to glorify himself in the eyes of posterity, did not
scruple to erase the names of former kings from off their
cartouches on their monuments and inscribe his own in
their place. That he has accomplished the end he had in

view by so doing there is not the slightest doubt, for no
monarch of Egypt is better known than he. But apart

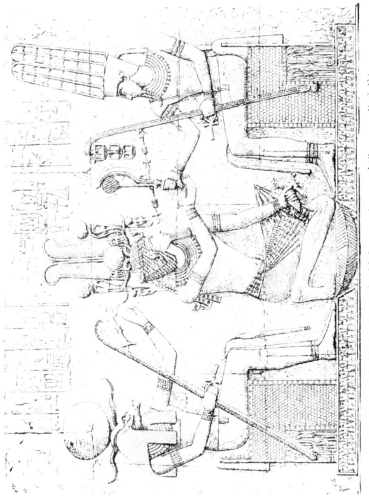

Fig. 95.—Seti with Attributes of Osiris between Amen and Choonm.   (P. & C.)

from this he was certainly a mighty chieftain, who "enriched the land with memorials of his name."

The greatest of his many battles he was always fighting) was fought with the Khita (Hittites), under the walls

of Kadesh, in the valley of the Orontes. His forces were

Fig. 96.—Entrance to the Hypostyle Hall of the Temple of Amen at Karnak. (M.)

almost defeated when by his personal valour he turned the tide of the battle and entirely routed the Khita Fig. 97).

The most famous building of his time is the rock-hewn

temple, the "Great Temple," that he built and dedicated
to Amen, Ptah, and Harmachis, which faces the Nile at
Ipsamboul, in Nubia.

On the façade of this temple are sculptured *in situ*
four seated colossal figures of Rameses, two on each side
of the doorway. From the soles of the feet to the top of

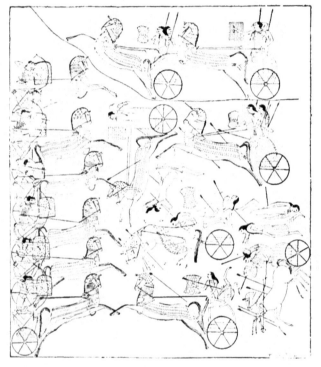

Fig. 97.—The Rout of the Khita ; Egyptians to the left, the Khita to the
right. (M.)

the pschent on the head measures sixty-five feet; they
are the largest statues in Egypt, and the workmanship is
careful in finish. Over the entrance is carved in relief on
the rock a colossal figure of the god Rā, and on either side
of it are single figures in low-relief of Rameses in the act
of adoration (Fig. 98).

Menephthah (B.C. 1300 — 1266) was the successor of
Rameses II. and his successor was Seti II. The latter

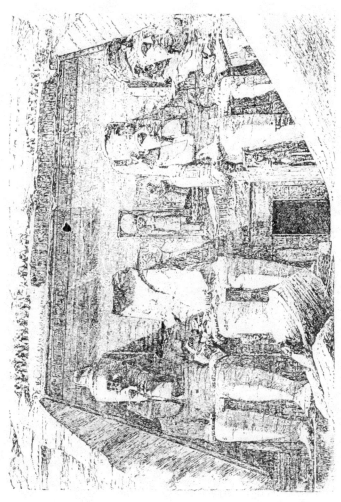

Fig. 98.— Façade of the Great Rock-cut Temple at Ipsambonl.

was the last king of the Middle Empire. With the commencement of the Twentieth Dynasty the New Empire

dates (about B.C. 1200—358). Towards the Twenty-second Dynasty (B.C. 966—776) Egypt began to pass into a state of dissolution. In the Twenty-fourth Dynasty (B.C.

Fig. 96.—Principal Hall in the Great Temple. (H.; P. & C.)

733—700) she was at the mercy of Assyria on the north and Ethiopia on the south. In 672 B.C. the Assyrian King Esarhaddon invaded Egypt and occupied the whole

of the Delta, afterwards capturing Memphis and Thebes,
which he pillaged. The Assyrian king died suddenly, and
Taharka, a native usurper, succeeded in driving out the
Assyrians, but soon after Egypt was again conquered by

Fig. 100.—Portrait of Rameses II. (Louvre; P. & C.)

Ashurbanipal, a powerful Assyrian King (B.C. 666). The
Assyrians, however, after a short time of occupation with-
drew from Egypt, owing to their troubles at home with
the Medes, who were laying siege to Nineveh, and Egypt

again revived. Under Amāsis the country enjoyed peace
for about forty years (P.C. 572—528). The Egyptians possessed a fleet at this time with which they advanced to the
Phœnician coast and took the city of Sidon, and also
annexed the island of Cyprus to Egyptian rule.

Egypt submitted to the Persian army under Cambyses
in B.C. 527, and was for more than one hundred years afterwards a mere vassal of Persia. The Twenty-seventh
Dynasty (B.C. 527—424) was composed solely of Persian
kings. A successful revolt broke out in the last Persian
king's reign, Darius II., when Egypt was free once more.

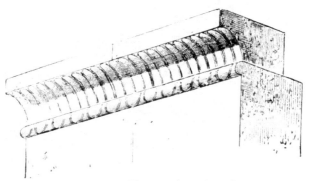

Fig. 101.—The Egyptian "Gorge."

Amenrut was the only king of the Twenty-eighth Dynasty,
and after the Twenty-ninth and Thirtieth Dynasties were
ended, the latter, by the conquest of Egypt once more by
the Persians under Artaxerxes III. (B.C. 340), we find the
country under Persian rule for the space of eight years.
About this time the Persian monarch was defeated by
Alexander the Great, which brought Egypt under the
Greek rule. At the death of Alexander Egypt was
governed by the Macedonian kings, the Ptolemies, from
330 to 30 B.C. After the Roman wars and the death of
Cleopatra, Egypt found itself a Roman province.

In A.D. 638 the Arabs under Omar conquered the country,

and it was ruled by them till 1517, when it passed into the hands of the Turks.

The Pyramids of Egypt have doubtless derived their

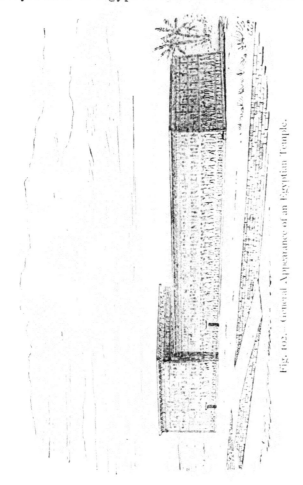

Fig. 102.—General Appearance of an Egyptian Temple.

shape from the prehistoric grave mounds. Although elaborately and ingeniously contrived for the concealment of the remains of the kings, and are stupendous monuments of building skill, they are not examples of architecture in the true sense of the word. Perhaps the earliest examples

of Egyptian architecture, properly speaking, are seen in the
ancient shrines, with sloping walls and flat roof, and having the peculiar cavetto cornice moulding called the

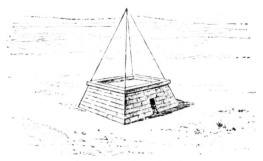

Fig. 103.—Square Building.

Egyptian "Gorge" (Figs. 101 and 109). Horizontality is
the great feature of Egyptian architecture, which is typically expressed by the illustration Fig. 102, an ideal
generalisation of an Egyptian temple.

As hardly any, or no, rain falls in most parts of Egypt,

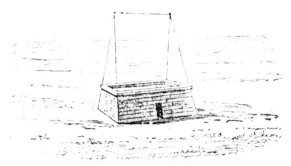

Fig. 104.—Oblong Building.

a sloping roof was not a necessity. The external walls in
the case of a square building are in the form of a trape-
zium, making the whole edifice of the shape of a truncated
pyramid, and pyramid-like in either the square or rectan-
gular-planned buildings (Figs. 103 and 104), except when

the end walls are vertical (Fig. 104), then it tends toward the ridge-form.

In regard to the scarcity of voids and narrow sloping doorways, the similarity in Egyptian buildings of every kind is very striking (Fig. 105). This absence of voids gives a dark and gloomy character to the buildings, when compared with the architecture of other countries. The horizontal element and solidity of construction impart a look of powerful strength and of deep repose to the Egyptian temple. Even the tall and slender obelisks placed in front of the mighty pylons have little, if any, effect in

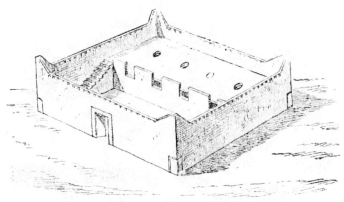

Fig. 105.—Model of an Egyptian House.   (P. & C.)

removing the horizontal appearance of the whole building We give the ground plan, perspective view, and front elevation of the great Temple of Luxor, as a typical illustration of an Egyptian temple from restorations by Chipiez (Figs. 106, 107, and 108). Its construction is described by Champollion as the "Architecture of giants."

This double-temple was the work of two kings. From the second pylon to the further end of the Temple is the portion built first, by the King Amenophis III. The other portion, from first to the second pylon, is the part built by

Rameses II. The sanctuary
is placed in the centre of a
hall, surrounded by small
chambers. It has two doors,
one at either end, and on the
axis of the building it has
a vestibule in front and a
hall beyond, supported by
twelve columns. Another
hall in front of the *Naos* (or
interior apartment) is supported by thirty-two lofty
columns. In front of this
again is a large square open
court. This court is con-
nected to the larger front
peristylar court by a grand
and lofty gallery, similar to
a hypostyle hall. It is
176 ft. long, enclosed and
covered, and richly deco-
rated like the hypostyle hall
at Karnak (Fig. 96). Four
colossal seated statues are
in front of the first pylon,
and two obelisks, one on
each side of the door-way.
Four large flagstaffs and a
double row of sphinxes in
front of the temple complete
the accessories to this great
edifice. The whole building
and obelisks were covered
over with bas-reliefs and
inscriptions.

The typical Egyptian
columns or supports are of

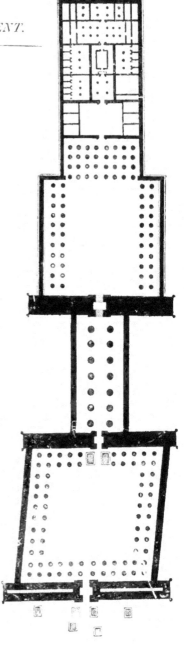

Fig. 106.—Plan of the Temple of Luxor.
(P. & C.)

Fig. 107.— Bird's-eye View of Luxor, as restored by Chipiez. (P. & C.)

Fig. 101.—Principal Façade of the Temple of Luxor, restored by Chipiez. (B. & C.)

Fig. 109.—Column of Thothmes III.; from the Ambulatory of Thothmes at
Karnak. (P. & C.)

two distinct and well-marked kinds, the *lotus-headed* and the campaniform or bell-shaped. The former is so called

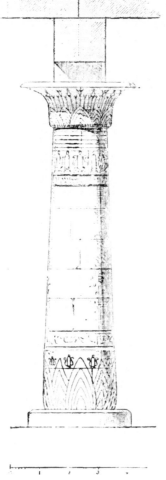

from its resemblance to a closed lotus-bud (Fig. 109), and the latter from its resemblance to a bell with the mouth uppermost (Fig. 110). An earlier and simpler form of column or support is the quadrangular pier Fig. 111), and the next development is the tapering quadrangular pier Fig. 112, both undecorated. Next we have the pier with a capital which, in profile, is a simple cavetto or " gorge," and square abacus (Fig. 113).

Between the abacus and the entablature or beam is

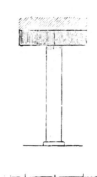

Fig. 110.— Column of the Hypostyle Hall of the Ramesseum ; from Horeau. P. & C.)

Fig. 111.—Quadrangular Pier (P. & C.)

a square thickness of stone ; this is the great defect in the Egyptian orders, and distinguishes the latter from the

Greek orders. This space between the abacus and the architrave is bad, both from a scientific and artistic point of view. It robs the capital of its legitimate appearance as a supporting member. This pier, with capital and the Hathoric pier (Fig. 114, with the head of the goddess Hathor, are both decorated.

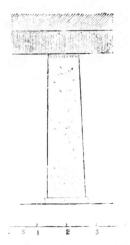

We next come to the octagonal (Fig. 115), and the sixteen-sided pillars (Fig. 116, which are almost Greek in their classic simplicity; the latter is fluted. All forms of Egyptian columns have either square slabs or circular discs as bases, on which the column rests. The two latter mentioned pillars are

Fig. 112.—Tapering Quadrangular Pier. (P. & C.)

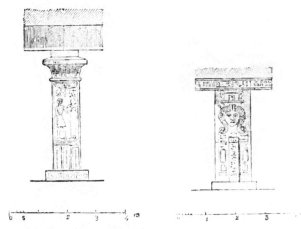

Fig. 113.—Pier with Capital. (P. & C.)   Fig. 114.—Hathoric Pier. (P. & C.)

exceptional, and therefore not typical Egyptian, in having the abacus directly under the architrave; the sixteen-sided

pillar is especially Doric-like in this respect, and also in
its fluted shaft (Fig. 116).

The supports known as "Osiride" pillars are chiefly of
the date of the Nineteenth Dynasty. They have a kind of
analogy to the caryatid Grecian pillars, but are unlike
them in respect that they do not support the entablature,

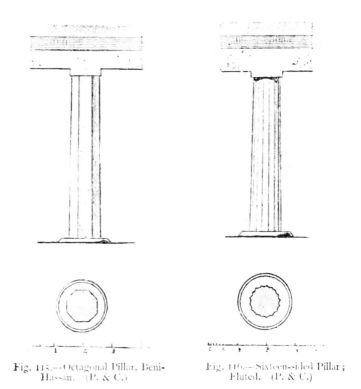

Fig. 115.—Octagonal Pillar, Beni-
Hassan.   (P. & C.)

Fig. 116.— Sixteen-sided Pillar;
Fluted.   (P. & C.)

as they are only placed in front of the quadrangular supporting pier for purposes of decoration, and are usually
meant as representations of the kings who erected the
temples they decorate, with a head-dress ornament consisting of the attributes of Osiris (Fig. 117).

Another variety of column has a fanciful combination of
floral forms for its capital (Fig. 118). This and others of

fanciful design are from the bas-reliefs and wall-paintings, and remind us of similar creations of the artist's pencil, as seen in the Pompeian wall decorations.

The upper parts of the capital are developments from

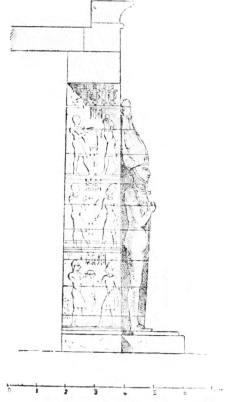

Fig. 117.—Osiride Pillar from Medinet-Abou. (P. & C.)

the calyx of the lotus, with the sepals curled outwards, and look very much like the first notions of the Greek Ionic capital, as indeed we shall find the Ionic volute to be a development of the lotus calyx more than anything else. An example of the faggot-shaped column, with its base, lotus-capital, and entablature, is given at Fig. 109.

The ornamental parts of this column were painted in bright yellow and blue, and, as a rule, the sculptured ornament of the Egyptian columns, architrave, and cornices were relieved by the painter in bright colours.

The illustration at Fig. 119 is that of the palm-shaped capital from Sesebi. This type of capital is a frank imitation of a bunch of palm-leaves tied by the circular bands around the top of a column. A later development of the palm capital shows the bell shape with a more complicated decoration,

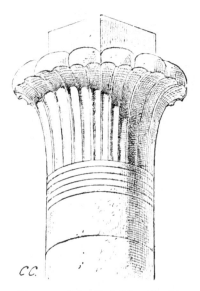

Fig. 118.—Column from Bas-
Relief. (P. & C.)

Fig. 119.—Palm-Capital from Sesebi.
(P. & C.)

and has the Hathor-headed abacus, surmounted by a *Naos* (Fig. 120)

EGYPTIAN ORNAMENT AND INDUSTRIAL ART.

A great part of Egyptian ornament and decoration is composed of symbolic forms, the remainder is made up of geometrical ornament, such as checkers, meanders, frets, rosettes, diapers of lotus and other forms. Natural forms of flowers and foliage were not copied direct, but only used in shape of geometric abstractions, and their arrangement as diapers in surface decoration was derived, in the first instance, from the older arts of weaving and matting. The old Egyptians were skilled in weaving both plain and figured fabrics, chiefly from flax and hemp fibre. The lotus form was pre-eminently the leading motive in Egyptian floral ornament. The papyrus (from which our word paper is derived) and the palm are next in importance as motives from which Egyptian ornament is derived.

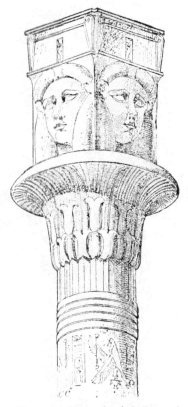

Fig. 120. – Hathor-headed Campaniform Capitals, Temple of Nectanebo, at Philæ. (P. & C.)

The lotus-plant (*Nymphæa nelumbo*), the variety in which the leaves grow up out of the water and do not lie on its surface, is shown at Fig. 121, and drawings, evidently from nature, at Fig. 122, from the tomb of Ptah-Hotep.

The lotus flower in ornament may be seen in the ceiling

decorations from tombs at Fig. 123, Nos. 3 and 5; at Figs. 118, 124; and in the painted frieze from Thebes (Fig. 125), where the similarity between this and the Assyrian lotus, fir-cone and daisy may be noticed (see Fig. 167).

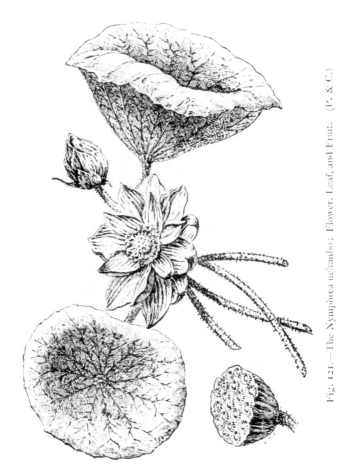

Fig. 121.—The Nymphœa nelumbo; Flower, Leaf, and Fruit. (P. & C.)

The bi-lateral rendering of the lotus plant is not common in Egyptian ornament, though it is the oldest form of the lotus known, as it occurs on the prehistoric pottery of Koptos, and on tombs of the Fourth Dynasty (Fig. 126), and earlier. Two lotus flowers are here seen tied together; the general outline of the flower is only rendered which would enclose the sepals and petals when seen in a side view.

The lotus flower and bud alternating in a border ornament may be regarded as the prototype of the Greek palmate borders. We are inclined to believe in Professor Goodyear's theory, that the egg and tongue decoration on the Greek ovolo moulding is nothing more than a disrupted lotus and bud ornament developed in transition through

Fig. 122.— Drawings of the Lotus from the Tomb of Ptah-Hotep. (P. & C.)

the Rhodian pottery decoration. The shells and the tongue were originally the lotus calyx, and the egg or pebble the lotus bud.

Other plants, as the thistle, convolvulus, daisy, vines, and grapes, &c., were used very much in decoration, especially during the Akhenaten period (Eighteenth and Nineteenth Dynasties), when the decoration was of a florid kind. The papyrus is seen in the ceiling ornament Fig. 123, No 6, at Fig. 127, and on the perfume spoon of carved wood (Fig. 151. The ceiling decorations (Fig. 123), from the Theban tombs, show the fine sense and feeling the Egyptians had for the appropriate decoration of flat

Fig. 123.—Specimens of Ceiling Decoration at Thebes; from Prisse. (P. & C.)   92

surfaces, and the judicious balance maintained in the
contrasting units of the ornament.

Fig. 124.—Lotus and Water Ornament.

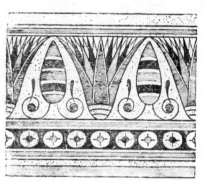

Fig. 125.—Painted Border; from Thebes,
after Prisse. (P. & C.)

In animal forms found in Egyptian decoration there are
a few distinct and typical varieties, that have been used

Fig. 126.—Flattened Form of Lotus-leaf Ornament; Front View and
Section I. (P. & C.)

times without number, both in painting and in carving in
the round, and in the bas-reliefs of stone, wood, and in

gold, silver, ivory, and bronze.   Among the most frequent
is the vulture, with outstretched wings, having sacred
symbols in his claws.   It has been used appropriately in

Fig. 127.—Hunting in a Marsh: from a Bas-Relief in the Tomb of Ti.   P. & C.

this form as ceiling decoration in the great temples at
Thebes, on a blue ground diapered with golden stars; the
ceilings thus are symbolic representations of the heavens
at night (Fig. 128).

Similar outstretched wings have been added to the scarabs or sacred beetles. These winged scarabs, together with similar winged-globe and uræus creations, have been

Fig. 128.—Vultures on a Ceiling. (P. & C.)

used as ceiling decorations in tombs and on mummy-cases, and sometimes the goddess Isis, or Nepththys, was furnished with these wings as guardian of the tomb (Figs. 129 and 130).

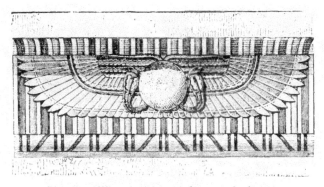

Fig. 129.—Winged-Globe with Uræus. (P. & C.)

The Uræus and winged-globe was a favourite decoration for cornices and for heads of doorways (Fig. 108). The colouring of the winged-globe decoration was generally, in the case of the globe, a red colour, as the emblem of the sun; the wings green, and the striped ground behind the figure was painted in alternating stripes of red, blue, and white, which produced an effective arrangement of colour.

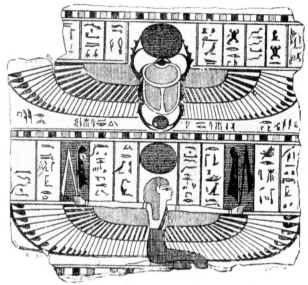

Fig. 130.— Painting on Mummy-Case. (P. & C.)

Fig. 131.— Hunting in the Desert. M.

The Egyptians excelled in the drawing of animals and birds in outline, and in bas-relief carvings of them, some examples of which are given at Figs. 131, 132, 133.

Many chimerical animals or monsters were used in Egyptian decoration, as sphinxes, or imaginary animals of the desert, which were really fanciful creations of the artist's pencil (Figs. 134, 135, 136, 137).

Their representations of lions always have an expression of dignity, though more mild in aspect than the Assyrian lion in art (Fig. 138).

Pottery, glass, and earthenware were manufactured in Egypt from the earliest times. The country was well supplied with good potter's clay; bricks were made and dried in the sun, not burned, and were used very much in

Fig. 132.—Antelope and Papyrus. (P. & C.)

building. The common pottery was unglazed, and their decorated pottery was in glazed earthenware, but not so highly decorated as many other objects of industrial art. Fig. 139 is a common pitcher of fairly good form, in red earth. The decoration on the enamelled earthenware dish (Fig. 140) is composed of bouquets of lotus flowers; and that on the larger basin or bowl is a design of lotus and mystic signs (Fig. 141). The three objects are in the British Museum.

Rosettes and plaques have been found enamelled in colours, and probably used for floor or wall tiles. The doorway to the stepped pyramid at Sakkarah is decorated with rows of convex-shaped rectangular plaques of

enamelled earthenware of a greenish-blue glaze. Some
are black in colour.

The Egyptians were particularly skilful in glass making,

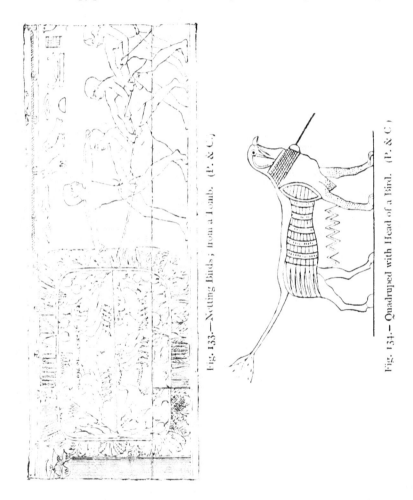

Fig. 133.—Netting Birds; from a Tomb. (P. & C.)

Fig. 134.—Quadruped with Head of a Bird. (P. & C.)

but they never produced quite a clear glass; it was always
slightly opaque, but generally bright and rich in colour.
Vases, cups, pateræ, statuettes, necklaces, goblets, brace-
lets, and, above all, enormous quantities of beads, which

Fig. 135.—Sphinx or Man-Headed Lion, in Black Granite, from Tanis. (P. & C.)

they used to make a network of to cover their dead. Great quantities of glass objects were exported in trade with the Phœnicians.

The Venetians during the Middle Ages imported soda

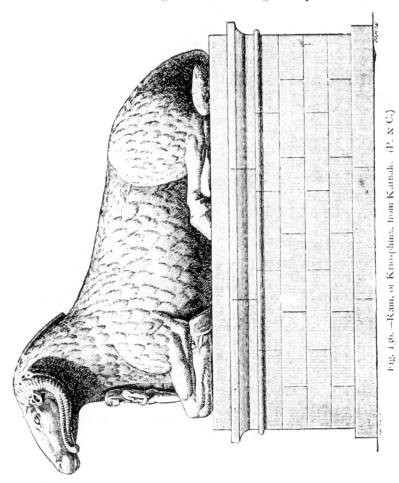

Fig. 136.—Ram, or Knoephius, from Karnak. (P. & C.)

in large quantities from Alexandria, for purposes of glass making, the soda of Egypt being famed for this purpose, as it was prepared from the many marsh-loving plants that grew luxuriantly in the Delta.

Gold had always been more plentiful than silver in ancient Egypt. It was found in the hills of Ethiopia, but silver had to be imported from Asia. This accounts for

Fig. 137.—Sphinx with Human Hands: Bas-Relief from Prisse. (P. & C.)

the great quantities of gold objects and ornaments that have been found in the tombs, and the scarcity of silver ornaments. The Egyptian goldsmiths made all kinds of

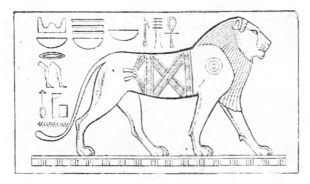

Fig. 138.—Lion from a Theban Bas-Relief. (P. & C.)

vessels and personal jewellery in gold, set with lapis lazuli and other precious stones. We shall have to be content with giving, as examples of this art, the famous pectoral

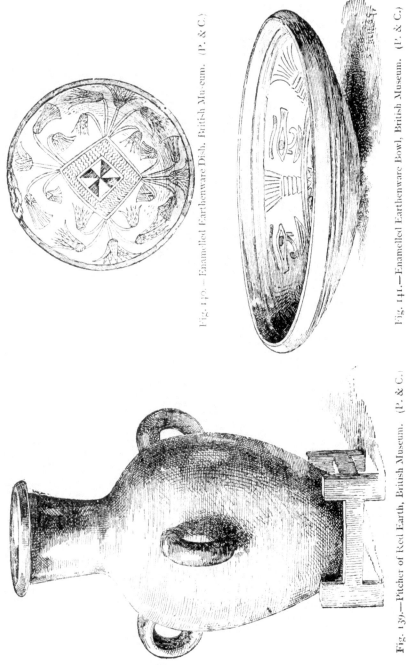

Fig. 139.—Enamelled Earthenware Dish, British Museum. (P. & C.)

Fig. 141.—Enamelled Earthenware Bowl, British Museum. (P. & C.)

Fig. 139.—Pitcher of Red Earth, British Museum. (P. & C.)

of Kha-em-uas, son of Rameses II. (Fig. 142), and the
golden hawk (Fig. 143).

The former is a splendid and unique specimen of a

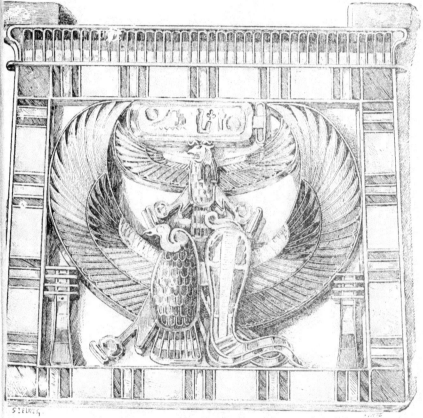

Fig. 142.—Pectoral: Actual Size. (P. & C.)

pectoral, or breast ornament for the dead. These pectorals
have been found in great numbers, made of wood, metal,
and earthenware. The general shape is that of a *naos*, or

little temple. The Kha-em-uas pectoral is made of gold inlaid with lapis lazuli, and is thus described by M. Pierret:

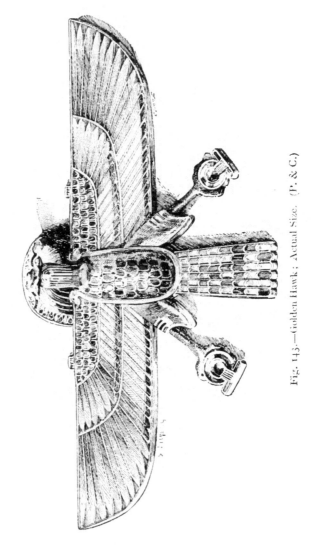

Fig. 143.—Golden Hawk: Actual Size. (P. & C.)

"Jewel in the form of a naos, in which a vulture and an uræus are placed side by side: above them floats a hawk

Fig. 144.—Fragment of an Ivory Castanet, Louvre.

with extended wings, in his claws are seals, emblems of
eternity.   Under the frieze of the naos an oval, with the
prenomen of Rameses II., is introduced.   Two *tet* (or *dad*,
symbol of stability) are placed in the lower angles of the
frame."   The golden hawk is a similar kind of ornament,
with crescent wings and seals in its claws, emblems of

Fig. 145.—Ivory Plaque; Late Work. (P. & C.)

reproduction and eternity.   The workmanship in these
articles looks like that of *cloisonné* enamels, but they are
not enamels.   The thin ribs of gold that surround the
lapis lazuli stones in the pectoral and hawk are *cloisons*,
but the stones are cut to fit into the spaces accurately, and
are therefore inlaid, while in the true enamels the enamel

is put in the cells and fused to the metal by fire afterwards.
Enamelling as known to the Chinese was not practised in
Egypt.

As ivory could be obtained from Ethiopia in great quantities, it was natural that the Egyptians would make good
use of it. It was a favourite material with the sculptors,

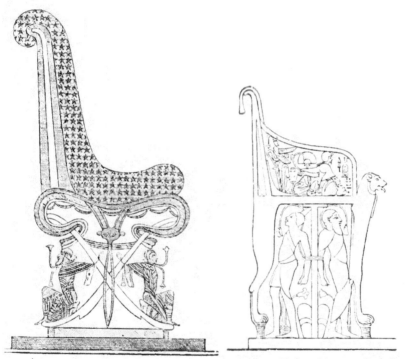

Fig. 146.—Egyptian Chair. (P. & C.)   Fig. 147.—Chair or Throne. (P. & C.)

and many fine examples of ivory carvings and incised
work have been found in the tombs. The incised outlines
on the ivory were usually filled in with black (Figs. 144
and 145).

Gold, silver, ivory, and ebony were worked in usually by
the same Egyptian artist, as we learn from an inscription
on a stele of Iritesen, an Egyptian sculptor, thus translated

by Maspero: "Ah! there is no one excels at this work except myself, and the eldest of my legitimate sons. God

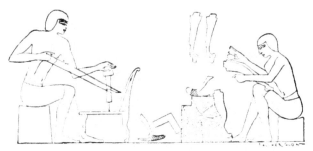

Fig. 148.— The Carpenters Making Chairs.   M.)

decided that he should excel, and I have seen the perfection of his handiwork as an artist, as the chief of those

Fig. 149.—Coffer in Wood.   P. & C.)

who work in precious stones, in gold, silver, ivory, and ebony."

Judging from the small remains left to us, the furniture and woodwork of the Egyptians must have been of an excellent description. We have evidence also of this in

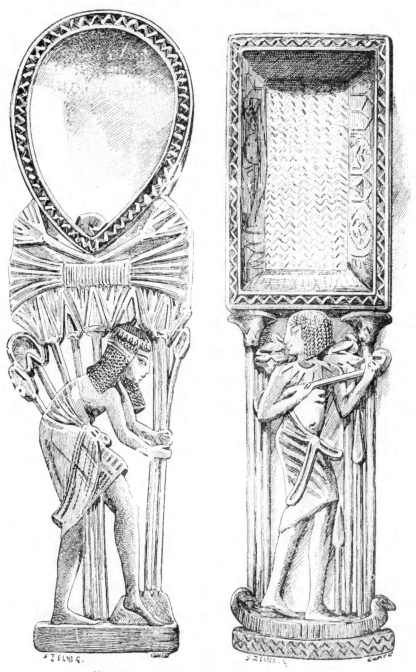

Figs. 150-51.—Perfume Spoons, Louvre. (P. & C.)

the wall paintings and bas-reliefs that give representations
of tables, chairs, and couches.   Some of the chairs or
thrones are of special beauty (Figs. 146 and 147).   A

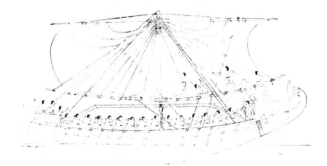

Fig. 152.—An Egyptian Ship, Sailing and Rowing.   (M.)

carpenter's shop showing the workmen making chairs is
seen at Fig. 148, and a coffer (Fig. 149). The feet of chairs
and thrones were usually imitated from those of animals.

Fig. 153.—The River Transport of a Mummy from Maspero.

In wood-carving nothing could be daintier than the
perfume spoons with figures and water plants decoratively
treated (Figs. 150, 151).

The Egyptian ships were singularly beautiful in their outlines, with their prows and sterns ending usually in a metal stalk and carved lotus flower or ram's head (Figs. 152, 153). The "bari," or sacred boat which transported the dead, decorated at each end with the carved metal lotus, and pavilion or chapel in the centre, with its freight of the mummy and the mourners (Fig. 152), is represented as it sails off towards Abydos, the city of the dead, to the west of Thebes, and the crowds of friends on the banks of the river will salute the dead, saying : " In peace, in peace towards Abydos ! Descend in peace towards Abydos, towards the Western Sea ! "

CHAPTER VIII.

THE Chaldeans or Babylonians and the Assyrians came from one great stock, the Assyrians being mostly colonists from Babylonia. The original inhabitants of Chaldea spoke a Semitic dialect. At an early date Eastern Chaldea was invaded by the Sumerians or Accadians, a Turanian race which is supposed to have come from the plateau of Central Asia. The two languages were used side by side, the Semitic as the common tongue, and the Accadian as a literary language. The earliest known king of Chaldea was named Eannadu (B.C. 4500). The Chaldeans advanced slowly along the Tigris and pushed their kingdom towards Assyria in the north, where they built the cities of Ashur (Kal'at Sherkât), Calah (Nimroud), and Ninua (Nineveh).

The northern portion of the Chaldeo-Assyrian empire asserted its independence about 1700 B.C., and Assyria became a separate kingdom. From B.C. 1275, when Tukulti-Adar I., the Assyrian king, conquered Babylonia, down to the destruction of Nineveh, B.C. 609, the Chaldean kingdom took a place of secondary importance, while Assyria became the greatest power of Western Asia.

Tiglath-Pileser I. (B.C. 1100), and Ashur-nasir-pal (B.C. 885), were amongst the greatest kings of Assyria. The latter was a great builder. He built the great palace at Calah (Nimroud), the place to which he removed his seat of government from Ashur. Assyrian art reached a high state of development in his reign. His son and

successor, Shalmaneser II. (B.C. 860-825) was no less
powerful; he extended his kingdom by wars from the
Persian Gulf to the Armenian mountains, and from Media
to the Mediterranean. Jehu, King of Israel, sent him
tribute. After his death Assyria declined and shrank
within its borders, but under Tiglath-Pileser III. regained
its lost ground again (B.C. 745). Sargon, the "Son of no
one" (B.C. 722-705, usurps the throne, makes great wars,
is the first King of Assyria that comes in contact with the
Egyptians. He built the great palace at Khorsabad,
which in late years has been excavated. Sennacherib, his
son, succeeded him, whose wars with Hezekiah, King
of Judah, are recorded in the Bible in the Book of Kings.
He built a great palace at Nineveh, many of the wall
slabs of which are now in the British Museum.

The death of the succeeding monarch, Esarhaddon, took
place before he had completed his great palace at Calah
(Nimroud). Another palace supposed to be his has lately
been excavated at Nineveh. It lies buried under the mound
of Nebi Yunus. The Assyrian kings were great builders
of palaces. Each one, it appears, thought it his duty
either to add a large portion to a palace of his predecessor,
or to build a new one for himself. Ashur-bani-pal, who
reigned for forty-two years (B.C. 668-626), was one of the
most powerful and most cruel of all the Assyrian
monarchs. His victory over the Elamites is depicted
on the sculptured slabs that enrich the Ninevite gallery of
the British Museum. At his death the Assyrian power
was broken up, partly by the Scythian hordes that swept
over that part of Asia, and partly by the Medes. Nineveh
was besieged by Cyaxares of Media, and by Nabopolassar,
an Assyrian general who held command in Babylonia. It
was at length captured and destroyed B.C. 609). The
whole empire was then divided between the Medes and the
Babylonians. The new Babylonian empire lasted seventy
years, and in the reign of its last king, Nabonidus, when
under the command of Belshazzar, his son, Babylon was

captured by Cyrus of Persia (B.C. 539). From this time
until its subjugation by Alexander the Great Babylon was
under the Persians.

The religion of the Chaldeo-Assyrian nation was the
worship of the sun, moon, stars, and the various powers
of nature. Their chief gods were Shamash, the sun; Sin,
the moon; Marduk, a sun-god, the carrier of prayers from
earth to heaven; Anum, the sky god; Bel, the god of the

Fig. 154.—A Winged Bull, Assyria. (M.)

earth; and Ea, the god of great knowledge: the last three
were the Trinity. Other gods were Dagon, the fish-god;
Ishtar, their Venus; Nabu, their Mercury and scribe of the
gods; Rammánu, the god of wind and thunder; and Negral,
the god of war and hunting.

The Assyrian and Babylonian people have a proverbial
name for being a warlike and cruel race, in opposition to
their contemporaries, the more peaceful and gentle Egyp-

tians. At the same time they have the reputation of being highly skilled in arts and sciences.

Fig. 155.-- Demons, from the Palace of Assurbanipal, British Museum. (P. & C.)

The greatness of the Chaldeans in astronomy, in astrology, and as wise men generally, is too well known to be repeated. Their skill in the arts of building, sculpture, in the use of metals, in pottery, tiles, gem cutting, painting, embroidery and weaving, excites our wonder and admiration.

The art of the Assyrians is intensely earnest and full of realism, vigorous in the highest degree, and true art of its kind. It is the art of a people who were brave and powerful, and of princes that were despotic and stern. The keynote of their art was *force*, whether displayed in its physical and realistic aspects, in the sculptural representations of ferocious animals, as their lions and dogs, or embodied in their mysterious and wonderful creations

of human-headed bulls, and other monsters and demons (Figs. 154, 155), or in the haughty self-consciousness of strength and power, with which their sculptors sought to invest the representations of the monarchs going forth to battle or to the lion hunt (Fig. 163); everywhere, in the

Fig. 156.—A Griffon in the Egyptian Style. (M.)

higher aspects of Assyrian art, physical force, or personal force of will, is the culminating point of expression aimed at in all their efforts.

The sculptured lion of the Egyptians is *couchant*, half slumbering; the Assyrian lion is *rampant* and roaring for his prey. The simile may be used to illustrate the characteristic difference of the Art of both countries. The Assyrian made his art minister to his worldly uses and delights, the Egyptian lavished his on the tomb and for the hereafter.

The Assyrian religion and the Chaldean magicians' and astrologers' exposition of its mysteries, doubtless gave the subject-matter for the creation of those strange combinations of chimeras, monsters, and bi-form deities that are so common in Assyrian art.

The griffons and other curious hybrid creatures of the

Middle Ages, and those that adorn the Gothic buildings of

Fig. 157.—Eagle-headed Divinity from Nimroud, with the Sacred Tree. (P. & C.)

our own days, can be traced to their birthplace in Assyrian art.

The great god of the Assyrians was named Assur, the

all-powerful god of battles. In his name all kinds of cruelty and torture were practised on heretics and apostates, and in his name, and to extend his kingdom of Assyria,

Fig. 158. –Figure of a Goddess in Act of Adoration, British Museum. (P. & C.)

the Ninevite kings found their excuses to make war with nations far and near. He seems to have been a later creation of the Assyrian gods, but became supreme as

Nineveh rose in power. He was supposed to have descended from Sin, the moon-god. The winged-globe,

Fig. 159.—The Winged Globe with the Figure of a God. (P. & C.)

with the god in the centre holding the bow and arrow, or thunder-bolt (Fig. 159), is by some thought to be a representation of Assur. A similar figure is seen at the

Fig. 160.—The Winged Globe; from Layard. (P. & C.)

top of the Assyrian standard, as the "Director of Armies" (Fig. 161). This figure in the centre of the ring or solar disk, who is evidently divine, by reason of his feathered

lower garment, and his wings that raise him in mid-air,
above all humanity, is quite likely to be the original type
of the later Persian supreme god, Athurâ-Mazda (see
Fig. 243), and the emblematic symbol of his divinity is
quite likely to have been designed and adapted from the
winged disk or "globe" of the Egyptians.

Fig. 161.-- The Assyrian Standard.
(P. & C.)

Fig. 162.—Dagon, the Fish-God.
(P. & C.)

The winged globe (Fig. 160) of the Assyrians is an imitation of that of Egypt; this emblem having found its
way into Assyria on many carvings in ivory and on
articles in bronze, carried hither by the trading Phœnicians
from Egypt, and the emblem in question was, according to
Perrot, appropriated by the Assyrians.

Fig. 163.— Assurbanipal Attacked by Lions, British Museum. (P. & C.)

In their ornament and decoration they were more free and natural than the Egyptians, and the execution was careful and refined, as witnessed by their bronze bowls, gem-engraving, and the patterns on the enamelled bricks.

The bronze gates from Balâwât in the British Museum are examples of highly skilful repoussé work. Their palaces must have presented a gorgeous and glittering appearance in their rich colouring and enamelled brilliancy. Although not a single specimen of Assyrian weaving has been discovered, we have abundant and sufficient evidence from the sculptured patterns of textiles and embroideries on the kings' robes and wall decorations that both weaving and embroidery must have been one of their most glorious arts.

The Asiatic love of colour would lead us to suppose that these embroideries were excessively rich in colour (Figs. 162A, 163A, 164, 165) as they were in design.

The details of this embroidery design (Fig. 162A) are well drawn, and the design is full of rich variety without heaviness or too much crowding. The king is seen twice represented in the circle doing homage to the sacred tree and to the winged disk ; and in other places he is between two genii or deities ; combats of lions and bulls, palmate borders, fir-cones, and spirals, with bands that divide the work in varied spaces, complete these rich designs in embroidery, which are among the very finest efforts of Assyrian decorative art.

Details of embroidery patterns are shown at Figs. 164, 165.

The sills or thresholds of the doors of the palaces were sometimes sculptured in low relief on large slabs of alabaster stone. The design is evidently copied from an embroidered carpet; perhaps the central part of the one given (Fig. 166) is a copy from a fabric woven in the loom, and the border, enlarged at Fig. 167, would have its original in embroidery.

The figure of the plan and elevation of part of a Chal-

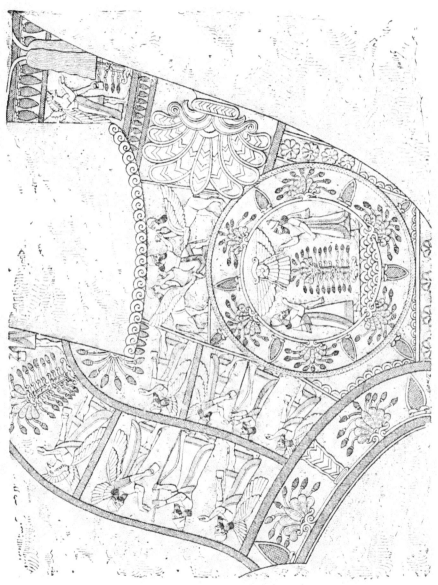

Fig. 162A.—Embroidery upon a Royal Mantle; from Layard. (P. & C.)

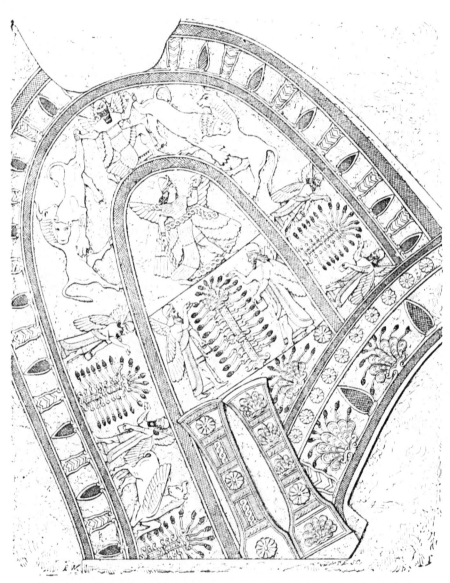

Fig. 163A.—Embroidery on the upper part of a Royal Mantle; from Layard.   P. & C.)

dean façade in enamelled bricks, from Warka, is decorated with patterns that, no doubt, had their origin in weaving and matting (Fig. 168). The surface of this façade is

Fig. 164.—Detail of Embroidery; from Layard. (P. & C.)

composed of terra-cotta cones, with their bases turned outwards. These bases were previously dipped in enamelled

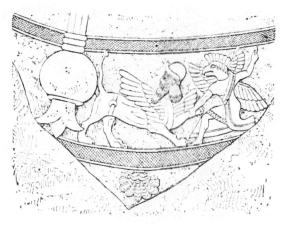

Fig. 165.—Detail of Embroidery; from Layard. (P. & C.)

colours before they were inserted into the clay cement; so they form a kind of terra-cotta mosaic work (*Loftus*).

The land of Chaldea was devoid of stone for building

purposes, but extremely rich in immense banks of clay, which was used for brick making from the earliest times in Chaldea. The Chaldean brick is rather more than one

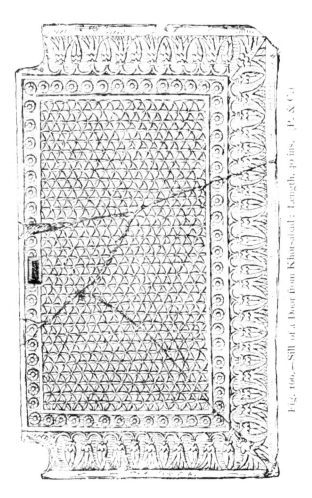

Fig. 166.—Sill of a Door from Khorsabad ; Length, 40 ins. (P. & C.)

English foot square, and about four inches in thickness; of a dark red colour to light yellow. Nearly all of them have an inscription with the name of the king, &c. (Fig. 169).

The brick from Erech, or ancient Warka, gives a good idea of one of the oldest forms of Chaldean writing known (Fig. 170). It consists of an abridgment of the representation of natural objects, as all alphabets in their original state were merely pictures or pictographs. This inscription shows the stage of conventional signs or

Fig. 167.—Fragment of Border of Fig. 166 ; from a Threshold of Khorsabad. (P. & C.)

ideographic writing before it underwent the change into the *cuneiform*, or wedge-shaped writing of the Assyrians.

Some of the bricks were made wedge-shaped, for use in the building of arches and vaults. The common bricks were sometimes used in the crude state, or unburnt, and burnt. Enamelled bricks were greatly used in Chaldea, but the clay of which they were made was softer and more friable. This was used purposely, so that the enamel would sink deeper into the soft material, and thereby make a more lasting surface protection.

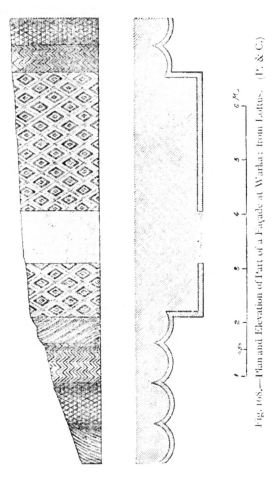

Fig. 108.—Plan and Elevation of Part of a Façade at Warka: from Lottus.   (P. & C.)

Assyria copied most of her art and sciences from her older sister in civilisation, and had the advantage over Chaldea in a good supply of building stone, that formed the substructural bed for the clay deposits. This was a sulphate of chalk known as alabaster, grey in colour, and easy to work. The great wall slabs used for the bas-

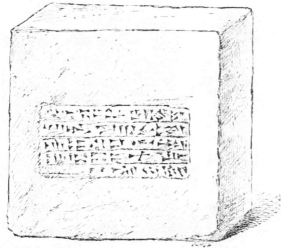

Fig. 169.—Babylonian Brick, 16 ins. square, 4 ins. thick. (P. & C.)

reliefs and the winged bulls and other statuary, were carved out of this material; but the Assyrians used bricks for the

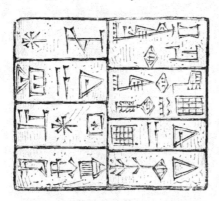

Fig. 170.—Brick from Frech. (P. & C.)

main structure of their buildings, like the Chaldeans. Timber was scarce in Assyria, but was used very much

in the palaces. It was brought from the mountains of
Upper Mesopotamia, on the left bank of the Tigris, and,
later, cedar and other woods were transported from the
forests of Lebanon for the beams of the palaces and
temples. All kinds of metals, burnished and unburnished,
were used as decorative accessories, especially by the
Chaldeans.

The historians' descriptions, the foundations that have
been excavated, and the sculptured buildings on the bas-
reliefs, are the materials, together with well-preserved

Fig. 171.—One of the Gates of the Harumat, Dur-Sarginu.   (M.)

fragments of architecture, which archæologists and architects have used to enable them to restore some of the
wonderful temples and palaces of ancient Assyria (Fig.
172 .

The bird's-eye view of the palace of Dur-Sarginu will
give a good idea of the typical Assyrian palaces (Fig. 174),
and the triumphal gate with its man-headed winged bulls
at the base and sides (Fig. 173), and also the other gate at
Fig. 172, both with their crenallated battlements, serve to
show the imposing character of these edifices. It will be
noticed from the bird's-eye view and the gateways that
the general character of Assyrian architecture was rectan-

gular in the highest degree. The arch and vaulted structures were known to the Assyrians, who used them to great

Fig. 172.—Interior of a Temple, after Layard's Restoration.

advantage (Figs. 175 and 250), and much more so than
the Egyptians, although the latter people occasionally
employed them.

The Chaldeans, as would naturally be expected, used
the arch construction very much in their brick buildings,
as it would be the only means of carrying roofs and upper
floors, where stone and timber could not easily be obtained
(Fig. 175).

The use of the column in Chaldea is proved by the bas-
reliefs before it developed itself in Assyria ; but in either
country it was not an important feature in the architecture, being mostly used for awnings supporting light tents

Fig. 173.— Triumphal Gate at the entrance of the Palace. (M.)

or tabernacles ; sometimes, indeed, used in a disengaged
way, as proved by the views of small temples on the bas-
reliefs (Figs. 176, 177, 178). The use of the column was
not in accord with the principles of their architecture, and
was only to be found in small porches, or in an engaged
way against outer walls and piers (Fig. 179). The only
capital found in a fragment, and restored by Place, is
shown at Fig. 181, and two bases (Figs. 180 and 182).
From these remains it is assumed that the shaft was
smooth and cylindrical.

An incipient form of the Ionic volute is seen at Fig. 177

in the capital of the small columns to the little temple (Fig. 176).

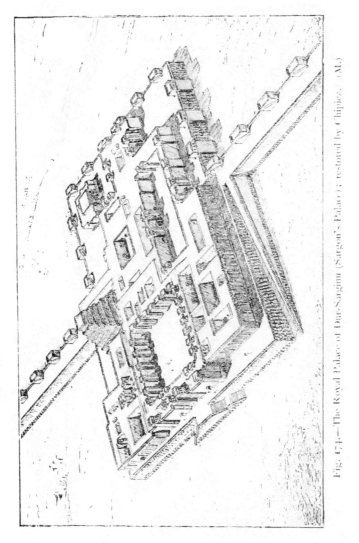

Fig. 174.—The Royal Palace of Dur-Sargina (Sargon's Palace); restored by Chipiez. (M.)

The kings of Assyria had in their palaces a great deal of luxurious furniture. The couches, chairs, and tables

were made of wood, with bronze fittings, and decorated
with ivory, gold, and lapis lazuli. The bas-relief in the
British Museum representing Assurbanipal and his queen
at a banquet (Figs. 183 and 184) will give a good idea of

Fig. 175.—A Bedroom in the Harem at Dur-Sargina (Sargon's Palace). (M.)

the extreme richness in design and decoration of these
sumptuous articles of furniture (Fig. 185).

Bronze sockets (Fig. 186) and all kinds of fragments
in metal and ivory fittings, and decorations corresponding to the designs on the bas-reliefs, all indicate that
the anathemas of the prophet Nahum (Nahum ii. 9) gave

a good picture of Nineveh's richness in the sumptuary arts. "Take ye the spoil of silver," he exclaims, "take the

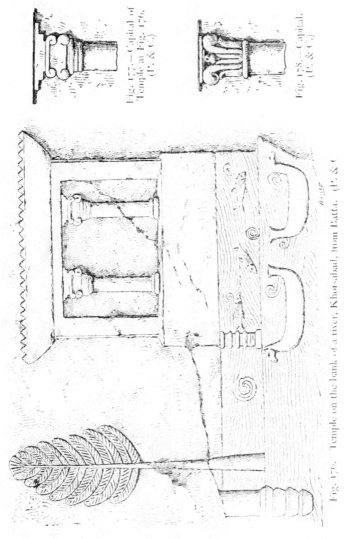

Fig. 177.—Capital of Temple at Fig. 176. (P. & C.)

Fig. 178.—Capital. (P. & C.)

Fig. 176. Temple on the bank of a river, Khorsabad, from Batta. (P. & C.)

spoil of gold; for there is none end of the store and glory out of all the pleasant furniture."

Animals have been represented with such faithfulness, especially in their most vigorous and ferocious aspects, by the sculptors of Assyria, that in any notice of Assyrian art

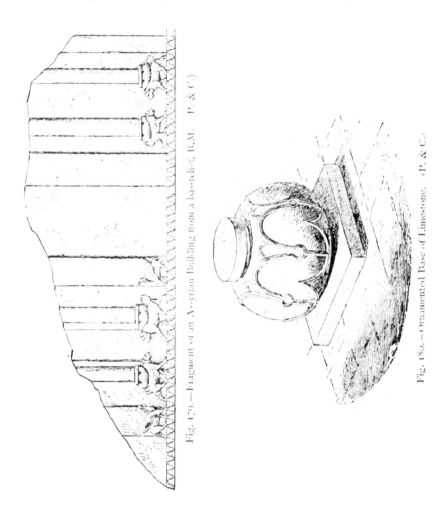

Fig. 179.—Fragment of an Assyrian Building from a bas-relief, B.M.   P. & C.)

Fig. 180.—Ornamented Base of Limestone.   (P. & C.)

they must have a place. Lions especially were rendered in all their ferociousness, and were the favourite game for kingly sport (Figs. 187, 188, 189). Lions were kept in cages,

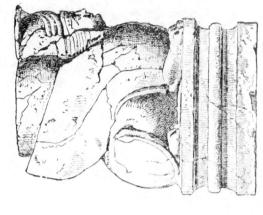

Fig. 182.—Winged Sphinx carrying Base of Capital. Layard. (P. & C.)

Fig. 183.—Assurbanipal and his Queen feasting in the gardens of the Harem after the battle. The head of Teuman, the Elamite King, hangs on the left on the sacred tree. (M.)

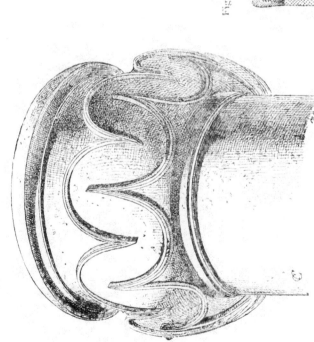

Fig. 184.—Assyrian Capital compiled from Place. (P. & C.)

Fig. 184.—The Feast of Assurbanipal. (B.M.) (P. & C.) Enlarged detail of Fig. 183,
showing the Assyrian Furniture. Drawn by Gautier

and let out when the monarch decided to have a day's
hunting (Fig. 187). Dogs were specially trained for lion-
hunting (Fig. 190.

We add two illustrations of the sphinx variety of fantastic animals ; one is the most remarkable creation of all
the fantastic animals of Assyria (Fig. 192). It has the
horns of a ram, a bull's head, a bird's beak ; body, tail, and

Fig. 185.—Assyrian Stool ; from Layard. (P. & C.)

fore-legs of a lion ; and the hind-legs and wings of the
eagle. The Andro-Sphinx (Fig. 193) from the robe of
Assurbanipal foreshadows the fabulous centaurs of Grecian
art. Other bi-form creations have been found in Assyrian
art bearing a close resemblance to the Greek centaur.

The purely ornamental forms from the vegetable world
that have been used in Assyrian and Chaldean art are
limited in number. The daisy or rosette is the commonest

Fig. 187.—Lion coming out of his Cage. (B.M.) (P. & C.)

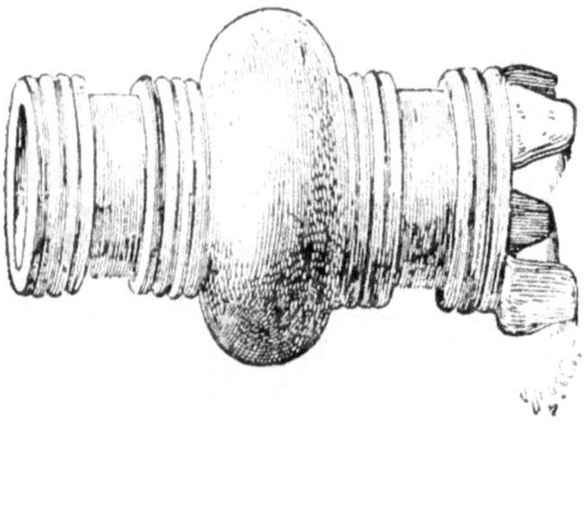

Fig. 186.—Bronze Foot of a Piece of Furniture.

(Figs. 194 and 198). In the illustration of the " Lion and
Lioness in a Park" (Fig. 188) the daisy is beautifully
though conventionally rendered ; the large leaves at the

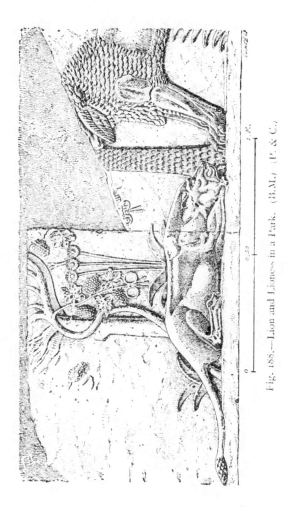

Fig. 188.—Lion and Lioness in a Park. (B.M.) (P. & C.)

bottom are typically the common daisy leaves ; the vine is
no less well executed, and the lioness on the same bas-
relief is treated with consummate skill. The vine is also

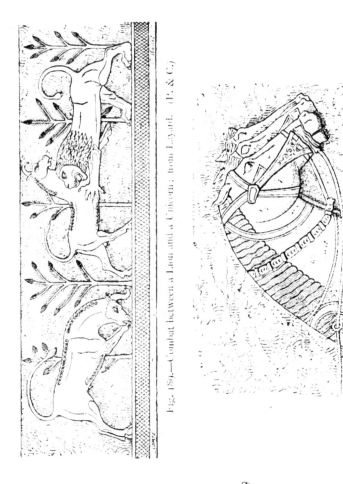

Fig. 189.—Combat between a Lion and a Unicorn; from Layard. (P. & C.)

Fig. 191.—Chariot Horses; from Layard. P. & C.

Fig. 190.—Dog used for Lion Hunting. (M.)

seen to great advantage in its conventional treatment at
Figs. 184 and 188.

There is an Assyrian ornament called the "knop and

Fig. 192. Fantastic Animal, drawn by Gauder. P. & C.

flower" ornament, which occurs in various forms and in
endless profusion in Egyptian, Assyrian, Persian, and
Greek, and even is copied down to Indian and Roman

ornament. It may be native, or some forms of it at least, to Assyrian ornament, but is undoubtedly Egyptian in its earliest source; we have spoken of it before in our notice of Egyptian ornament as being derived from the lotus page 90). It appears on the rich border of the carved threshold (Fig. 167); the flower there is undoubtedly a lotus, and the bud or "knop" may be a representation of a "fir-cone," or may be meant for the closed lotus-bud. Another form of the same elements occurs at Fig. 195, in a beautiful design enclosed in a square, forming one of the central patterns of a similar sill or threshold, and this form

Fig. 193.—Andro-Sphinx, Robe of Assurbanipal; from Layard. (P. & C.)

of it would doubtless also be used for a ceiling decoration of the palaces. A bouquet of similar flowers is seen at Fig. 196 of the date of Assurbanipal (885-860 B.C.). It is very difficult to say whether this bouquet represents the lotus or not, as, according to the testimony of Layard, the lotus flower is only to be found on the most recent of Assyrian monuments dating from the eighth and seventh centuries B.C., at the time when Assyria had invaded and occupied the Delta of Egypt. If not the lotus flower, something very like has been found on monuments in Assyria much older than these dates.

As the result of some recent scientific examinations into the origin of pattern, some investigators have decided that

the "knop and flower" patterns of Assyrian ornament
(Figs. 167, 195, and 198) are but evolutions of tassels, and
knotted fringes of matting and embroideries, just because

Fig. 194.—Detail from the Enamelled Archivolt, Khorsabad ; from Place. (P. & C.)

they bear a not very clear resemblance to such trimmings
as we see on the tabernacle on the Balâwât gates (Fig.
197), &c. We admit that there is a fancied resemblance in

VOL. I.   L

Fig. 195.—Rosette of Lotus Flowers and Buds. (P. & C.)

Fig. 196.—Bouquet of Flowers and Buds ; from Layard. (P. & C.)

many ornamental forms to patterns that have been evolved
from constructed articles, especially from woven and matted
examples, but it is an insult to the intelligence of an artist
to ask him to believe that the beautiful and clearly distinctive floral bud and palmate borders in Egyptian,

Fig. 197.—Tabernacle from the Balāwāt Gates. B.M.. (P. & C.)
Date, B.C. 859 to 824.

Assyrian, and Greek art have resulted from tyings and
knottings of the fringed ends of mats, when one can clearly
see the daisy—in some cases turned to a disk—the palm,
and, above all, the lotus, almost naturally drawn and
modelled; even the connecting lines of flower and buds,
where scientific connection with the fringed-end idea seems
the strongest in the eyes of the evolutionist, will be found
on examination to be always used in the exact reverse way

to that which is formed by the constructive joinings of the knotted fringe. (See Figs. 198 and 167.)

It will require an amazing quantity of scientific proof to get rid of the lotus in Egyptian ornament, and much also to turn it and the daisy into tassel knots in Assyrian ornament, when we have overwhelming evidence as to the natural representations of such floral forms, as well as the conventional designs derived from them, on the very oldest monuments in both countries.

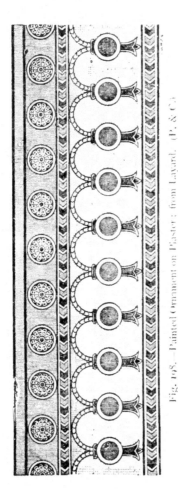

Fig. 198.—Painted Ornament on Plaster: from Layard. (P. & C.)

The "Sacred Tree," or "Tree of Life," is often represented in Assyrian art, and under different forms, but generally with a king or some divinity on either side of it, paying homage Figs. 157, 162A, 208.

An enlarged portion of it is seen at Fig. 199.

The exact meaning of the "Sacred Tree" has not yet been satisfactorily explained, but, at any rate, it seems likely enough that it represents a palm-tree, shown by the palmate head and by the conventional markings on the trunk, no doubt meant for the bark roughening lines. The surrounding palmates may be meant to represent a leafy enclosure for the sacred tree in the centre, or the whole thing may be a conventional picture of a sacred grove.

Owing to the comparative lateness of the universal use of
the lotus in Assyrian art, we can well imagine that this

Fig. 199.—Upper Portion of a Tree of Life: from Layard. (P. & C.)

flower form was introduced into Assyria by the articles in
bronze, ivory, and other material by the Phœnician traders,

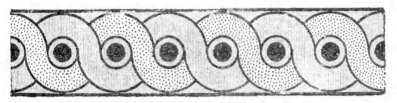

Fig. 200.—Guilloche Ornament on Enamelled Brick. (B.M.) P. & C.)

that were both of Egyptian and Phœnician design, as
there was scarcely an article of commerce on which the

lotus was not represented in those early days of Phœnician trade 900 to 300 B.C.

Fig. 201.—Ivory Plaque; Actual Size.   Drawn by Gautier.   (P. & C.)

Another very characteristic ornament of the Assyrian decorations is the double-interlacing meander, or guilloche

(Figs. 200 and 201). It is generally found in combination with the other ornaments just spoken of, both on tiles and in ivory engraving. It is sometimes called "cable ornament" or "snare-work," from the appearance it has to a rope or cable twisted around the eyes of posts. It has been used very much by the Greeks and Romans.

The art of ivory carving and engraving was practised in Assyria, judging from some plaques and carvings that have been found that are distinctly Assyrian in motive and design (Fig. 201), and from many elephants' tusks that have come to light from the ruins of the buried palaces; but it has been clearly established that the art was first introduced into Assyria by the importation of the Egyptian plaques and other carvings, and also by the imitations of Egyptian articles made by Phœnician artists, and probably sold to the Assyrians as the product of Egypt.

Fig. 202.— Ivory Plaque found at Nimroud. (B.M.) (P. & C.)

Fig. 202, a small plaque, is quite likely to be one of these imitations of Egyptian design with the lotus-tree of life which rests on a support or top of a capital. This form of lotus capital is found everywhere in Cyprus, and in all countries where Phœnician trade extended. It is distinctly Egyptian in origin, and more than likely is the

origin of the Ionic volute capital of the Greeks. The small
and beautifully carved sphinx (Fig. 203) is one of the
many Egyptian ivories that had found its way to Assyria,
and is immeasurably superior in workmanship to any of
the Assyrian carvings.

It may be remarked here that the Assyrian artist excelled in the flat or engraved treatment of his designs in
nearly every branch of art, but was inferior in workmanship to the Egyptian in carved work in the round ; though

Fig. 203.—Ivory Fragment in British Museum ; Actual Size.   Drawn
by Gautier.   (P. & C.)

in expressing intense life, virility, and movement, especially in the representation of animals, he was superior to
the Egyptian artist.

There is one important product of Assyrian art that
deserves notice—the exquisite bronze bowls, cups, and
platters, made in repoussé and finished off with the
engraver's burin (Fig. 204, 205). In these products we
may recognise the renaissance of Assyrian art, based on
the art of the Egyptians. That they must have had their
origin in Assyria no one can doubt, when we think that

the working in bronze was so well known in Assyria and Babylonia ; for example, we quote the magnificent Baláwât plates, of repoussé bronze, of Shalmaneser II.

Fig. 204.—Bronze Platter, 9 ins. diameter. (B.M.) Drawn by Wallet. (P. & C.)

(B.C. 859—824) now in the British Museum ; and although the designs on some of them are distinctly Egyptian (Fig. 204), not one specimen of such bowls or platters has yet been found in the Valley of the Nile.

Fig. 205.—Bronze Cup, diameter 11 ins. : from Layard.

It may be reasonably assumed that the Egyptian motives
were copied from ivories or painted vases brought to

Assyria by the Phœnicians, and that those master workers in bronze, the Assyrians, copied such designs on their platters and cups, and afterwards introduced their own distinctive designs, as may be seen in Fig. 205, a design which is Assyrian in every detail, with no Egyptian trace. Designs like the latter disprove the theory that these bronze bowls and dishes were altogether made in workshops of Tyre and Byblos, but undoubtedly the Phœnician artists—who really invented nothing—may have in their turn copied these designs on their wares, when they found such handy and portable goods might be easily transported,

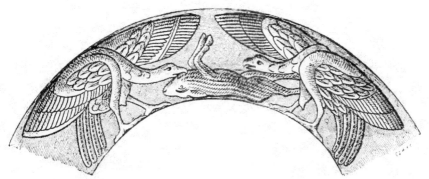

Fig. 206.— Border of a Bronze Cup ; from Layard. (P. & C.)

and would be sure to find a ready market in other countries bordering on the Mediterranean, as we shall see when treating of Phœnician Art. The importance of the design on such handy and indestructible articles on the art of the Greeks, Cypriots, and Etruscans, not only from the workmanship point of view, but from the themes portrayed on them suggesting ornament, and other subject matter, perhaps religious motives as well, to the rising civilisation of the countries named, can hardly be exaggerated.

In painting on plaster (Fig. 198) or enamelling on tiles (Figs. 194 and 200) and bricks, the Babylonians and Assyrians used very few colours, not more than five or six, but they used them with great advantage and decorative effect, and always in flat tints. Their painted figures were, as a rule, not intended for any other meaning than their geometric ornament, and merely used as units in the ornamental scheme (Fig. 194). The colours were: blue from the lapis lazuli; yellow, an antimoniate of lead and a little tin; white, an oxide of tin; black, an animal charcoal; red, an oxide of iron; and another blue from the

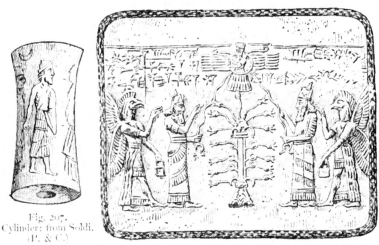

Fig. 207.
Cylinder: from Soldi.
(P. & C.)

Fig. 208.—Assyrian Cylinder. Worship of Sacred Tree.
B.M.) (P. & C.)

oxide of copper completes, as near as possible, the range of their palette.

The nearly universal colour of the groundwork was blue, a deep dark blue from the lapis lazuli. At Khorsabad M. Place found a mass of powdered blue, over two pounds in weight, that was found to be made from the lapis lazuli for the purpose of enamelling. The main portion of the decoration was yellow, but often white was used with black outlines, and red sparingly. A green tint was less common, but was supposed to be obtained from a mixture of the yellow and copper blue oxide.

Remains of pottery are not very plentiful, and the forms

have nothing distinctive that calls for special notice. The vessels, such as vases, cups, and buckets of bronze, are elegant in form and decoration (Fig. 209).

Jewellery and personal decoration have only been found in a limited quantity, and not of a very good quality in design or material: the bas-reliefs furnish our best information on what existed in these articles.

Gem cutting and cylinder engraving were arts very much practised in Babylonia and Assyria (Fig. 208). The

Fig. 209.—Bronze Bucket: from Layard. (P. & C.)

cylinders usually were engraved with subjects of a religious character. The illustration shows one of the best engraved Assyrian cylinders that has yet been found. It represents the king and deities at the worship of the Sacred Tree, and the God Assur. In the hands of the deities may be seen the bronze buckets shown at Fig 209.

This subject is supposed to be a copy from a bas-relief. The material of these cylinders was generally of serpentine, chalcedony, agate, black marble, jasper, &c., and they were used to impress clay documents with, in a similar way as in the use of ordinary seals (Fig. 207).

CHAPTER IX.

THE origin of the Phœnician people remains in obscurity. According to Herodotus, we learn that they came as an Eastern branch of the Canaanitish peoples, of which race the Greeks were also a part, and who settled at the foot of Lebanon, on the Syrian sea-coast, between Mounts Carmel and Casius.

The Phœnician and Hebrew languages resembled each other very closely, and from this it has been argued that the Phœnicians belonged to the Semitic race of the Hebrews. Ancient Phœnicia was a narrow strip of land, 130 miles long by only a few miles in width at its widest part. The three principal towns in ancient times were Tyre, Sidon, and Joppa; three others of importance were Arvad, Gebal or Byblos, and Accho or Acre.

Arvad in the north, was, like Tyre in the south, built on a rock some little distance from the mainland. Tyre was for a long time impregnable on its rocky seat, with a channel of about three-quarters of a mile dividing it from the coast of the mainland. Owing to its peculiar position, it could defy all unmaritime nations, and it was not until Alexander the Great built an isthmus connecting it with the Phœnician coast that it fell. The inhabitants of Gebal or Byblos were, according to Rénan, more Jewish-like than any other Phœnician people.

Sidon was the first town of Phœnicia to rise to importance, and Tyre afterwards, with greater vigour, rose to power and greatness; and both, from being originally colonies of poor fishermen, became the famous ports which sent forth ships to all points of the Mediterranean, and even to the British Isles, carrying all kinds of merchandise to barter for silver, gold, and tin, as well as for other raw materials from the barbarians beyond the seas, and carrying these raw materials back to supply the artists and artificers of the East. No two cities of the ancient world did so much for the spread and progress of human civilisation as the maritime cities of Tyre and Sidon.

Like the rest of Phœnicia, Sidon, the first in power,

Fig. 210.—Phœnician Merchant Galley; from Layard. (P. & C.)

accepted without resistance the supremacy of Egypt. This was indeed to her great advantage, for the ships of Sidon could fly the Egyptian flag in any part of the Mediterranean or other seas, and so exist secure under the protection of the mighty monarchs of that great country. In return for this protection the Phœnicians carried on a successful trade with Egyptian goods, thus benefiting themselves, and their masters to even a greater degree.

The Phœnician fleets were, in fact, at the entire disposal of the Egyptians, who possessed, in the early days, no fleet of their own.

Sidon was sacked and taken by the Philistines about B.C. 1000 or 900, and from that period Tyre rose in supremacy. The first Tyrian king known by name was Abibaal, the contemporary of David; his son was Hiram, the friend of Solomon.

Afterwards Tyre, with its close intercourse with Egypt, established colonies on the Delta of the Nile, the most renowned of which was called the "New City," *Kart-*

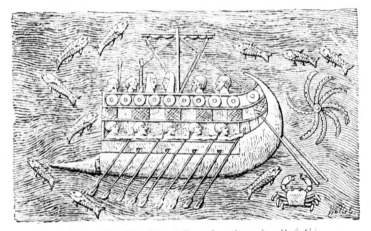

Fig. 211.— Phœnician War Galley; from Layard.   P. & C.)

hadast, called by the Greeks Carchedon, and by the Romans Carthage.

This daughter of Tyre rose to great prosperity, but never forgot her allegiance to the mother city. Their combined fleets sailed to, and founded, colonies in Sardinia, Cyprus, the Grecian Archipelago, and to Spain, doing enormous trade with both East and West. The Phœnician ships that are known to us from the relief representations are of two kinds, the round-prowed galleys, or cargo-carriers (Fig. 210), and the ram-stemmed vessels, or war galleys (Fig. 211). There is no record that has been found of their larger sea-going "merchant-men" ships.

The growing power of the Greeks and Etruscans, and their improvement in shipbuilding, was a new competition

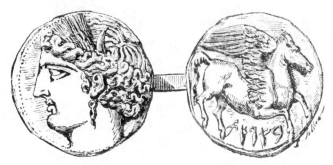

Fig. 212.—Carthaginian Coin, Silver. (P. & C.)

with the ships of Tyre in the East, and at length forced the Tyrians to find new markets in the West.

The staple trade of the Tyrians had now become that of metals, the chief of which was tin, owing to the great

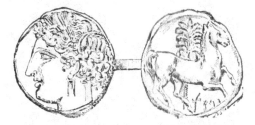

Fig. 213.—Carthaginian Coin, Electrum. (P. & C.)

demand for it in the manufacture of bronze in this period.

Their ships went as far as the Scilly Isles, to Cornwall, and to Ireland. Diodorus mentions that the inhabitants of Great Britain were much softened in their manners by their intercourse with the "strangers" who came to their

shores for tin. It is supposed that the strangers alluded
to were the Phœnician Carthaginians.

Fig. 214.—Votive Stele, from Carthage, with Sacred Emblems.   (P. & C.)

In the fourth century B.C. the Carthaginians waged a war
against the Sicilian Greeks, and carried off the statues of

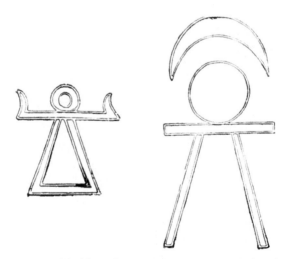

Fig. 215.—Sacred Emblems, from a Carthaginian Votive Stele. (P. & C.)

gods from their temples, and went so far as to copy their
money the early Phœnician coins being copies of Greek

ones (Figs. 212, 213). The votive stele (Fig. 214), from
Carthage, shows the Greek Ionic-like columns, with the
"blessing hand," and a collection of sacred Phœnician
emblems. Greek architects were employed in Carthage
about this time. Phœnician architecture in every case
consisted of borrowed forms from surrounding nations.

The sacred emblems (Fig. 215) are supposed to represent the cone-shaped stones, *betylæ*, from Bethel, the

Fig. 216.—Coin of Byblos, with Sacred Cone, enlarged. (P. & C.)

"House of God," the great worship of the Phœnicians.
The sign at the top is meant for a rude idea of the head
and arms of a god (Tanit, face of Baal?). The figure on
the right is the cone again, with the emblems of the
goddess Astarte (Aphrodite), the lunar signs. The sacred
cone is seen surrounded by the temple court on the coin
of Byblos (Fig. 216).

The small statuettes of the Phœnician gods and god-
desses (Fig. 217) were the originals from which the Greeks
developed their sculptured figures in the round. Among

the gods of the Phœnicians were : Baal, *the Master*, the *Bel* of Assyria, which seems to be a generic title for any chief divinity of a town or place, such as *Baal Peor, Baal-Sidon, Baal-Tsour*, or the *Baal* of Tyre ; *Tanit*, or the *face of Baal*, worshipped at Carthage ; *Moloch*, or *Melek*. Melkart-Baal-Tsour was the full name of the Great God of Tyre, which means "Melkart, Master of Tyre." *Baalat* was the title for "mistress," the goddess who shared the throne of Baal. Sidon-Astoret was the *Baalat* of Sidon, the goddess Astarte, the Istar of the Assyrians, and the Aphrodite or Venus of the Greeks and Romans (Fig. 217). She was a favourite divinity with the Phœnicians, and more personal than any of their other divinities. She was nature itself, the great goddess of life, presiding over creation and also destruction. This Syro-Phœnician goddess of the Sidonians was adopted by Cyprus, Cythera, Paphos, and Eryx, in Sicily. She is also supposed to be the Moon-Goddess. The dove was sacred to

Fig. 217.—Astarte, terra-cotta, height 10½ ins. (P. & C.)

her, and was offered to her in sacrifice; a Phœnician statuette (Fig. 217) represents her with a dove in her hand. The Phœnicians had many other minor gods.

A terra-cotta model of a small temple is peculiar in
design (Fig. 218); it was found in Cyprus, and may have
been the model of the shrine sacred to Astarte.   As before
mentioned, Phœnician architecture, from the few remains
of it that have been found, consists of borrowed forms from
other nations, and if any development even in the ornamental forms is noticeable, it can generally be traced to the
rising influence of the Greeks, especially in Cyprus and
Carthage.   The tomb at Amrit (Fig. 219) is, on the other

Fig. 218.—Model of a Small Temple, in terra-cotta, Louvre. (P. & C.)

hand, decidedly Assyrian in every detail, and is a happy
example of architectural proportion.

The fragment of an entablature from a temple at
Byblos (Fig. 220) is of a later date, and has for design and
decoration of the moulding the strongly marked features
of Græco-Roman work, with the addition of the Egyptian
winged globe and asps.

Cyprus was a Phœnician dependency ; many vases, and
a great multitude of other objects of art and treasures,
have been brought to light from tombs and from the

subterranean chambers of former temples, mainly through the instrumentality of General di Cesnola.

Fig. 219.—Tomb of Amrit, restored from Renan. (P. & C.)

The series of capitals (Figs. 221 to 224) show strongly the principle of the Ionic volutes. The first (Fig. 221) is

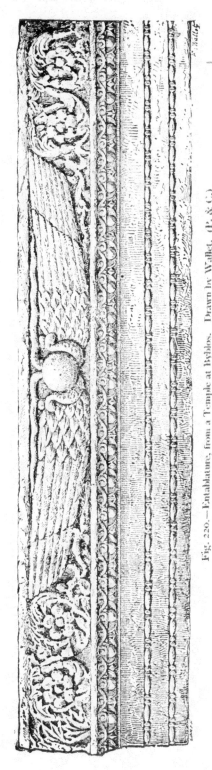

Fig. 220.—Entablature, from a Temple at Byblos. Drawn by Wallet. (P. & C.)

the simplest, the next (Fig. 222) has the triangular point between the lower volutes that we see in so many lotus forms in Egyptian work (see Fig. 202), and has besides the curious double boat-shaped volutes above, with other lotus-buds under the abacus. Another capital (Fig. 223) has all the elements of the Erectheum Ionic capital, but arranged in a totally different order, and is more Byzantine than anything else. The capital found at Kition, in Cyprus, is decidedly Ionic Greek, but in its earlier stage, just before the period of the fully developed Ionic (Fig. 224). It can hardly be doubted that the first two of decidedly Egyptian elements are derived from the lotus, and may certainly be taken as the forerunners of the pure Ionic Greek. The capital from Kition belonged to a temple of Astarte, that once stood on the mound at Kition.

The capital found at Golgos (Fig. 225) is distinctly an early form of Greek Doric.   If little remains of Phœnician

Fig. 221.—Cypriot Capital. (P. & C.)

Fig. 222.—Cypriot Capital. (P. & C.)

architecture have been found, on the other hand many objects of minor art have been brought to light, bearing on their face the unmistakable stamp of Phœnician workmanship.

Some of the bronze bowls and platters, and cups of silver, and also carvings in ivory, although generally

Fig. 223.—Capital at Djezza, limestone. Drawn by Saladin. Height, 26 ins. (P. & C.)

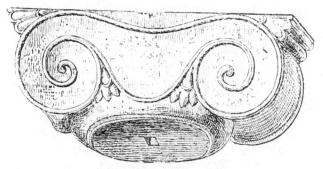

Fig. 224.— Capital from Kition, height 18 ins. Drawn by Saladin. (P. & C.)

composed of Egyptian or Assyrian design, were really the work of Phœnician artificers. The latter were not slow in copying the motives of the above-named nations, but the workmanship, especially in bronze and silver, was their own. The Phœnicians were highly skilled in metal work, and we have proof that they were employed in the building and decorating of the Temple at Jerusalem. The bronze and silver bowls and platters were carried to all countries where the Phœnicians had trading transactions, and they have been found at Mycenæ, Etruria, Cyprus, Sardinia, &c. As stated before in our notice of these objects in Assyrian art, the Assyrians were the first to make these articles from copies of Egyptian design, and then producing others with purely Assyrian designs.

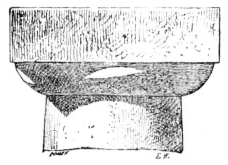

Fig. 225.—Capital from Golgos (Ceccaldi).   P. & C.)

The Phœnicians in their turn imitated both, and did a great trade with them. The silver platter (Fig. 226) was found, in 1876, in the Necropolis of ancient Præneste, in Latium, and in the same tomb was found a quantity of vases, diadems, and jewels, all of Phœnician workmanship. On this platter a clearly engraved inscription occurs in Phœnician characters, giving the name of the first owner, Esmunjair-ben-Asto. The Phœnician inscriptions, and above all, the want of method or arrangement of themes or motives on the articles, stamp them to be of Phœnician origin. The silver platter has more meaning in the use of the Egyptian motives than some others, but the hiero-lygphics are not to be relied on as correctly Egyptian.

The silver-gilt cup or patera from Curium (Fig. 227) is a fair illustration of this mixture of Egyptian and Assyrian ideas put together from a multitude of stock-in-trade

Fig. 226.—Phœnician Platter, Silver, diameter 7 ins. Drawn by Wallet. (P. & C.)

subjects or patterns. The centre piece is Assyrian, and also the cable ornament. The inner row of animals are Assyrian in feeling, but an Egyptian sphinx is introduced

amongst them ; but the outer border is the most curious of
all, as it contains six or seven distinct Egyptian scenes,
each divided by the tree of life or palmates, taken at hap-

Fig. 227.—Patera from Curium, diameter 8 ins. (P. & C.)

hazard from designs of bas-reliefs. The Phœnician goldsmith, evidently not understanding the story of these
Egyptian mysteries, used them merely as decorative units.

The workmanship is admirable; first the work is beaten up in repoussé and then chased afterwards, and may be described as a mixture of the two methods.

A beautiful Egyptian design of a cow and calf in a papyrus brake forms the centre medallion of a Phœnician cup found at Caere (Fig. 228).

The Egyptian vessels figured in the tomb of Rekhmara (Fig. 229) are mostly made in metal and are of Phœnician

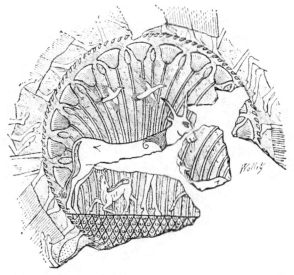

Fig. 228.—Centre Medallion : from a Cup from Griffi. (P. & C)

design. They would be sold to the Egyptians, as the former supplied the latter in most articles of metal workmanship; many rims and handles of elaborate workmanship have been found, but scarcely any whole forms of these vases, though we have many of their forms preserved in Greek and Etruscan work.

In articles of personal jewellery the Phœnicians were as skilful as the Greeks and Etruscans; it was only in the matter of higher motives in design that the Greeks excelled

the Phœnicians. We give one or two specimens of their
jewellery at Figs. 230 to 233.

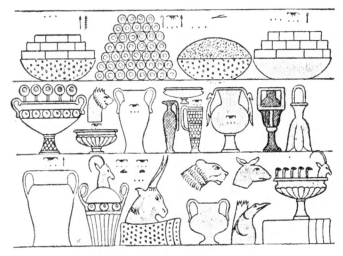

Fig. 229.—Vessels figured in the Tomb of Rekhmara ; from Wilkman.

Cyprus was inhabited from the earliest time with a
mixture of races in which the Greek or Hellenic element
was represented, and though nominally a Phœnician

Fig. 230.—Gold Bracelet ; from Tharros. (B.M.) (P. & C.)

dependency, the Greek superiority of artistic genius
asserted itself at a very early date in the art of the country.
Some of the architectural features already noticed, notably

the Ionic capitals, may be given as examples of this; and
another very important branch, the minor art of pottery,
may furnish further examples of the Greek art tendency,
though infused with a mixture of Phœnician influences.

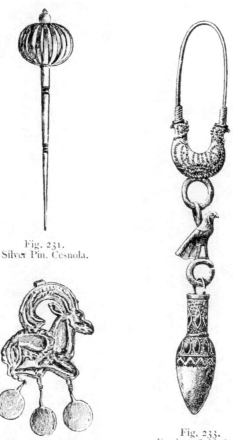

Fig. 231.
Silver Pin. Cesnola.

Fig. 232.—Pendant, Wild
Goat, Gold. (B.M.)

Fig. 233.
Earring. Gold, from
Cesnola.

Cyprus has always been particularly noted for its ceramic
products. The island is rich in potter's clay of two kinds—
a black earth, and a red kind. The oldest kind of Cyprian

known is of a good shape, and is generally furnished with
handles according to the uses of the vase. The making
and fitting on of handles is only achieved when the art of
the potter has been well advanced.

The two vases (Figs. 234, 235) are of the oldest dates, and
are decorated purely in the oldest form of geometric ornament. The one with the handle is particularly good in
form, and has the decoration incised like sgraffito work.

Fig. 234.—Bottle with Incised Ornament, from Cesnola. (P. & C.)

Fig. 235.—Bottle with Geometric
Decoration. (P. & C.)

Fantastic shapes of animals made as vases and drinking
vessels were very common in Cyprus. Although not many
of them can be called beautiful, still it required considerable skill and knowledge to model them (Fig. 236).
The goat-shaped vessel is very lifelike. The bowl or
crater (Fig. 237) has the lotus flower and geometric bands
and divisions for its decoration; it is painted with light
brown and red on a cream-coloured ground. The decoration from a cup is more elaborate, it has a new element in
the shape of some kind of water bird arranged Assyrian-

like on each side of the sacred tree, and has a sun sign
filling up a space close to one of the bird's legs (Fig. 238).
Another very interesting and beautiful vase is the
Œnochoé (Fig. 239). Another bird is painted on this, and
at the same time the geometric checkers and lines still
cling to it as part of the decoration. On this vase, also,
may be seen two moon signs, and the sacred sun sign, the

Fig. 236.—Vessel in the Shape of a Goat. (P. & C.)

fylfot, or swastika, repeated four times. These sacred
signs are often found on Cyprian pottery. The latter vase
in shape and decoration is more Greek in feeling than
most Cyprian vases. The larger Œnochoé (Fig. 240) has
the human figure with some kind of water fowls; it has a
sacred sign on its lips. Though the subject recalls Egypt,
the design and execution might have been done by a

clever Greek artist. The style of execution and drawing on these vases may be a little archaic, but the design and bold manner of execution is eminently correct and could not be better for the decoration of pottery.

The discovery of glass making has been attributed to the Phœnicians, but this is not correct ; the Egyptians made glass articles, and used glass in their vitreous enamelled tiles and bricks long before the Phœnicians had any connection with Egypt. It was most likely because

Fig. 237.—Bowl in the Piot Collection, height 6¾ ins. (P. & C.)

the Phœnicians traded so much in glass, and for the reasons also that they had large glass manufactories at Tyre and other places, that they have received the credit from early times of being the inventors of glass. The oldest dated glass bottle or vase in the world is one from Egypt, and now in the British Museum. It bears the name of Thothmes III. (B.C. 1600). The body is turquoise blue with yellow details of decoration and hieroglyphics; the handle is dark blue with yellow and white markings.

The Phœnicians at a later period were extensive makers of glass articles, and made glass of three kinds, the clear

Fig. 238.—Detail of the Decoration of a Cup. (P. & C.)

and transparent, but always with a slight greenish hue, the coloured and transparent, and the opaque.

A great quantity of glass bottles, statuettes, vases,

plaques, and beads have been found in Cyprus. The bottles and vases that were prized most highly were decorated chiefly in alternating lines of bright colours, such as blues, greens, yellows, white, and purple. Beads, cones, amulets, scarabs, heads of animals, and statuettes, as well as bottles and vases, were made both by Phœnician and Egyptian workmen, some cast in moulds and some blown. There is a cup in the French National Library called the cup of Chosroes II., made of glass, and decorated

Fig. 230.—Œnochoé, New York
Museum. (P. & C.)

with artificial gems. The finest work of art in glass is the famous Portland vase in the British Museum. The decoration on this vase is in relief in cameo glass.

The small cylindrical perfume bottles in glass known as *alabastrons* are of the highest antiquity; they were usually placed in the hands of the dead.

In the art of weaving and making textiles the Phœnicians are not credited with making anything different from the Orientals or Egyptians, and perhaps supplied themselves with the Egyptian muslins and linens, and had their rugs and carpets from the East, which were famed then as now for their soft nature and brightness of colouring. We have evidence from Homer that the Sidonian slaves were very skilful at embroidery. " With threads of gold, or with a colour contrasting with that of the ground, they drew fantastic beasts of every kind."

These embroideries would likely have similar decoration to that which is found on the metal platters, and perhaps imitations of those decorations we see on the embroidered

robes of the Assyrian kings' mantles (Figs. 162A, 163A), and
the scheme of decoration would likely be a division of the
field into bands and circles, each filled with Egyptian or
Assyrian motives.

In Cyprus, we can easily infer that the textiles would

Fig. 240.—Œnochoé. New York Museum. (P. & C.)

be strongly influenced, as other manufactures were, by
Egyptian art. The Phœnicians were noted for their
famous purple dye obtained from the *Murex* and *Purpura*
families of shell-fish. This purple dye was of world-wide
renown. Its great advantage was that on its exposure to
light and sunshine it became more fast and more intense
in colour, which is contrary to most dyes. It was very

costly by reason of the difficulty in extracting it from the fish, and of the enormous quantities required to produce even a small quantity of the dye. The city of Tyre had

Fig. 241.—Intaglio on Chalcedony. (P. & C.)

extensive factories for the manufacture of the Tyrian purple. It is not obtained now from the shell-fish, as, of course, many other ways and cheaper have been found to produce a similar colour.

The Phœnicians were adepts at ivory-carving, shell-engraving, and gem-cutting (Fig. 241), as many examples of these arts have been found, but we regret that the limitations of this volume prevent us from going into these subjects as fully as we might wish.

CHAPTER X.

PERSIA occupies what is known as the tableland of Iran,
and is a plateau bounded on the north by the Elburz
Mountains, Armenia, and Afghanistan; the Bol-ur and
Hindu-Kush in the east; the heights that are parallel to
the Indian Ocean in the south; and the Persian Gulf, the
chains of Zagros, and Ararat in the west.

The Zagros Mountains separated Persia on that portion
of the Iran plateau from Assyria, which was known as
part of Media. The Assyrians under Tiglath-Pileser
scaled these mountains and conquered the Medes.

The Medes have always been considered with the
Persians as forming part of one nation, being closely
related to each other in language, religion, manners, and
customs.

The Medes were the first to emerge from barbarism,
owing to their nearness to the Assyrians. After the conquest of Babylon (B.C. 539) the Medes and the Persians
descended from their mountains into the valley of the
Tigris, under Cyrus, the first Persian king of the Achæ-
menidæan dynasty. The name Achæmenidæ was given by
the Greeks to the descendants of a native chief called
Akhamanish, and one of the oldest families of Persia.
Cyrus marched through Asia Minor to Asiatic Greece,
seized all the cities on his way, and made them pay
tribute. Under Cambyses (B.C. 527) the countries of Syria,
Palestine, Phœnicia, Assyria, Babylonia, and Egypt—
nearly all the old-world civilisation from the Mediter-

Fig. 242.—Naksh-i-Rustem, General View of the Rock-cut Tombs.   (F.C.)

Fig. 243.—Persepolis. Tomb on the North-east. Elevation. (F.C.)

ranean to the Indus—belonged to the Persian Empire.
Hostilities were kept up between the Asiatics and
Hellenes for two hundred years, until Alexander the
Great ended them at the battles of Issus and Arbela
(334-330 B.C.). For nearly a century Persia was under the
vassalage of the Greeks, but still kept her ancient
customs and her ancient cult of fire-worship, the national
religion, although this was in a great measure undermined
and weakened by the teachings of the Greek conquerors.

The Greeks were, in turn, overthrown by the Parthians,
a northern Asiatic tribe who ruled in Persia down to
B.C. 226, when the native Sassanidæ family of the south
restored Persia to her former freedom, and installed again
the ancient worship of Ahurâ-Mazda, and also tried to
restore the art of the First Dynasty. The Greek and
Roman influence was, however, too strong at this period
to be entirely shaken off, in spite of the renewed display
of patriotism. For instance, a great quantity of Greek
furniture, utensils, and figures of Greek gods must have
found their way into Persia during the reign of the
Seleucidæ—the Greek rulers—and must have influenced
the native Persian art; besides borrowed ideas from the
art objects and other things that the Persians at a former
time pillaged from the Greek temples and carried home
with them. When the Arabs finally overthrew the
Sassanid Dynasty and conquered Persia, the state religion of fire-worship was proscribed, but the Moslem
religion never took the same hold in Persia as it did in
other countries, the Persians adopting the secular form of
it—the Shiah—as opposed to the more devout form, the
Sunni. To this reason is assigned the independence of
Persia to the present day amongst the other Moslem
countries of the world.

It was during the period of the First Empire that the
greatest works in architecture first appeared in Persia.
It is clear from the remains of this period that the national
architecture of Persia was composed of a mixture of

Fig. 244.—Funeral Tower at Naksh-i-Rustem.　(D.)　(P. & C.)

Assyrian, Egyptian, and Greek elements, blended together in an original way. The artists and architects who produced the national Persian style were hardly native Persians, as there was no previous style of any importance in Persia on which such great works as the famous palaces could be founded or developed from. It is, therefore, quite likely that the artists and architects were of Phœnician or Greek nationality. Indeed, records of Greek names appear on the buildings as architects of some of the palaces of the best periods, and ancient history mentions the names of more than one Greek sculptor that was brought to Persia for this purpose by the victorious kings, and induced to work for them by being well treated and cared for. Many of the Greek artists were also political refugees who found employment and a hearty welcome in Persia.

It was when Cyrus had become master of Western Asia that the Persians began to think of building the famous palaces at Persepolis, Susa, and Pasargadæ. Most of these palaces and the tombs were built of a close-grained limestone that is found very plentiful in the mountainous country of Persia. The royal tombs were, as a rule, cut out of the living limestone rock (Fig. 242). They are of the time of Darius, and are all of one type that seems to have been invented by one mind, and, after the first was cut, *speos*-like, out of the native rock—probably that of Darius itself—the rest were copied faithfully from it. The great height from the ground of the tomb itself was arranged for safety from violation. The sculptured figure of the king is represented near the top, in the act of worshipping the sacred fire seen on the right ; at the centre of the top of the field is seen the emblem of the god Ahurâ-Mazda and the sun disk (Fig. 243). An older form of tomb, the " built " tomb, is seen at the right of the rock-cut tombs, and a larger illustration of this rectangular cemetery is seen at Fig. 244. The latter type of tomb belongs to the time of Cyrus.

We must not look for much in the way of religious

architecture in Ancient Persia. Where temples in other countries were required, fire-altars took their place in Persia (Fig. 245). These altars, by reason of their uses,

Fig. 245.—Fire Altars, Naksh-i-Rustem. (F.C.) (P. & C.)

were generally found in "high places," on summits of hills and on rocks.

The fire-altars at Naksh-i-Rustem are really one with the rock on which they stand. Remains of a fire-temple

have been discovered at Ferûz-abad, which is supposed
to have had a roof; but the ends of the temple would

Fig. 246.— Persepolis ; Staircase of the Palace of Darius.   (D.) (P. & C.)

be open, with the sacred hearth on the top and centre
of a lofty flight of steps, on a quadrangular plan.

The buildings in Persia of the Achæmenidæ Dynasty, both palaces and tombs, are of the pillar and beam, or the architrave system of construction. The horizontal

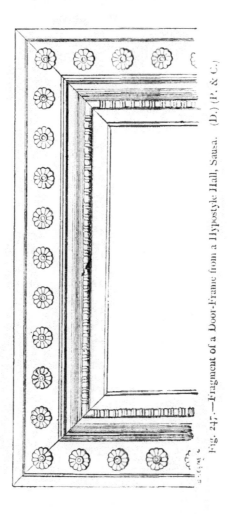

Fig. 247.—Fragment of a Door-Frame from a Hypostyle Hall, Sausa. (D.) (P. & C.)

ceilings were of wood, and were panelled very elaborately, and rested on stone supports. The doorways and windows are square-headed, upholding a lintel (Fig. 248).

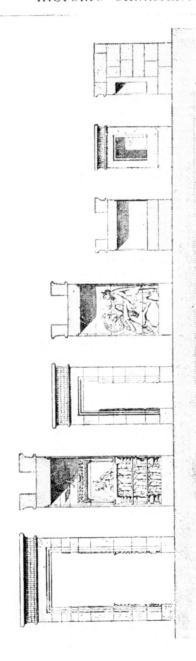

Face and Profile of Principal Doorways.   Face and Profile of Lateral Doorways.   Profile of Window.   Face of Window.   Face of Cornice.   Profile of Niche.

Fig. 248.—Elevations and Sections of Doorways and Windows of a Palace at Persepolis.   (F.C.) (P. & C.)

The doorway, at Fig. 249, of a royal tomb, is a very
rich specimen of a decorated Persian doorway. The

Fig. 249. — Persepolis, Doorway to Royal Tomb. (D.) (P. & C.)

Egyptian "gorge" is seen in the cornice, but the Persian
treatment of this feature is shown in the channelled

VOL. I.   O

grooves, with imbricated markings between each channel. The rosettes, too numerous here to be in good taste, are

Fig. 250.—View of a Group of Domed Buildings, from an Assyrian Bas-relief. Layard. (P. & C.)

evidently borrowed from the Assyrians. The door-frame, from Susa (Fig. 247), restored by Dieulafoy, is, on the contrary, a beautiful example of good proportion and restraint in decoration. It would pass for an example of Greek work in its classic simplicity.

The walls of the palaces were usually crenellated or embattled (Figs. 246 and 261).

The staircase walls and other parts of the buildings were often covered with tiles made of a white cement, and

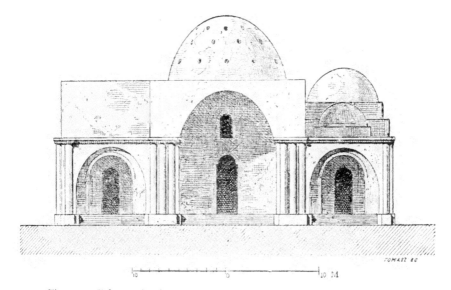

Fig. 251.—Palace at Sarvistan, Principal Façade. (F.C.) (P. & C.) Example of Domed and Vaulted Structure.

enamelled in colour decoration. These have been found chiefly at Susa. The principal parts or body of the building were of stone or brick, and the upper parts were supposed to be of wood. This is correctly inferred by the stepped notches still to be seen in the antæ, or corner piers of stone, which must have been cut in this way to receive the ends of the ceiling beams (*Perrot & Chipiez*). Wood was a scarce material in Persia, and must have been brought from the Elburz Mountains at a great cost of time and labour ; but this would be nothing to a king like Darius, whose revenue was reckoned at about £27,000,000 of English money.

Fig. 253.—Base of Pillar at Susa. (D.) (P. & C.)

Fig. 252. — Column with Volute Capital, Persepolis.

Remains of Persian buildings of another order, the vaulted structures (Fig. 251), have been found at Sarvistan and Ferûz-abad, in the province of Fars (Ancient Persia), which some archæologists have ascribed to the time of the Sassinid Dynasty, the construction of which is supposed to

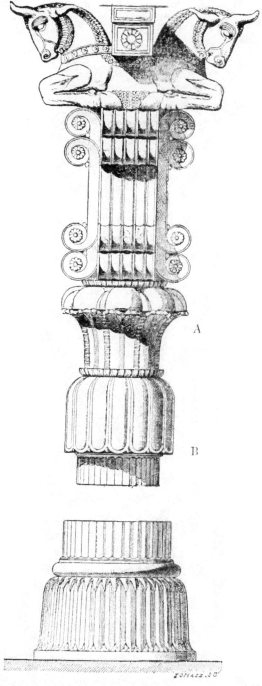

Fig. 254.—Base and Capital from Persepolis ; Propylæa.   (F.C.) (P. & C.)

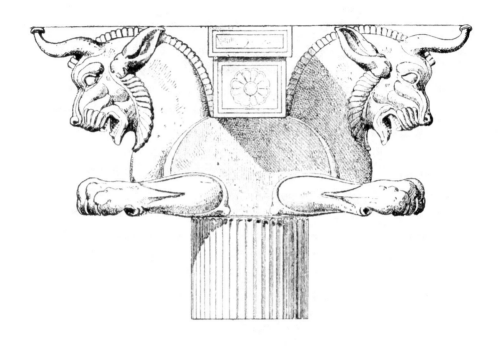

Fig. 255.—Capital and Base from Hypostyle Hall of Xerxes, Persepolis
(F.C.) (P. & C.)

have been derived from their prototypes, the domed and vaulted buildings of Assyria (see Fig. 250).

Fig. 256.—Upright of Royal Throne, Naksh-i-Rustem. (F.C.) (P. & C.)

The most distinctly Persian feature in all the architecture of Persia is undoubtedly the column with its double-bull-headed capital (Fig. 254). Archæologists are divided

in opinion as to whether it is derived from Egyptian or
from Assyrian sources. If it is a borrowed idea, the

Fig. 257.—Staircase Wall of the Palace of Xerxes at Persepolis. (F.C.) (P. & C.)

Persians may certainly be credited with developing the
supposed idea into something wonderfully unique and
interesting as a capital. The name *Zoophoros* (life-bearing)

has been given to it. Perrot and Chipiez (from whom the illustrations are taken) say that the capital was in design an inspiration from the Assyrian national standard (Fig. 161), while Dieulafoy ascribes to it an Egyptian origin. The former appear to have the best of the argu-

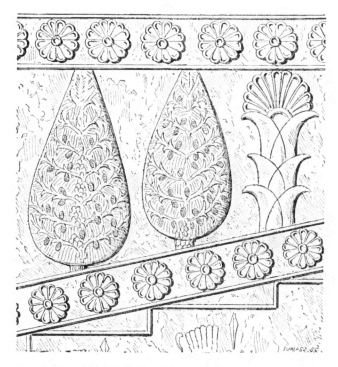

Fig. 258.—Crowning Wall of Staircase, Palace of Xerxes, Persepolis.

ment, for there is nothing in Egyptian ornament that comes so near it as the animals of the Assyrian standard, as regards position, but the supposed resemblance of idea even is not very clear in this case.

The base of the Persian bull-headed columns is almost as unique in its way as the capital. It is of the shape

known as *Campaniform*, and consists of an inverted bell
of beautiful contour, richly decorated with falling leaves,
a torus moulding and fillet connecting it with the shaft
(Fig. 253).

Another capital has, instead of the bull heads, a lion's
head, with the horn of a unicorn. This capital is wanting
in the volutes and lower capital. It is as poor, in this
respect, as the voluted capital is doubly rich, and can

Fig. 259.—Temple in a Royal Park.   (B.M.) (P. & C.)

hardly be called beautiful (Fig. 255). It belongs to the
hypostyle hall of Xerxes, at Persepolis.

The shaft of the Persian column is channelled or fluted
in nearly all cases, and the number of flutings is very
great, being from thirty-two to fifty-two, while the
Egyptian column has never more than sixteen, and the
Greek from sixteen to twenty-four. The great characteristic of the Persian column is its slender and airy
appearance. At Persepolis the total height is twelve

diameters of its shaft. Some are even more slender than this. The Egyptian averages, in contrast, from five to six diameters, and the Greek seven to nine. The Persian column had its origin in timber supports.

Besides the unique capitals and bases in Persian art

Fig. 260.—Enamelled Ornament on Bricks from Susa. Drawn by Gautier. (P. & C.)

there is not much of the ancient Persian ornament and decoration that does not strongly partake of foreign influences. The upright support of the royal throne (Fig. 256) is distinctly Assyrian in feeling, and the upper horizontal moulding is very like Greek work. A moulding is seen on the upper rounded edges of the staircase (Fig. 246) and on the inner portion of the parapet wall (Fig. 257) of an elongated egg shape, which is one of the rare exceptions of ornament that is really Persian.

The Assyrian daisy, patera, or rosette is a very characteristic ornament in Persian decoration (Figs. 249, 258). This is also a typical ornament in Greek architecture. Two well-known ornamental forms of Assyrian ornament occur on the crowning wall of the staircase of the Palace of Xerxes (Fig. 258), the cone-shaped pine-tree form, and

Fig. 261.—Upper Part of Parapet Wall, Susa. (P. & C.)

the palmate-crowned tree stem. The prototype of the former may be seen as an ideal rendering from nature of the cypress or pine-tree (Fig. 259) in the Assyrian illustration of a royal park. The contour of this ornament may have reminded the Persian fire-worshippers of the flame shape, which circumstance may have accounted for their fondness for using it so much. The other adjoining palmate ornament is distinctly Assyrian; as also are the daisy borders. A common form of ornament is seen on the enamelled bricks from Susa (Fig. 260) consisting of a double palmate or lotus form of flower, alternating and joined to concentric circles to form a band. Below is an Egyptian chevron rather out of proportion to the rest of the design. The whole thing has a decided Egyptian look, and may be a copy of the enamelled ornament of that country.

The Persian palaces were richly decorated with

Fig. 262.—Lion, from the Lion Frieze in Enamelled Bricks at Susa. (P. & C.)

enamelled bricks and tiles, in strong blue, orange, white, and brown colouring, as the archer's and lion's friezes from Susa (now in the Louvre) testify. These two works are reproduced in colours in Perrot and Chipiez' "History of Art in Persia." The upper part of the crenellated parapet wall of the staircase at Susa gives an idea of the extreme

richness of the decoration in glazed tiles with enamelled
covering (Fig. 261). The Persians learnt their art of

Fig. 263.—Head of one of the Lions from the Frieze at Susa.   (P. & C.)

enamelling tiles and bricks from the Chaldeans, and they
have never lost it. Under the Moslem rule in the fourteenth
and fifteenth centuries, the tiles and majolica that were
made for the decoration of the mosques reached a high stage

of perfection, especially in the colouring. This beauty is seen more particularly in the deep azure grounds, and in their treatment of conventional flower decoration that has never been surpassed in any country. This subject will be further treated in the future notice of modern Persian ornament.

In animal and figure design, the Persians closely imitated the Assyrians and Chaldeans, but were not so successful in their general treatment of them. The lion was one of the most favourite animals in Persian art. The lions in the " lion frieze " at Susa were represented with more than usual vigour and ability. This frieze remains the finest work of Persian design that is yet known to us, and probably was the work of a Chaldean artist employed by the great Persian king, Darius, to decorate his palace at Susa. (See Figs. 262, 263).

CHAPTER XI.

THE early inhabitants of Greece were the Pelasgians, a people who had the reputation of being great builders. At Athens, around the Acropolis, and at other places, remains of huge walls, made of unsquared stones laid in mud, have been found; these are the remains of the Pelasgian walls. The oldest historians were not disposed to make any difference between the Hellenes and the Pelasgians, but see in the former a continuation merely of the old Pelasgi stock. The Dorians came from the mountains of Thessaly, and steadily gained an ascendancy over tho other tribes of Greece.

The Ionians in the East gave an Oriental colouring to Hellas, both in manners, customs, and in art. There were three dialects in the language of the Greeks: the Doric, broad and soft; the Ionic, melodious and rich; and the Æolic, a mixture to which nothing of a special character is given, except that it is the nearest to the Latin.

The Greeks were a light-hearted and joyous race: they worshipped their gods in everything they did—in running, wrestling and dancing, in building, carving, and painting, in writing and reciting of poetry; their whole life was one of intense artistic devotion, and all their works of art were so many prayers to their gods. Whatever may have been the racial differences of the Hellenic peoples, they united all their physical and intellectual efforts to perfect their civilisation. They emerged from archaic barbarism step by step, to such a refinement of culture that has had no parallel in the history of nations.

It would be impossible to give an outline of Grecian or Roman art without describing at least the outlines of their religious beliefs as shadowed forth in their myths and in their plastic representations of the same. It would be advisable, therefore, to sketch, in as brief a manner as possible, some of the superior deities and their attributes, in order to understand better the art that was the glory of Greece and the grandeur of Rome.

The Theogony, or myths that relate to the origin of the Greek gods, includes that of the Romans, since the latter did not trouble themselves with the inventing of any origins for their gods, but simply borrowed them, as they did all their art, direct from the Greeks, merely substituting Latin names for their borrowed deities, instead of the original Greek ones.

Zeus (Jupiter) was the Supreme god of the Greeks, chief of the Olympian deities, the "Sky Father," the ruler and controller of the universe, dispenser of the thunder and lightning, rain, hail, and fertilising dew. Before the birth of Zeus, the Greek poets tell us that Ge (the earth) first emerged from Chaos, and separated itself immediately from Tartarus (the abyss beneath), and that Eros, or love, then first sprang into existence. Ge (the earth) then begat Uranus (the mountains and the heavens), and Pontus (the sea).

By the union of the earth and Uranus, the twelve Titans came into existence. They represented the elementary forces of nature ; there were also from this union the three Cyclops, thunder, lightning, and sheet-lightning, and the three Centimanes (hundred-handed), which are supposed to represent the stormy winds, the stormy sea, and the earthquakes.

By union with Pontus, the earth became the mother of many fabulous sea-deities. Other deities, offspring of the Titans, are Helios, the Sun ; Selene, the Moon ; Eos, the dawn. From Cœus and Phœbe, deities of the night, are Leto (dark night) and Asteria, (starry night). Cronus and Rhea, of the family of the Titans, had six children, the youngest of whom was the great god Zeus. He was rescued from the fate of being swallowed by his father, as his five brothers and sisters had been, and was brought up secretly in a grotto, on Mount Dicte, in Crete, was nursed by nymphs and the she-goat Amalthea, whilst the bees brought him honey to eat. Thus the youthful Zeus grew up in secrecy until he became a mighty god. The first of his exploits was to attack his father, and compel him to restore to life again his five brothers and sisters. He then found it was necessary for his supremacy to fight the Titans, who disputed his authority, which he did from his stand on Mount Olympus, in Thessaly, while the Titans fought from the opposite Mount Othrys. This fight lasted for ten years, and ended in the defeat of the Titans.

After this battle Zeus shared the ruling of the world with his two brothers, Poseidon (Neptune) and Hades (Pluto); the former he set as ruler over the sea, and the latter as king of the infernal regions. About this time the earth had produced another enemy to vex the peace of Zeus— Typhœus, a monster with a hundred fire-breathing dragons' heads, which Zeus was obliged to fight also. After a mighty battle the thunderbolts of Zeus prevailed, and the monster was cast into Tartarus, or as Virgil and Pindar have it, into Mount Ætna, in Sicily, where he still shows his anger at times, by breathing out fire and flames against the majesty of heaven. Another battle still is recorded to the credit of Zeus before he was able to enjoy his undisputed dominion over the world, that is the battle with the Giants, when they attempted to scale the sacred Olympus by "piling Ossa on Pelion." Zeus and his adherent gods were again victorious, and remained ever after the undisputed lords of Olympus.

The story of the battle with the Giants, the Giganto-Machia, formed a favourite subject for illustration with the

Greek sculptors. The cameo of Athenion depicts Zeus in his chariot, and the Giants attacking, having snakes for their legs (Fig. 264).

Zeus was the national god of the Greeks, and was first worshipped on high places and mountain tops long before any temples were raised to his honour. He was worshipped all over Greece, and one of his earliest shrines was at Dordona, in Epirus. The greatest of all his shrines was at Olympia, on the northern banks of the Alpheus. It was here that the Olympian games were celebrated.

It was also here that the great statue of Zeus was set

Fig. 264.—Cameo of Athenion.

up, which was the work of the renowned Greek sculptor Phidias (B.C. 500—432). This famous statue of the supreme god of the Greeks was a seated figure on a lofty throne, and was more than 40 feet high. It was made of, or probably covered over with, plates of ivory and gold (chryselephantine); the ivory plates covered the exposed parts of the flesh. In his right hand he held a figure of Victory, also made of ivory and gold. The sculptor sought to give his statue a look of sublime majesty, as the ruler of gods and men, and, at the same time, a kindly expression of benevolence, as the gracious father and dispenser of good gifts to mankind. Thousands are said to have come from great

distances in order to gaze on this masterpiece of the
greatest sculptor of Greece. It remained in its place for
more than eight hundred years, and was supposed to
have been destroyed by fire in the time of Theodosius III.
The coins of Elis have a seated figure, and the head of Zeus
on them (Fig. 265).

A supposed copy of the head of the god is in the Vatican
Museum. It was found at Otricoli in the last century
(Fig. 266).

The worship of Jupiter was also universal in Italy;

Fig. 265.—Coins of Elis with the Phidian Zeus (after Overbeck).

many temples have been erected to his honour. The most
famous of these was the one erected by Tarquin on the
Capitol at Rome. It had a statue of Jupiter, the work of
the Greek artist Apollonius, made of ivory and gold, and
said to be a copy of the Phidian Zeus.

Zeus is credited with a numerous family. He produced
Pallas Athene from his own head; the birth of Athene is
supposed to have formed part of the subject of the
sculptures on the pediment of the Parthenon (Temple of
Athene at Athens) the remains of which are in the British
Museum, but unfortunately the central figures of the
pediment are wanting which depicted the event.

One of his goddess-wives was Themis, of the Titan family, whose children are the Fates. Dione was his Dodonian wife, by whom he had as daughter Aphrodite (Venus). The Arcadian Zeus had for his wife Maia, who

Fig. 266.—Zeus of Otricoli, Vatican Museum.

was the mother of Hermes (Mercury). By Demeter (Ceres) he had a daughter Persephone (Proserpina), the flower goddess. By Eurynome, the Graces, and by Leto (Latona) Apollo and Artemis (Diana).

Later mythology recognises Hera (Juno), his sister,

to be his only legitimate wife (Fig. 267), and by her he had his children Ares (Mars), Hephæstus (Vulcan), and Hebe.

His earthly mistresses were Semele, daughter of Cadmus,

Fig. 267.—Head of Hera, perhaps after Polycletus.

King of the Greek Thebes, and mother of Dionysus (Bacchus) and others; Leda, Danaë, Alcmene, Europa, and Io.

The Roman Jupiter had at first no family, nor wives,

but later, when the Greek influences were more strongly developed in Roman mythology, he was made to be the son of Saturn, and had Juno for his wife, and Minerva (Athene) for his daughter.

Hera (Juno) is the feminine counterpart of Zeus (Jupiter). She represents air or atmosphere, is the queen of heaven, and is the guardian goddess of marriage ties with both Greeks and Romans. The peacock, goose, and the cuckoo as the herald of spring, are sacred to her. The beautiful head (Fig. 267) of Hera is supposed to be the work of Polycletus, a celebrated Greek sculptor.

Pallas Athene (Minerva) is the great virgin goddess of wisdom, of the dawn, and of war. According to some Greek accounts she sprang forth to life from her father's head (Zeus) fully armed with helmet and spear, chanting a war song, at which event the whole earth and sea trembled with commotion. She is represented in sculpture as the war goddess, in flowing robes with helmet and spear, and wearing the dreadful ægis, the breastplate of mail, with the snakes and head of Medusa, that "turned all men to stone who gazed on it" (Fig. 268). The serpent, the owl, and the cock are sacred to her.

Apollo was the favourite son of Zeus, and was a great god with both Greeks and Romans. He is the god of light, of music, and of healing. He is sometimes the god of death, sending out his arrows of sunshine that often breeds pestilence, as well as giving health. His favourite instrument is the lyre, which he plays at the feasts of the gods. His sons were Orpheus, the god of music, and Asclepius (Æsculapius), god of healing. Delphi was the chief seat of his worship, where a gorgeous temple was erected to him.

There the priestess Pythia uttered the oracles that were supposed to come to her ears alone, from out of a cleft in the rock under the sacred tripod, from which also issued gaseous vapours. These oracles were sacred words of advice or warning for those who came to consult them.

Other oracles of Apollo were at Didyma near Miletus, at
Clarus, and at Thebes.

Fig. 268.—Athene Polias (Villa Albani).

The Roman Emperor Augustus erected a great temple
to Apollo on the Palatine Hill, in which was placed the

celebrated statue of Apollo Citharædus (Apollo with the lyre), a work by the famous Greek sculptor Scopas. The statues of Apollo are of two kinds : one represents him as a conquering deity, strong and handsome, of youthful beauty both in face and body (Fig. 270); the other is in the more benign character of the Pythian lute player, with long flowing garments of a feminine nature, and with a

Fig. 269.—Pallas Athene, Naples.

pleasing expression. Scopas and Praxiteles made many statues of Apollo; copies of some of these are still in existence. These sculptors flourished about B.C. 400. The celebrated statue of the youthful Apollo known as the Apollo Sauroctonus (the lizard slayer) is a work of Praxiteles.

Aphrodite (Venus) was "born of the sea foam," as some

say near to the island of Cyprus, where she was first supposed to touch the land; many temples were built to her worship in this island. She was the goddess of love

Fig. 270.—Apollo Belvedere, Vatican.

and beauty, and of the generative and creative forces in nature; the goddess of spring, and all kinds of fertility, both in celestial and terrestrial regions. She was the

favourite deity of the Grecian mariners, and was worshipped in Cyprus and the isles of Greece more than any
other divinity. Iris in the *Tempest*, in referring to Venus,
says—

> " I met her deity
> Cutting the clouds towards Paphos, and her son
> Dove-drawn with her."

The story of her love for Adonis, and of his death and
coming to life again, is but the decay of nature in autumn,
and its resuscitation in the spring. The Seasons and the
Graces are her attendants, who dress and adorn her. She
is accompanied by Eros and Hymen, the gods of love and
marriage. Venus of the Romans is the goddess of spring,
and the month of April was held sacred to her by the
early Italians. She was also, with them, the goddess of
love and marriage.

The best artists of Greece put forth all their powers in
painting and sculpture in their representations of the sea-
born Aphrodite, and if we except Zeus himself, there is no
other divinity of the Greek mythology that has served so
much as a model for the loveliest creations of the plastic
genius of the Greeks. The grandest conception of the
goddess as a work of art is the Venus of Milo, found in
1820 in the island of Melos (Milo) (Fig. 271), and now in
the Louvre. The grandeur and majesty of this famous piece
of sculpture is beyond praise. It ought to be seen in the
Louvre, to be appreciated at its worth, as drawings and
casts do not give an adequate idea of its beauty. The
Medicean Venus is a work of the Athenian artist Cleo-
menes, of the later Attic school, in the second century B.C.
A statue of Venus Anadyomene (rising from the sea), of
"Venus crouching in the Bath" (Vatican collection), and
of "Venus loosing her Sandal," are all of this later and
declining period of Greek sculpture, where the goddess is
represented undraped and more realistic in conception.
Venus had many attributes. The dove, sparrow, and the
dolphin, and in plants the myrtle, rose, apple, poppy, and

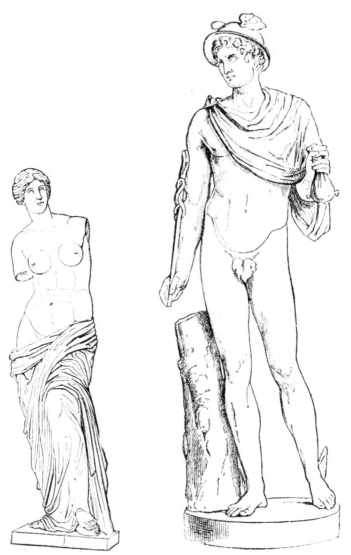

Fig. 271.—Venus of Milo.   Fig. 272.—Statue of Hermes, Capitol.

lime-tree, were sacred to her, but varied according to the
locality and times.

Hermes (Mercury) is the god of shepherds and of

Fig. 273.—Diana of Versailles.

pastures, and also of commerce and trade. When a child
he invented the lyre from a tortoise-shell which he was

forced to give up to Apollo. He is represented with
wings on his cap and feet, and a herald's staff as the
messenger of the gods, and with a well-filled purse as an
emblem of trade (Fig. 272).

Fig. 274.—Melpomene, Vatican.

Artemis (Diana) was the twin-sister of Apollo, and was
at first the goddess of the moon. Her favourite amusement
is the chase, but in the statue (Fig. 273) from the Villa

Hadrian, now in the Louvre, she is represented as the protectress of wild animals.

Mnemosyne (Memory) is the mother of the Muses. The nine Muses are — Clio (history), Melpomene (tragedy) (Fig. 274), Terpsichore (dancing), Polyhymnia (religious service), Thalia (comedy), Urania (astronomy), Euterpe (lyric poetry), Erato (erotic poetry and geometry), and Calliope (epic poetry and science generally).

Dionysus or Bacchus is, with both Greeks and Romans, the god of wine, of vineyards, and of autumn blessings. Naxos was the chief seat of his worship. It was on this

Fig. 275.—Dionysus and the Lion, from the Monument of Lysikrates.

island that he met and married Ariadne, the daughter of Minos, King of Crete, who had been deserted here by Theseus, her former lover. The story of Dionysus punishing the Tyrrhenian pirates who took him prisoner, intending to sell him as a slave, and of his changing himself to a lion and so terrifying the sailors, who jumped overboard and were changed into dolphins, is the subject of the fine relief on the frieze of the Lysikrates monument (Fig. 275 and Frontispiece).

The lion, tiger, bull, and ram are his favourite animal attributes Among plants, the vine, the ivy, and the laurel were sacred to him.

Bacchanalian subjects and festivals of Dionysus occupy a large and important place in the art of Greece, Rome, and Pompeii.

Nice, Victoria, or Victory is always represented with

Fig. 276.—Victory, Munich Collection.

wings, a palm branch, and holding a laurel wreath, and, as would be expected, was more extensively venerated at Rome than in Greece. In the latter country her statues are generally of a small size, and she is an accompanying goddess to Athene and Zeus (Fig. 276).

CHAPTER XII.

ART IN PRIMITIVE GREECE.

IT was not only on their temples and images of their gods that the Greeks put their best efforts in art; but in their vases, jewellery, furniture, and humbler utensils of the household and of every-day life, we find the Greek artist pouring out some of his richest fancies, and the same spell of beauty is cast over them all. And did not Pericles, the son of Xanthippus, eulogise his countrymen in his famous speech on those who had fallen in the Peloponnesian War, as "lovers of justice and wisdom," " philosophers, lovers of *beauty*, and foremost among men " ?

In Egypt, Assyria, and Persia we find all the artistic knowledge of these countries was lavished on the temples, and to the glorification of their autocratic rulers ; but scarcely any remains are found that would imply a fostering of the minor arts among the common people. On the contrary, in Greece art impregnated the life and work of all classes, from the highest to the lowest in the state. This was only possible when entire freedom prevailed, as it did in the mass of the Greek people

Some of the oldest monuments of primitive Greece have been found at Mycenæ, Troy (Hissarlik), and Tiryns. These consist of domed tombs, such as the tomb of Agamemnon, or the so-called " Treasure-house " of Atreus, and others, as the rock-cut tombs. The site of ancient "Troy divine" was discovered by Dr. Schliemann in the year 1875, under the mound of the modern Hissar-

Fig. 277.—Perspective View of the Lion's Gate.   (P. & C.)

lik, in the Trojan plain, in the north-west corner of Asia
Minor. The character of the stone, clay, wood, and lime

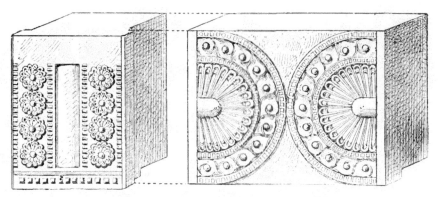

Fig. 278.—Alabaster Frieze, Tiryns. (P. & C.)

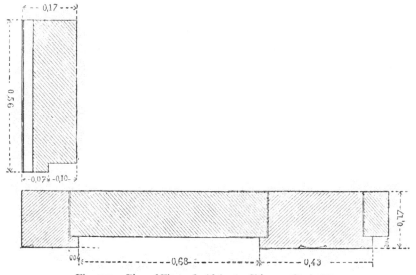

Fig. 279.—Plan of Fig. 278, Alabaster Frieze. (P. & C.)

materials, and similarity of the construction, enable the
archæologist to place the remains found at these three
places as belonging to the same epoch of time and style

of art which has been called Mycenian. The oldest
monument of Greek sculpture yet discovered is supposed

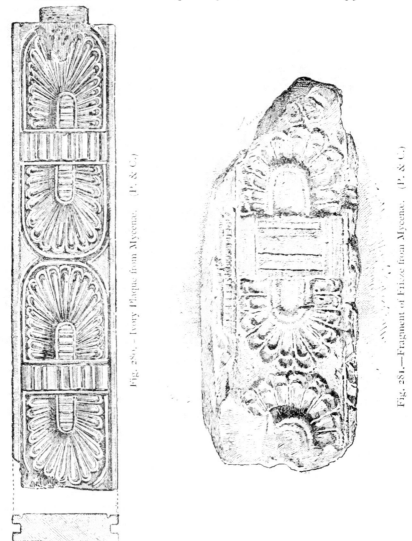

Fig. 280.—Ivory Plaque from Mycenae.   (P. & C.)

Fig. 281.—Fragment of Frieze from Mycenae.   (P. & C.)

to be the Lion's Gate of the Mycenian Acropolis (Fig. 277).

Pausanias thus alludes to Mycenæ and Tiryns :—"A portion of the enclosure wall still remains, and the principal gate, with the lions over it. These (the walls) were

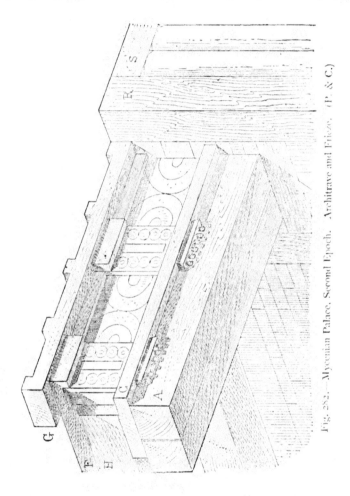

Fig. 282.— Mycenian Palace, Second Epoch. Architrave and Frieze. (P. & C.)

built by the Cyclops who made the wall at Tiryns for Præteus. Among the ruins at Mycenæ is the fountain called Perseia, and the subterraneous buildings of Atreus and his children, in which their treasures were stored."

The sculptured lions are still there, so is the spring
Perseia, and the wonderful treasure-house of Atreus is still
the best preserved of all the domed tomb buildings of
Mycenæ.

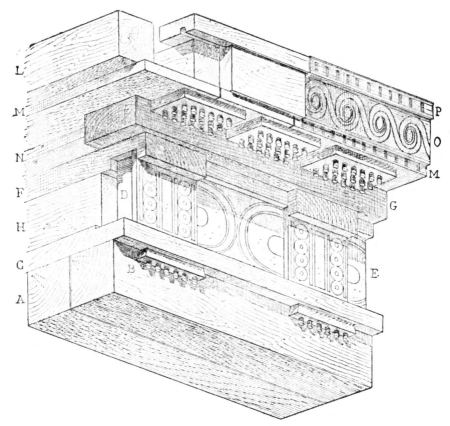

Fig. 283.—Mycenian Palace, Second Epoch. Restoration of Entablature. (P. & C.)

From the remains of Mycenian architecture, Messrs.
Perrot and Chipiez have ingeniously restored some of the
wooden construction of the palaces of that early period,
and have assumed that, from these early wooden construc-

tions of Mycenæ, the Greeks developed the renowned order of Doric architecture. We have seen that, in most

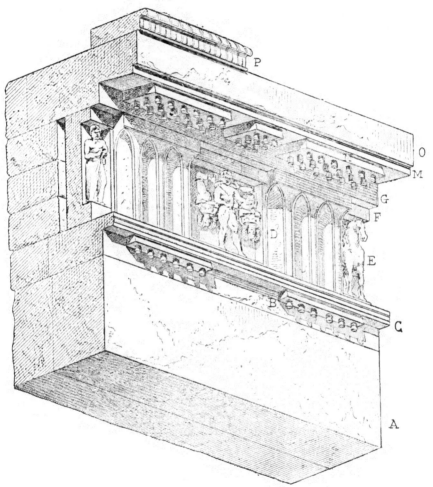

Fig. 284.—Entablature of C. Selinous Temple. (P. & C.)

countries, stone architecture, in its earliest stages, was but copies of the earlier wooden construction. The Doric order seems to have been no exception to this rule, for here again the stone-cutter has borrowed from the carpenter. To go back for some of the supposed beginnings of the Doric frieze, the alabaster frieze, shown in plan and elevation at Figs. 278 and 279, has been found in the ruins of a palace at Tiryns.

The pattern of this frieze is the same as that which has been frequently found on other fragments from Mycenæ.

Fig. 285.—Vase of Woman's Form, Troy. (P. & C.)

It resembles the Doric triglyphs and metopes in consisting of a double design ; two semicircles back to back, divided by a vertical rectangular band, which is subdivided by a vertical central division, having rosettes arranged vertically on either side. Two similar designs are seen on the ivory plaque (Figs. 280 and 281) and fragment of frieze from Mycenæ. The same design appears also on the red porphyry fragments of the façade decoration on the Mycenian beehive tombs.

An illustration from Perrot and Chipiez shows an assemblage of the component parts of this frieze pattern, with a portion of the architrave in wood (Fig. 282).

Fig. 286.— Vase from Troy.   (P. & C.)

We refer the reader for a fuller description of the transition of the Doric entablature from the Mycenian wood construction to Perrot and Chipiez' "Art in Primitive Greece," Vol. II. We extract a portion in explanation of the illustrations (Figs. 282 and 283), where the analogy between the wooden construction of the former and the stone construction of the latter is clearly established.

Fig. 288.—Three-Handled Amphora, Ialysos. (P. & C.)

Fig. 287.—Pilgrim's Bottle, Ialysos. (P. & C.)

In Fig. 284 we have the entablature of the C. Temple of Selinous (one of the oldest examples of Doric architecture), rendered famous by the archaic sculptures embellishing its metopes. There is not one of all the members we have passed in review but which appears in it. Thus, a pair of stone beams, corresponding with the like number of timbers in the Mycenian wood frame, constitute the architrave; and under listel C surmounting it, peers, flush with the triglyphs, the small plank B.

Its lower section is adorned by the ornament known as guttæ, the origin and meaning of which had hitherto been unsatisfactorily explained. The guttæ are cylindrical in shape detached from the walls, and in every respect

Fig. 289.—Vase with Geometric Decoration. (P. & C.)

identical with the wooden pegs which occur in this situation below the timber entablature. These same pegs again appear above the frieze in the semblance of another ornamental form, the "mutules" which, until lately, had seemed every whit as strange and problematical as the guttæ. The stone table N, in the lower surface of which the guttæ are carved, is no other than our old wood-plate, which in the Mycenian carpentry work exhibits these same saliences or pegs, and served to fix the lining of the joists below. If the Selinous mutules are sloped, it is because they are associated with a ridged roof; but as a flat covering has been assumed for Mycenæ, it involved— without prejudice to the system—a horizontal position for the mutules. As regards the frieze, both here and in every Doric building, it invariably consists, like the alabaster frieze, of pillars D alternating with slabs E. The function of the pillars (triglyphs) is to maintain the slabs (metopes) in place.

Fig. 290.—The Marseilles Ewer. (P. & C.)

Comparison between these two figures will further show all the details, with slight modifications, to be practically similar. Thus, the whole of the Doric order, the basis of all Greek architecture, including the column, longitudinal

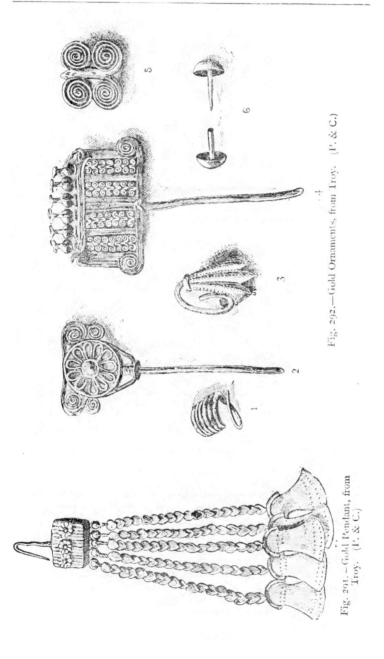

Fig. 292.—Gold Ornaments, from Troy. (P. & C.)

Fig. 291.—Gold Pendant, from Troy. (P. & C.)

beams, and joists supporting the roof, as well as the
secondary decorative construction, had its origin in wooden
construction, and there is hardly any doubt but that the

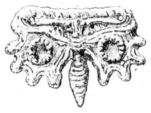

Fig. 203.— Gold Plate Ornament, from Troy.

Mycenian palace was its prototype. The Greeks of later
days forgot the borrowing of the timber construction, and

Fig. 204.—Gold Disc.   (P. & C.)

have given names to some parts, such as "guttæ" (drops),
which ought to be more correctly pegs.

Great quantities of pottery and objects of industrial art
in metal—more especially in gold—have been found in

the excavations at Mycenæ, Tiryns, and Troy. The earthenware pottery is generally decorated in colours of brown, red, and greyish white. The patterns are very simple, bands and squares arranged in rows, some animal forms, leaves with wavy stems, and spirals; some of the pottery is decorated with marine animals, such as the octopus, cuttle-fish, argonaut, and with seaweed. Some curious shaped vases of woman forms (Figs. 285, 286) have been found by Dr. Schliemann.

Fig. 295.—Gold Disc. (P. & C.)

A pilgrim's bottle from Ialysos decorated with circular bands, and an amphora with three handles, from the same place, decorated with bands and lily forms with curled-back petals, are very beautiful, and a small vessel with geometric ornament are all of the same character (Figs. 287, 288, and 289). The most beautiful form of Mycenian pottery is the Marseilles vase or ewer, in the Borély collection (Fig. 290).

The decoration is a brown-black on a light ground, and

consists of the argonaut shellfish and seaweed. It is likely to have been a copy from a metal object owing to its shape, which is characteristic of metal.

In metal-work generally, and in the inlaying of gold and electrum in a bronze ground, the Mycenian artists have produced some splendid work. There are six chromo-

Fig. 296.—Gold Cup, Troy. (P. & C.)

lithographs in Messrs. Perrot and Chipiez's "Art in Primitive Greece" of bronze Mycenian daggers inlaid with gold and electrum of various shades : one has the representation of panthers hunting birds on a river-bank—the river is stocked with fish ; another has a lion hunt by armed men ; a third, lions hunting gazelles ; a fourth has running lions ; a fifth, spiral ornamentation ; and the sixth a free rendering of lilies both on handle and blade. The art and workmanship of them all are of a high order.

Some gold ornaments from Troy (Figs. 291 and 292) show their skill in hand-wrought jewellery.

The golden butterfly (Fig. 293) and the two gold discs (Figs. 294 and 295) are stamped on the metal, and were

Fig. 297.—Gold Ewer, Troy. (P. & C.)

used as dress decorations; they were found in great quantities in the tombs of the women at Mycenæ. One is an octopus design, and the other a butterfly.

The gold cup (Fig. 296) and ewer (Fig. 297), found at Troy along with many others in silver, gold, and bronze, give a fair idea of the beauty of shape and design of such articles of this period. They show marks of injury by fire

CHAPTER XIII.

ALTHOUGH Egypt and Assyria are justly credited with the creation of the models and the invention of the methods that subsequently aroused to life the artistic genius of the Greeks, yet the fact remains that, from all the wealth of artistic forms bequeathed to succeeding ages by the nations of hoary antiquity, prior to the Grecian period, nothing has survived except those forms which Greece has selected from her predecessors, and after remodelling them by her own standards of beauty and fitness, has left them as imperishable models of art for all nations that follow her. All historic art and architecture, whether classic or what not, since the days of Pericles, is based on Greek art, notwithstanding the many modifications which we see in Byzantine, Saracenic, Romanesque, and their offshoots. All of them owe their life and vitality to Greek traditions and to Greek principles.

We have seen that in the earlier Greek buildings, such as Mycenian palaces, timber construction must have largely entered into the architecture of that period, and it is quite likely that timber was used for the greater part of the Greek domestic dwellings, which may account for no remains of them having been found.

The rock-cut tombs of Lycia, in Asia Minor, afford to us a further proof of timber construction which may have been in use in the Early Greek period in Europe, and these tombs of Lycia tend to throw a side light on the probable forms of Greek construction that existed between the date of the Mycenian buildings and that of the oldest Doric remains that are at present known, for the Lycians had free intercourse with the Ionians and European Greeks. The

Fig. 298.—Lycian Rock-built Tomb at Pinara. (P. & C.)

earlier Lycian tombs are of a great antiquity, and the same form of tomb has been used in Lycia down to periods when Greece was far advanced in art (Figs. 298 and 299).

The Lycians formed a connecting link with the Anterior
Asiatics and the Ionian Greeks. Their origin and their
language were Asiatic, but the greater part of their art was
the product of Hellenic artists from Ionian Greece, and,
therefore, the Lycians must have been intimately connected
with the Greeks, and must have played an important part
in the development of Hellenic culture.

Fig. 299.—Lycian Rock-built Tomb at Pinara. (P. & C.)

The Greek temples were in some respects related to the
Egyptian temple. The pillar and beam construction was
copied from Egypt, and also the rectangular plan. The
great distinction between the two was that rows of columns
were placed outside the temples of the Greeks, which gave
to them a light and airy appearance, while in contradistinction the Egyptians had their rows of columns inside

the great hypostyle halls and galleries of their temples which gave to them the effect of oppressive gloominess. Broadly speaking, the Greek temple was something of the model of an Egyptian temple turned inside out.

The interior of a Greek temple was simply a rectangular *cella* or cell where the statue of the god or goddess was set up, and sometimes a smaller chamber behind called the treasury. The smaller temples consisted of the cella only. A row of lighter columns sometimes supported the roof of the cella, as in the case of the Parthenon. It was only in the case of the larger temples that we find more than one cell, while the Egyptian temple was often a maze of large and small chambers, the multitude adding to the mystery sought for in all Egyptian architecture. The Greek temples were usually placed on a basement of steps, and built on elevated positions. The Greeks sought all publicity in the honouring of their deities, and in pleasing the passer-by with the sight of their beautiful buildings, on which their best decoration was shown on the outside.

Greek architecture dates from the end of the Archaic age down to the death of Alexander the Great, from about B.C. 600 to B.C. 333.

It is usually divided into three Styles or, as they are called, "Orders," namely, the Doric, the Ionic, and the Corinthian. The Doric represents the European phase of the Greek style, the Ionic and Corinthian having more of the Asiatic features. The three orders were in use in Greece at the same time, that is to say, a more severe and correct phase of the Doric—the older order—was used after buildings in the newer orders had appeared. Thomson, in his " Ode to Liberty," has alluded to the orders in the lines—

> " First, unadorn'd
> And nobly plain, the manly Doric rose ;
> The Ionic then, with decent matron grace,
> Her airy pillar heaved ; luxuriant last,
> The rich Corinthian spread her wanton wealth."

The Greeks made use of the vertical and horizontal line in their architecture; the curved line was not used, except, of course, in decoration. The half-diameter of the column was the module or unit by which the whole building was measured, and the column was limited in height according to the diameter of its base. This did not preclude freedom in design; on the contrary, freedom was allowed and practised to such an extent that hardly two Grecian buildings of any one order were alike in proportion or design. Even the mouldings were varied in curve and proportion; these members that were with the Romans merely segments of circles, were in section with the Greeks either parts of the curve of the ellipse or parabola, and in many cases were designed by freehand. Some very subtle devices to overcome natural optical effects when viewing the buildings have been discovered by Mr. Pennethorne and Mr. Penrose, more especially in the Parthenon.

It is well known that the *entasis*, or slight swelling made in Greek columns, which makes a convex line of their profiles, is done to prevent the column from looking hollowed in the centre, which it would do if it were perfectly straight; but in addition to this the architects above named have discovered in the Parthenon a correction in the vertical lines, to prevent the apparent tendency which all high vertical lines have to spread out at the top, in the making of the columns to incline slightly inwards; and the steps of the basement and horizontal lines of the architraves are found to be slightly curved upwards in the middle to prevent the tendency that all long horizontal lines have to droop in the middle.

Thus we learn how admirably painstaking, and how well the Greeks applied their profound knowledge to their architecture, as they did in everything else.

The joints of their marble masonry were as a rule so fine and accurate in the fitting together, that it has been said a razor edge could not be inserted between them.

The Greek Doric order (Fig. 300) is without a base; the

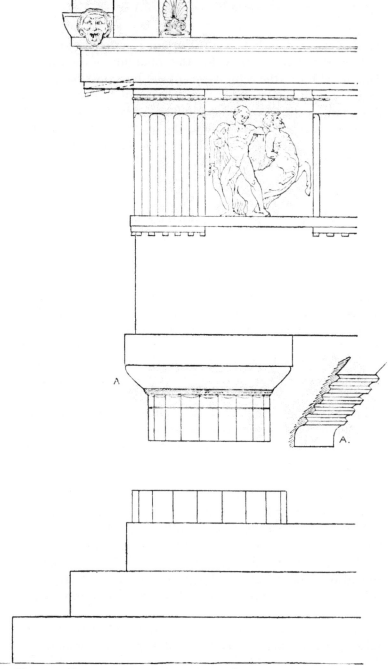

Fig. 300.—The Parthenon.   Greek Doric, enlarged Section of Annulets at A.

shaft of the column has twenty flutings ; sunk lines or rings
encircle the shaft a little below the moulding of the capital.
This moulding—the echinus—is of the best possible profile
that a supporting member could have ; it is divided from
the shaft by three or five annulets. Above the echinus
rests the square tile-like cap—the abacus—which carries
the architrave. The latter is a marble beam with square
ends, and above the architrave is the frieze separated by a
band *(taenia)*. The frieze has triglyphs alternating with
metopes. The former consists of channelled pier-like
forms one over and one between each column, and the
metopes are square panels between two triglyphs on which
are usually found sculptured subjects. At the bottom of
each triglyph, separated by a fillet, is a row of pegs, cylindrical or conical in shape, called " guttæ " or drops.

Above the frieze the cornice projects, which in profile
consists of a flat band—the corona—and the crowning
member, an ovolo moulding. Under the projecting eave of
the cornice are slanting slabs of marble—parallel to the
roof tiles—placed one over each triglyph, and one over
each metope. These are called mutules, and they have
rows of guttæ on their under surface.

The crowning members of the cornice are carried around
the sloping lines of the triangular pediments at each end
of the building. On the pediments were sculptured the
figure subjects that had usually some relation to the
divinity to whom the temple was dedicated ; as, for
example, on the Parthenon pediment the story of the birth
of Athene was the subject executed and designed by
Phidias, who also was the sculptor of the celebrated
Panathenic frieze that adorned the outer part of the cella of
the Parthenon. Ictinus was the architect of the Parthenon
and also of the temples of Apollo Epicurius at Bassæ and
at Phigallia, both in Arcadia. The Parthenon was finished
about B.C. 438.

The Greek Ionic order in its capital and ornaments is
quite distinct from the Doric, and has more mouldings.

Fig. 301.—Temple on the Ilissus; Greek Ionic.

The general plan of the temple is the same as in the Doric, but the proportions of the various parts are more slender. It has been generally thought that the Ionic volute was a development of the volutes from the Persian capital at Persepolis, but it is more likely, as before stated (on page 87), that their prototype is found on capitals derived from the Egyptian lotus. The architrave is sometimes plain and sometimes divided into three facias. The frieze was usually occupied with sculpture, and the base of the column was composed of a double torus, with a hollow between; the lower torus was plain, and the upper one fluted (Fig. 301).

The Temple of Diana at Ephesus, the Erectheum, and the Mausoleum of Halicarnassus were among the finest examples of the Ionic order.

The Corinthian order was more Roman than Greek, though of Greek invention, and was a rich type of architecture that suited the growing vanity for love of display with the Romans, who eagerly appropriated it in the second century B.C., and erected many fine buildings in this order; but often enriching the mouldings and all plain spaces almost beyond recognition.

The most perfect and truly beautiful example of the Greek Corinthian is the small Choragic monument of Lysikrates at Athens (Frontispiece). Its praises and merits have been spoken and written of by almost every architect of eminence; it may be said of it and of the Parthenon that for proportion, and for marvellous unity of parts, and also for the perfect marriage of sculpture with architecture, no buildings have ever been erected to equal them.

The bell of the Corinthian capital, as in the Lysikrates monument, is surrounded at the base by a row of water-plant leaves; acanthus leaves spring from these, and out of the latter spring volutes (*cauliculi*), the larger ones of which meet at the upper corners; the four smaller ones meet in the middle, and from the junction of the upper

Fig. 302.—Capital of the Lysikrates Monument; Greek Corinthian.

middle ones an upright palmate appears; rosettes are
placed between each of the eight acanthus leaves.   The
abacus is moulded and curved in plan.   The capital, as a

whole, is designed in a masterly way, so as to give the utmost variety and contrast of beautiful forms (Fig. 302). The frieze is sculptured with figures which illustrate the story of Dionysus and the Tyrrhenian pirates (Frontispiece).

The Etruscans were a race of people who settled in the west of Italy, between the Arno and the Tiber, at a very early date. Their origin is uncertain, but they are supposed to have come from Asia Minor. They were known as great builders, and were well skilled in all the arts. In their larger works of fortifications and great walls they used stones of an enormous size (Cyclopean). Many places in Italy still attest to the presence of the Etruscans by the remains of these Cyclopean walls.

They were considerably advanced in architecture and the minor arts at the time when Rome was first beginning

Fig. 303.— Etruscan Door from Perugia.

to show its signs of power, and were the architects and builders who executed all the works for the early Romans. The Etruscans used the arch very much in building, a feature that the Greeks, although they were acquainted with its use, did not think it necessary in their trabeated system of building. It was, on the other hand, a very favourite feature with the Etruscans, from whom the Romans learnt the use of it. The Tarquins were an Etruscan family who were masters of Rome in the sixth century B.C., and it was under these Emperors that the great sewer, known as the Cloaca Maxima, was built, part of which is still in existence.

This work consists of an arched waterway built in three concentric rings of large wedge-shaped stones (*voussoirs*). The Etruscans constructed temples, palaces, and dwelling-houses, all of which have perished or have been destroyed, and only a few remains of their walled cities survive. The gate of Perugia (Fig. 303) is the remains of a characteristic Etruscan building. The arch is seen in perfect construction, and the Doric frieze; above is seen a little Ionic column. Etruscan architecture was mostly a kind of Doric with a round shaft. According to Vitruvius the Etruscan temple consisted of three cells, with one or more rows of columns in front, the distance between the columns, or intercolumniation, being much greater than in Greek temples. Sometimes the temple consisted of a circular cell only and a porch, like the later development of this form in the Roman temple at Tivoli, and the Mausoleum of Hadrian. Many Etruscan tombs have been found, consisting of rock-built and detached structures. Some of the rock-built tombs at Castel d'Asso have beams and rafters cut out of the rock in imitation of wooden construction, and also figures cut out in high relief all around the chambers. Great quantities of vessels in pottery and metal-work objects, and also jewellery, have been found in recesses of the walls and roofs of these chambers. The temple of Jupiter Capitolinus at Rome was an Etruscan building. The Etruscan religion was dark and full of superstition; their gods were mostly deities of the thunder and lightning and subterranean spirits rather than divinities of comfort and mercy, and the Romans adopted most of them in their mythology. The Romans having mastered the principle of the arch, made very good use of it. The greater number of their principal buildings were erected in a mixture of the arch and trabeated system.

The Roman Doric and Ionic orders were ill-proportioned in their various members, bad in profiling, and also very heavy in appearance. The Theatre of Marcellus is an example of the former in its lower columns, and the Temple of Fortuna Virilis an example of the latter.

The Tuscan order is noted for a more elegant development of the Etruscan smooth column, and a great

Fig. 304.—Roman Corinthian, half Capital of Mars Ultor.

projection of cornice. A good example of this order may be seen in the portico of St. Paul's Church in Covent Garden, London, designed by Inigo Jones.

Fig. 305.—Roman Corinthian, Entablature, Capital, and Base of the Pantheon.

The Corinthian order received better treatment at the hands of the Romans; some of their buildings are fine examples of this order.

Some of the Roman Corinthian capitals are well designed, and have a very grand and imposing effect, as that of the Mars Ultor (Fig. 304) and the Pantheon. The Mars Ultor capital is undoubtedly fine and rich in the extreme; that of the Pantheon is more restrained; and in both of them is used the olive-leaf variety of acanthus, each tine or leaflet of which is hollowed out; and thus the whole capital in a full light would have a sparkling effect of light and shade, so that even at a great height and distance from the eye none of the modelling would be lost to sight.

The Roman Corinthian has more mouldings, and has modillions or brackets in the cornice instead of the usual Greek dentils (Fig. 305). The entablature from the Temple of Jupiter Tonans (Fig. 306) is an example of the inordinate love of over-richness and display that was so characteristic of the Romans.

The Baths of Caracalla and of Diocletian are the only ones that have remained to us in any state of preservation, and show from the remains what splendid examples of public buildings they must have been. They were built of brick mostly, and lined with stucco on which frescoes were painted.

The Baths of Caracalla, at the foot of the Aventine Hill, were erected A.D. 217. They covered a rectangular piece of ground about 1,150 feet each way, and were a great assemblage of bath-rooms, public and private, of cold, vapour, and hot baths; swimming and other kinds of bath, gymnasium hall, libraries, reading-rooms, assembly halls, &c., all comprised under the one roof, surrounding the open courtyard in which was the principal swimming bath, in a building 730 ft. by 380 ft. in dimension. In the centre and at the back of this group of buildings was a circular hall, with a domed roof, called the Solar cell, the

walls of which were lined with brass. Some of the finest of
Roman statuary adorned these halls. The principal hall
of the Baths of Diocletian, erected at the beginning of the
fourth century A.D is called the Ephebeum, and is still

Fig. 306.—Roman Corinthian. Entablature of Jupiter Tonans.

used as the Church of Santa Maria Degli Angeli. It is
almost 300 ft. long by 90 ft. wide, and was restored by
Michelangelo. Its roof consists of three great cross vaults
supported by eight granite columns, 45 ft. in height.

Another class of buildings that the Romans were fond of was the amphitheatres. Remains of them have been found throughout the Roman Empire, the most stupendous of which was the Coliseum or Flavian Amphitheatre.

Fig. 307.—Bas-relief on the Arch of Titus. (P. & C.)

It was begun by the Emperor Vespasian and finished by his son Titus, and its ruins still attest to its greatness.

It is elliptical in plan, is four stories in height; the three lowest are pierced with eighty openings, semicircular arched, with columns and piers between. The first story is Doric, the second Ionic, and the third Corinthian. Each column and pier is raised on a stylobate, and the columns carry entablatures continuously around the building.

An almost solid wall is the feature of the fourth story, which has a series of Corinthian pilasters, and projecting brackets for carrying the awning poles. The façade is

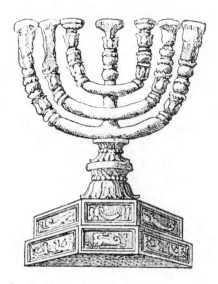

Fig. 308.—Jewish Candlestick, Arch of Titus. (P. & C.)

built of stone quarried from the neighbouring hills, and the interior portions are built of brick. The dimensions are 620 ft. in length, 513 ft. wide, and 162 ft. in height. Double corridors run around the building on each floor, and it had seats for more than 80,000 spectators. Chariot races, mimic sea-fights, when the arena would be flooded artificially with water, gladiatorial combats, and fights with wild animals and bulls, were among the amusements of the Romans that were performed in the amphitheatres.

Other monuments, such as triumphal columns and

Fig. 309.—Roman Composite Order, from the Arch of Titus

arches, were erected by the Emperors to commemorate their victories, and these were of the most elaborate and rich description. The column of Marcus Aurelius, known as the Antonine column, and the column of Trajan set up by that Emperor in Trajan's Forum at Rome in commemoration of his victory over the Dacians, are the two best known of these commemorative monuments. The latter column has been reproduced, and a cast of it may be seen in the South Kensington Museum. The original is nearly 133 ft. high, and is richly sculptured with bas-reliefs on marble slabs fastened together in a spiral form around the central structure. The order is Doric, the shaft being set up on a large pedestal with very fine sculptures of figures, armour, and inscriptions.

The triumphal arches are rectangular masses of masonry with arched openings, sometimes with one arch and sometimes three, a large one and two smaller ones, as the arches of Constantine and Septimus Severus ; and sometimes smaller ones had piers and pilasters with a lintel entablature instead of an arch, as in the Goldsmith's Arch in Rome. The arch of Titus (erected to commemorate the taking of Jerusalem A.D. 70), which is one of the finest of these monuments, is interesting for two reasons: one is that it has reliefs on it recording the capture of Jerusalem, with the representation of the seven-branched golden candlestick of the Temple (Figs. 307, 308), and the other is that the arch itself is one of the finest examples of the architectural order that was created by the Romans—the Composite—(Fig. 309), which is a grafting of the Ionic on the Corinthian.

The decoration of this order is extremely rich in character: the lower half of the capital has the Corinthian leaves, while the upper half is almost the whole of the Ionic voluted capital added ; the cornice has both the Ionic dentils and the Corinthian modillions. The arch of Septimus Severus and the Baths of Diocletian are of the Composite order.

CHAPTER XIV.

GREEK AND ROMAN ORNAMENT.

GREEK ornament—as found on the carved mouldings, friezes, acroteria, antifexes, and capitals, or, as in the painted variety, found on vases, plain mouldings, bands, plates, and other surface decorations, or incised on the bronze cistæ and mirrors—was of a severe and refined order, almost all of which had its birthplace in Egyptian and Assyrian forms, that in the first instances were used

Fig. 310.—Greek Frets.

in a symbolic sense, but under the hands of Greek artists had lost all their former meaning, and were developed and partly transformed into a wealth of purely æsthetic forms.

The simplest forms were frets or the so-called key pattern (Figs. 310, 311, and 315).

The word meander is sometimes applied to the Greek

frets ; this is not correct, as the word implies a curved line, not a rectangular one.

The guilloche, snare-work, or cable ornament, is used

Fig. 311.—Greek Carved Fret.

on flat bands, and also as the decoration of torus mouldings (Figs. 312 and 313).

The Greeks used the honeysuckle pattern in an endless variety of forms both in carving and in painting, examples of which are at Figs. 314 and 315.

Fig. 312.—Treble Guilloche Ornament.

The ivy was used very much in borders of their painted vases (Fig. 316).

The ogee moulding was usually decorated with the water-leaf and tongue ornament, and the ovolo with the characteristic egg and tongue, and the round fillets with

beads and reels. A fine example of this group of decorated mouldings comes from the Temple of Minerva Polias
at Athens (Fig 317).

Fig. 313.—Double Guilloche.

An elongated type of the egg and tongue comes from
the Erectheum (Fig. 318).

The Greeks seldom used large scrolls in ornament; an
exception is the scroll ornament from the roof of the

Fig. 314.—Anthemion (carved), from Apollo Epicurius.

Lysikrates monument, and in the Corinthian cauliculi or
volutes (see Fig. 302).

The Greek variety of acanthus foliage is seen in the
capital from the same monument.

Roman architectural ornament was simply Greek with a few variations, not always improvements. It was less refined, but in some cases, especially in the examples

Fig. 315.—Greek Border with Fret Bands.

of large acanthus scrolls on friezes, panels, and pilasters (Fig. 319), and in their large capitals, the ornament was designed with great skill and virility. They used the

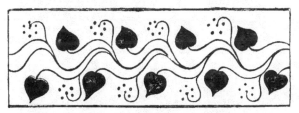

Fig. 316.—Greek Ivy Meander Border.

softer-leaved variety of acanthus—the mollis—while the Greeks used the spinosus, or prickly-leaved variety.

The decorations of the Roman mouldings were less elegant than those of the Greeks, owing to the contours being segments of circles where the Greeks used forms like conic sections, and the execution was less artistic in the Roman mouldings (Figs. 320, 321, 322).

The domestic architecture of Greece is guessed at by

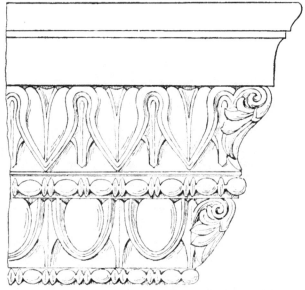

Fig. 317.—Decorated Mouldings from the Temple of Minerva Polias ; Ogee Ovolo, and Beads.

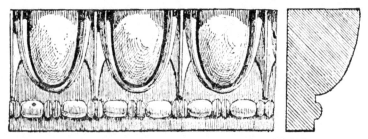

Fig. 318.—The Ovolo, with Egg and Tongue, from the Erectheum.

the remains of Pompeii and Herculaneum, which, though Roman provincial cities, were in style and decoration a fair reflection of Greek art. The remains of the art found

Fig. 319.—Ancient Roman Panel, Florence.

in these cities have been styled Greco-Roman. The destruction of Pompeii was in the year A.D. 79.

The general arrangement of a Roman house was rectangular in plan, with, and sometimes without, a

Fig. 320.—Ovolo and Astragal Mouldings; Roman.

vestibule in front. The front door opened on a passage called the *prothyrum* which led to the *atrium*, an open court partly roofed; the opening was in the centre, and was called the *impluvium*; exactly under it in the floor was a

Fig. 321.—Ogee and Fluted Cavetto Moulding; Jupiter Tonans.

tank called the *compluvium*; this received the rain water. In large houses the atrium roof was supported by columns, then the atrium was sometimes called the *cavædium*, at the end of which opened out three rooms ·

the larger and central one was called the *tablinum*, and the two side ones *alæ ;* these were the rooms where the family records, documents, histories, deeds, &c., were kept. A passage led from the atrium to the principal private reception-room, called the *peristylium*, which had a roof partly open to the sky. This room was the finest in the house, and was richly decorated with rare marbles, bronzes, and fresco paintings where the owner was wealthy. Round the peristyle were arranged the smaller rooms, such as the parlours called *exedræ*, the chapels *lararia*, and the picture galleries *pinacothecæ*. Kitchens and other offices

Fig. 322.—Ogee Decorated, and Astragal: Jupiter Stator.

were behind, as also were the various sleeping-rooms. Some of the rooms were badly lighted, and had to depend for the light from the doors or artificial light, but in some cases windows, rather small in size, were placed high up in the walls.

The walls of the Pompeian houses were richly decorated in strong colouring, where vermilion, black, green, and orange predominated. The subjects were figure groups, animals, birds, and grotesques of all kinds, encased in fantastic architectural framings (Fig. 323). Sometimes a dead wall of the yard would be painted elaborately to represent a garden. Sculpture also decorated the apart-

ments, the floors were in mosaic, and the ceiling richly
panelled and decorated.　Roman, Greek, and Pompeian

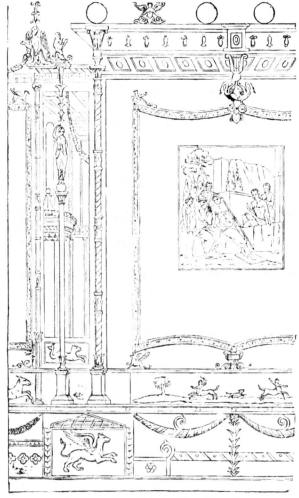

Fig. 323.—Mural Painting from Pompeii.

ornament will again be noticed in the second volume
under the minor arts of these countries.

CHAPTER XV.

AN Aryan race of people came into India about B.C. 2000 across the Upper Indus. They settled in the first instance in the Punjab, in the watershed of the Sutlej and the Jumna, and finally in Oude and the east. After one thousand years they lost their purity of race by mixing with the aboriginal natives.

About this time the prophet Sakya Muni, or Buddha, arose, and apparently succeeded in converting nearly the whole of Northern India to Buddhism. He died in B.C. 543, and three hundred years after his death, or about B.C. 250, King Asoka proclaimed Buddhism as the state religion, and for about one thousand years after it continued as the state religion of India, although at the present day there are said to be no native Buddhists in India.

Historic art in India began in Asoka's reign. The earlier rock-tombs and other architecture of Asoka's time are evidently stone copies of still earlier wooden constructions.

Monuments consisting of edict columns or *lats*, peculiar to this period, have been found in isolated positions erected to the honour of Buddha in the neighbourhood of Allahabad and Delhi; they are above thirty-three feet in height, and have a curved, inverted, bell-shaped capital on which probably stood a wheel, the emblem, or a lion, the symbol, of Buddha. This capital is similar in form to the base of a Persian column, and some of the ornamentation around the neck of the column is composed of Greek and Assyrian forms, all of which proves that the early Indian art owes something to Assyria, Persia, and Greece (Fig. 324). Probably this came about by the subjugation of Persia by Alexander the Great, who is said to have pushed his conquests as far as the banks of the Indus.

The next great immigration that we hear about is that of the Southern Dravidian people, who crossed the Lower Indus to Guzerat, and in course of time had settled themselves in the southern angle of India, in the Madras Presidency. They were a great building race of people. Another immigration took place in the first or second century B.C., and continued for some centuries after the

Fig. 324.—Ornament from Asoka's Pillar, Allahabad.   (B.)

Christian era. These people occupied nearly the western half of India, and erected buildings from Mysore in the south to Delhi in the north. This architecture is known as the Chalukya and Jaina styles. The fourth great immigration was that of the Mohammedans from the eleventh to the fourteenth centuries.

The four principal styles of Indian architecture are the Buddhist, the Dravidian, the Northern Hindoo, and the Chalukyan or Jaina.

In addition to the edict-pillars as illustrations of Buddhist architecture, many solid mounds of masonry, called topes, dagobas, or stupas, are found in some parts of the Punjab and north of India. These are relic-mounds, erected over the supposed relics of Buddha and of Buddhist priests, and are sometimes erected alone to the honour of Buddha. One of the most important is the Sanchi Tope in Bhopal, Central India (Fig. 325). Mr. Ferguson, in his "Study of Indian Architecture," describes this remarkable monument as follows : "It was built probably (the tope) B.C. 500, the stone railing B.C. 250, and the gateways A.D. 19 to 37. The principal part of the building consists of a dome 106 feet in diameter and 42 feet in height. The fence by which this tope is surrounded is extremely curious. It consists of stone posts 8 feet 8 inches in height, and a little more than 2 feet apart, surmounted by a plain architrave, and between every two uprights three horizontal cross-pieces of stone are inserted.

Still more curious are the four stone torans or gateways, one of which—the eastern—is shown at Fig. 325. It consists of two square pillars covered with sculptures, and with bold elephant capitals, rising to a height of 18 feet 4 inches. Above these are four lintels slightly curved upwards in the centre, and ending in Ionic scrolls ; they are supported by continuations of the columns, and three uprights are inserted between the lintels. All this construction is covered over with elaborate sculpture, and surmounted by emblems. The total height is 33 feet 6 inches." Sir G. Birdwood says : "The symbols are the *trisula*, the *wheel*, and the *lion*, representing the Buddhistic triad, Buddha, the law, and the congregation. The ground plan of the stupas or topes, with the return railings and the projecting doorways or entrances, form a gigantic swastika ('auspicious'), the mystic cross (fylfot) of the Buddhists." Ferguson says the Buddhist dagoba is a direct descendant of the sepulchral tumulus of the Turanian races, like those found in Etruria, Lydia, and among the Scyths of the Northern Steppes.

It is plainly seen that the details of Buddhistic ornament are derived from Greek and Assyrian sources mixed with Buddhist emblems ; a few native ideas may be seen in the construction, and in the substituting of the Indian elephant

Fig. 325.—The Sanchi Tope, Bhopal, Central India.

for the Assyrian or Persian bull. A fine cast of the Sanchi
gateway may be seen in the South Kensington Museum.

As an example of Hindu or Brahminical architecture the rock-cut temple at Ellora, called the Kylas, or "Paradise," is one of the finest and most wonderful (Fig. 326). The interior of the temple is not only cut out of the solid rock, but the exterior also, with its wonderfully rich square porch, and its two great square pillars or deepdans (lamposts) left standing in front, all literally cut out of the solid rock.

The interior, which has excited the wonder and admiration of all travellers, is rectangular in plan; the pillars

Fig. 326.—Brahminical Rock-Temple at Ellora.

are square and very short in proportion to their breadth; the bases are composed of plinth, circular hollows, and a torus moulding; the square shaft is fluted, the upper extremity of which is convex and ornamented with foliage; and above this are rings, neck, and a capital in the shape of a depressed sphere. Above the capital are bracket supports, on which the beams rest. The roof is panelled, and each panel has a central floral decoration. The Kylas was supposed to have been cut out of the rock by the Southern Dravidians. The Hindu or Brahminical

temples of the earliest type exhibit a marked imitation of
timber construction in almost every detail (Fig. 327).

Brahminical architecture has three varieties — the
Dravidian, which is common to the Dakhan, south of the
Kistna; the Chalukyan, between the Kistna and the
Mahanuddi; and the Indo-Aryan, which prevails in

Fig. 327. - Temple of Biskurma at Ellora.

Hindustan. The Dravidian temple is characterized by a
horizontal system of storied towers, and has a grand and
imposing look of solemnity. Examples of Dravidian
architecture occur in the temples at Seringham, Tinnevelly,
Madura, Perin, Vellore, &c.

The Chalukyan is distinguished by its star-like plan
and pyramidal tower. The great double temple of Siva at

Hullabeed, Mysore, is an example of this architecture. It is remarkable for its rich system of sculptured friezes. The building is raised from the ground by a terrace five or six feet in height; above this is an extraordinary frieze of two thousand sculptured elephants; the next frieze above is composed of lions, then a band of rich floriated scroll-work; above this is a frieze of horsemen, then another band of scroll-work; and over this appears the frieze with the conquest of Ceylon by Rama; other friezes and bands above this are divided by mouldings, and have celestial birds and beasts; a scroll-work cornice over all supporting a rail divided into panels, in each of which are two figures. Windows of pierced stone are over these, and groups of sculptured gods of the Hindu pantheon at regular intervals. The usual towers are wanting in this wonderful building, and doubtless would have been added afterwards had not the work been stopped owing to the Mohammedan invasion in A.D. 1310. Other temples of the Chalukyan style are seen at Somnathpur, at Baillur, in Mysore, and at Buchropully.

The Jainas sect makes its appearance in India about the seventh or eight century. They did not believe in the divine inspiration of the Vedas, or sacred books of the Hindus, but as long as they observed caste and acknowledged the gods of the Hindu pantheon—which they strictly did—the Brahmans did not question any other of their particular beliefs, and refrained from persecuting them. If the Buddhists, for instance, had only conformed to the observance of caste, they would never have been driven out of India by the Hindu devotees of caste.

The Jainas are peculiar in their worship of their four-and-twenty saints called "Jins."

The architecture of the Jainas began when the Buddhist was dying out. One of the characteristics of Jaina architecture is the horizontal archway, and another is the bracket form of capital (Fig. 328).

Jaina temples are found at Palatina and Girnar in

Gujarat, and the famous "Tower of Victory," erected to commemorate the victory of the Rajput raja Khambo over Mahmud of Malwa, A.D. 1439.

An interesting illustration of the transition of Indian

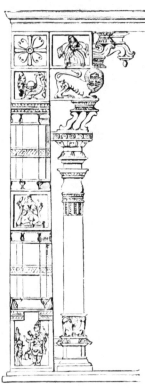

architecture to Mohammedan forms occurs in the Mosque of Moháfiz Khan, at Ahmedabad. This mosque was built in the sixteenth century, and is Hindu in character, with a Saracenic influence in the decoration and other details. The great omissions in the sculptures are the animal and figure forms, so dear to the Hindu artist, but the Moslem religion forbids the representation of these, and in place of figures in the window spaces we see some of the first indications of Saracenic tracery, executed most likely by Hindu workmen. These windows are typical of, and similar to, the exceedingly fine tracery of the windows of the Buddha at Ahmedabad, which consist of beautiful stems and floral tracery.

Fig. 328.— Pillar and Bracket, Doorway of a Pagoda.

From the eighth to the eighteenth centuries India was subject to the invasions of the Arabs, the Afghans, and Mongols, who devastated the country and sacked and pillaged many of the finest Hindu shrines, and, on the other hand, built some magnificent mosques and palaces, in which the Saracenic influences are predominant.

The palace of Delhi was built in 1627-1658 by the Mongol Emperor Shah Jehan, the king who built the present city of Delhi, which city contains the finest examples of the Mohammedan style in India. The Dewanne Khas, or principal hall of the palace of Delhi (Fig. 329), is a very rich and ornate example of this style. It is vaulted like a Gothic cathedral and is inlaid throughout with rich marbles and mosaic work. It has a niche inlaid

Fig. 329.—Interior of the Palace at Delhi: Seventeenth Century.

with precious stones in which once stood the famous peacock throne of Delhi. The throne was made in enamelled work, in the shape of a peacock with a spread-out tail, and was set with diamonds and precious stones to imitate the natural colours of the peacock. It was carried off by Nadir Shah at the sacking of Delhi, A.D. 1738. Around the frieze of one of the halls of this palace runs the famous inscription, " If there is a heaven on earth, it is this, it is this."

One of the loveliest and most impressive buildings in India is the Taj Mehal at Agra, on the river Jumna. It is in Mohammedan style with domes and minarets, and is erected on a platform 300 feet square and 18 feet in height. It was erected by the Emperor Shah Jehan about 1645 as the tomb of his favourite wife. The Emperor himself is also buried in the Taj. On the centre of the platform is the tomb, 186 feet square, with the corners cut off; over this rises the dome, 58 feet in diameter and 80 feet in height. The outside of the building is faced with white marble, inlaid with beautiful designs in coloured marbles and precious stones. The effect of this beautiful building in its dazzling whiteness surrounded by luxuriant vegetation, as seen under a moonlit sky, is said to be enchanting and beyond description.

The industrial arts of India will be noticed in the second volume of this work.

CHAPTER XVI.

CHINESE AND JAPANESE ARCHITECTURE.

THE architecture of China does not possess what we might call a serious character. Founded mainly on Buddhistic elements, as far as the more important efforts of their temple architecture is concerned, the only original development that marks the Chinese structural design is the pagoda tower—in itself really a Buddhistic idea—but the Chinese have the credit of carrying it further in their Taas or Pagodas by placing story upon story until sometimes a great height was attained; as, for example, in the great porcelain tower at Nankin, which is 200 feet in height, consists of nine stories, and is 40 feet in diameter at the base. Each story diminishes in size, and the concave roof of every lower story is in front of the receding one above. Varnished pillars, resting on a deep stone basement, support the verandah-like roof of the lowest story, and a fence of gilded trellis-work surrounds the lower half of the pillars. The eaves of the roofs curl upwards and end in points from which bells are suspended. Carved dragons peer out from under the rafters, and the whole building, inside and out, as well as the roof tiles, is faced with white porcelain slabs or tiles fastened to the inner brick structure; some parts—the roofs especially—are painted in alternating bands of green, yellow, and red.

The greater part of the Chinese houses are wooden constructions, and have movable walls of various materials, which slide in framework. The walls do not support the roof, which is, as a rule, supported on posts, independent of them.

In the gateways to the Confucian temples some attempts at architectural construction are seen, where a column would have a proper capital and a base, and a lintel or arched opening would appear. These Pae-lus or triumphal gates have the usual fantastic curled roofs so peculiar to Chinese architecture (Fig. 330).

The genius of the Chinese as great builders and engineers is expressed better in their works of public

Fig. 330.—Gateway of the Temple of Confucius, Shanghai.

utility, as in their finely-constructed bridges, their canals, and more particularly in the Great Wall, built to protect their country from the incursions of the Northern hordes, and which is a monument at the same time to their native love of exclusiveness from surrounding nations.

The Great Wall was built about B.C. 200, is 1,400 miles long, 15 to 30 feet in height, 25 feet thick at the base, and slopes upwards to 20 feet in width at the top. It has bastions or towers of defence at intervals, which are 40 feet square at the base, and the wall is carried over hills and

mountains regardless of all obstacles. Their country is a
network of canals, some of which are 700 miles in length.

Notwithstanding all this, they are no further advanced
in architecture than they were two thousand years ago, or,
indeed, in hardly any of the arts. At the same time the
Chinese are remarkably skilled in porcelain manufacture,
silk weaving, embroidery, colour printing, ivory and jade
carving, enamelling, metal-working, casting, and decorative painting. Their ornament is very conventional and
rich in colouring, but their ornamental forms are limited,
and their decoration so full of repetition that it becomes
very monotonous when judged by a European standard.

The architecture of Japan differs very slightly from that
of China, as it is either an offshoot from the older civilisation of China, or has been derived from the same sources,
through the Buddhist religion. Some changes have
occurred in the architecture of Japan in recent years owing
to the more extended use of stone in their buildings, which
has been brought about by their interchange of ideas with
Western nations.

Their Buddhist temples are similar to the Chinese, with
their curious turned-up roofs, but the Shinto temples are
usually covered with roofs that have great projecting
eaves, which do not turn up at the angles. The porches or
gateways (Torii) to the temples are built in stone, but in
imitation of their earlier wooden construction ; they are
of the pillar-and-beam order, and recall somewhat the
construction, on a smaller scale, of the " torans " or gateways of the Sanchi Tope in India (Fig. 325).

The Japanese carve their wooden rafters, beams, posts,
lintels, and stringcourses very skilfully, with conventional
ornament, dragons, and grotesque animals. The better
class of Japanese dwellings are usually of two stories ; the
lower story has a verandah, and the upper one is recessed
back, and is smaller than the lower, which produces a
pleasing effect. Their walls are, like the Chinese, more or
less movable partitions.

Japanese ornament and industrial art (which will be treated in another place) is more virile, has more variety, and is more artistic in execution, though governed less by architectural arrangement, than the art of the Chinese. The Japanese are, however, every day becoming more impregnated with Western ideas, and, as a consequence, their wonderful artistic feeling and native refinement of design, execution, and colouring are in a fair way of losing those seductive qualities that hitherto have characterized the artistic productions of these interesting people.

CHAPTER XVII.

EARLY CHRISTIAN AND BYZANTINE ARCHITECTURE.

FOR the first three centuries after the birth of Christ the early Christians suffered much persecution and martyrdom. The new religion was ridiculed and despised, and the converts of the new faith were obliged to hold their meetings and to worship in secret, which they did in the narrow but extensive catacombs in which they secretly buried their dead. The catacombs are found chiefly in the neighbourhood of Rome and Naples, and are cut in the dark soft tufa stone, in the nature of long passages, winding and doubling in their labyrinthine twistings. Some of these passages are so narrow as to barely admit of one person to pass in height or width. On either side of these narrow ways are cut out openings just large enough for the bodies of deceased persons to be deposited.

The body of the deceased was thus thrust into the narrow tomb, and with it was buried a flask of sacred oil. The entrance was then closed with a stone, on which would be engraved the name or initials of the dead.

Some of the catacombs were hollowed out in places into lofty and capacious chambers and niches. These were used as chapels for the early Christian worship, the walls and ceilings of which were decorated with paintings of a very primitive character.

The more important of these catacombs in which chapel-like rooms are found are those of S. Calisto, S. Sebastiano, S. Lorenzo, and S. Agnese, at Rome; and at Naples those of S. Mario della Sanita, S. Gennara de Poveri, and S. Maria della Vita.

Constantine became Emperor of the Romans (A.D. 312 — 337), and in the course of his reign embraced, or professed, Christianity, and proclaimed it the state religion. After this event freedom was allowed the converts of the new faith to celebrate their love-feasts in a public and open manner.

It was found difficult all at once to provide the necessary buildings for this purpose, and we hear of the heathen temples and great halls of the Roman baths being used as Christian churches—the Pantheon at Rome was used for this purpose—but few of these buildings were large enough or of the right shape to hold large masses of the faithful, and at the same time to provide for the celebration of the worship by the bishops and priests in presence of the congregation, besides the objection of having the odour of heathenism still clinging to them. The supposed model for the early Christian churches was found in the halls of justice and commerce of the Roman times. It is doubtful, however, whether the early Christian architecture owed so much to the basilica form of justice halls as has been so generally supposed.

The general plan of the basilica churches was rectangular, with a semicircular portion added to the back, as the plan of the apse; in the front was the atrium, a free quadrangular fore-court surrounded with pillars. This was usually roofed on the four sides, with an opening in the centre, like the atrium of a Roman house.

Next to the atrium was the narthex, or porch, which led to the church direct. Sometimes there was only the narthex without the atrium.

A central avenue, or nave, with two aisles, and the semicircular apse at the end of the nave, was the usual interior form of the early basilicas.

The nave was wide and lofty, and was usually divided from the aisles by two rows of columns, and from the apse by a large semicircular arch.

The capitals of the columns carried the arcaded upper

story, in the walls of which were the windows that lighted the church. In the oldest type of the basilica there was no window in the apse, so this portion of the church was bathed in a mysterious twilight, adding a poetic charm to the gold mosaics with which the roof of the apse was decorated.[1]

Sometimes windows were introduced into the low walls of the aisles; the aisles were covered with shed-like wooden roofs, which were supported on trussed frame-work.

Sometimes the trusses were ceiled, and on the ceilings were painted scriptural subjects. The wall spaces of the second story in the nave were also occupied with paintings of sacred subjects. The floor of the apse was raised higher than that of the nave, and was approached by steps; seats were placed around the wall of the apse for the priests, and in the centre was the elevated throne for the bishops. A portion of the nave space was sometimes appropriated for the choir, screened off by a marble structure, and at either end of the choir were placed the "ambos" or pulpits (Fig. 331).

Fig. 331.—Ambo or Pulpit from St. George's at Salonica.

The altar was in the centre of the apse, generally over the tomb of a Christian martyr, and underneath all, or sometimes a portion only of the church, was the crypt.

The nave usually had three entrance doors, and the aisles one or more each. As the heathen religions, and consequently the ancient temples, fell into disuse, there was plenty of building materials ready formed and dressed, which the architects of the new buildings appropriated for their own purposes in the erection of the basilicas. This accounts for the great number of Roman Corinthian and Ionic columns found in the buildings of the early Christian architecture, and we often find that when an ancient column was too short, it was simply raised on a higher base, and if too long it was cut down to fit its new position. It was generally in the later basilicas that this occurred, as might be expected, for the earlier basilicas are richer and better decorated in their beautiful details, seeing that the early Christian builders had the first choice of the rich ornamental work of architectural sculpture that had belonged to the ancient Roman temples. The church of S. Apollinare in Classe at Ravenna may be cited as one of the most finished and most beautiful of the early basilicas, which was erected with much of this old material. Although the Christian architects and artists were slow in producing new forms of plastic art, as long as they could adapt the existing fragments of architectural sculpture to their uses ; on the other hand, the art of painting and decorating by mosaic pictures on the great spaces of the walls and ceilings of the basilicas was developed to a high degree of monumental splendour, and brilliant effects were gained by the use of gold and bright colours.

Mosaics as wall decoration in the basilicas were suggested by the paintings in the catacombs. These primitive paintings were borrowed in their form and essence from ancient mythological works. At first, some of the earliest efforts at decoration in the catacombs consisted merely of monograms and symbols, such as the Greek letters Alpha and Omega, and the initials or monogram of Christ.

The use of these doubtless arose from the desire to deprecate anything that savoured of the images of heathendom, but evidently the early Christians soon arrived at the idea that painting might be admissible in a church where sculptured images could not be tolerated—the latter reminding them too much of the sculptured deities of the ancients—and consequently we find that the painted subjects from the heathen Pantheon were adapted by the artists who decorated the catacombs, but the figure of Christ was introduced where formerly a Roman god was the personage, thereby giving the mythological subject a new Christian meaning. In the catacombs of S. Agnese Christ is represented as the "Good Shepherd," carrying on his shoulders the lamb that had been lost (Fig. 332); and in the catacombs of S. Calixtus, on a wall painting, he is portrayed under the type and figure of Orpheus, charming all nature with his music (Fig. 333). In the central octagonal panel he is represented with a harp, surrounded by the beasts and birds of the field. In the eight compartments around the central panel, four landscapes alternate with four figure subjects :— Moses striking water out

Fig. 332.—Painting from the Catacombs of S. Agnese.

of the rock, and opposite, Christ raising Lazarus, who is represented as a mummy; Daniel in the lions' den, and opposite this, David with the sling. The heathen subjects of Cupid and Psyche, and others, have been used to represent Christian symbols. In sculpture, there are some remains of early Christian art in which the figures of Christ and his Apostles are clothed in the dress, and worked somewhat in the spirit, of the antique. The sarcophagus under the pulpit of S. Ambrogio at Milan is a good example of this kind of art. Some ivory carvings of this period have been executed as tablets, with scriptural sub-

jects, after the manner of the Roman Consular diptychs.
These ivory carvings, that exhibit a true spirit of the
antique in their design, are not to be confounded with the
later Byzantine diptychs that were executed in a more
archaic style.

During the fifth century, and even in the latter part of
the fourth, we see the more cheerful spirit of the antique

Fig. 333.—Wall Painting from the Catacombs of S. Calixtus.

character dying out, and the art of the time exhibits a
greater importance and attention which is given to large
masses, while smaller or minor surfaces are left empty, and
decorative detail suppressed. There is an apparent striving
to render the figure of the Redeemer—the chief personage
—larger and more important in the scale of the decoration,
and at the same time to give him more individuality. As
the technical qualities of the Christian art diminished, the

majesty and sublimity of the Great Teacher was expressed
in a more spiritual conception of his divinity.

Several examples of decoration illustrating this phase of
Christian art occur in the wall paintings in the catacombs of
S. Ponziano at Rome. The face of Christ in these representations is full of earnest and mild serenity ; the right
hand is raised as if in blessing, and the left holds the book
of life.

In the fourth century, mosaic was used in the basilicas
as a means of decorating the apse and walls, as the
Romans before had used it in their floors and dados.

In the hands of the early and inexperienced artists, the
character of the material in mosaic had a great deal to do,
but not all, in the creating of the type of angular and rigid
forms of the figures, which was transmitted to all subsequent Christian mosaics. At the same time there was the
intense desire to make the figures of Christ and of other
sacred personages of a sorrowful and austere character.
We can, however, trace in these figures the magisterial
dignity that invests the sculptured figures of the Emperors
and Senators of Roman art.

In Italy, the Christian mosaics assumed more and more
a decided breaking away from the traditions of the antique.
Large masses as single figures were symmetrically
arranged, ornamental details were suppressed, and bands
with inscriptions framed the large spaces of the walls and
the apse. The figures were more isolated, attenuated,
severe of expression, and leaving much to be desired in
their anatomical construction or in the natural movement
of the body; but all this tended to give them that expression of devotional simplicity aimed for by those early
mystics, who only looked on the world as a " vale of
tears." In the vaulted roof of the funeral chapel erected
to the memory of the daughter of Constantine at Rome—
Sta. Costanza—some of the earliest mosaic work is to be
found, consisting of an antique treatment of the vine and
tendrils used in a symbolic sense; and in another chapel,

that of the Empress Galla Placida, at Ravenna, similar
work is seen, mixed with symbolic signs, as the hart—
"panting for water brooks "—a symbol of the soul thirst-
ing for salvation. This chapel was erected A.D. 440.

After this time, and towards the end of the fifth century,
we find the characteristic features of Christian art more
insisted in : such as the colossal portraits and figures of
Christ, the isolation of single figures, the symmetrical
grouping of crowds of smaller figures, and of the repre-
sentatives of the angel, bull, eagle, and lion, as winged
symbols of the Evangelists, all rendered the more impressive by the architectural spacing, and the plain blue
ground which surrounded most of the figures. Two
churches may be mentioned that contained fine examples
of the above type of early Christian mosaics ; one is the
great basilica of St. Paul, without the walls at Rome,
built under Theodosius and Honorius about A.D. 386, and
the other that of St. Cosmo e Damiano in Rome. The
great mosaics in the apse of the latter church were executed between A.D. 526 and 530 by Pope Felix IV. The
floors of these churches are made of what is known as
"Opus Alexandrinum," the finest and grandest floor decoration that exists (Fig. 334. Circular slabs of porphyry
and serpentine marble sawn in disks from antique columns
are laid down, and twisted interlacings and rings surround
them as bands composed of triangular bits of white, black,
or coloured marble, forming simple and effective patterns
in a quiet harmony of colour. Some of this work may be
seen in Westminster Abbey.

In the early part of the sixth century Christian art in
Italy was at a low ebb, as by this time nearly all the
antique remains and culture had been used up ; but fortu-
nately, the Eastern and Western Churches were not as yet
divided in doctrine, and a fresh life had been imparted to
Italian art from the Byzantine culture of the Eastern
Empire.

Besides the basilica form of building, another antique

form of early Christian architecture was developed, called a " baptistery," which generally took the form of a detached building, with a circular or polygonal plan. In some cases the baptistery adjoins the atrium of the basilica, but often is a detached building of considerable importance. The structure is supposed to have been suggested by the circular portion of the Roman baths, and consists

Fig. 334.—Opus Alexandrinum Pavement, San Marco, Rome.

of a circular row of columns supporting the upper structure; the central portion is surrounded by a low cloister-like aisle, and the fountain is in the middle of the building. The circular building known as the Church of Santa Costanza in Rome—the funeral chapel before mentioned—the octagonal baptistery of Constantine, and the fine baptistery at Ravenna, are examples of this kind of

building.   Another beautiful example is the octagonal
baptistery of the Lateran, belonging to the fifth century; it
has eight large antique columns, which support an architrave, upon which rest another series of eight smaller
columns, carrying another architrave and the domed roof.
The whole building has a pleasant and agreeable effect of
extreme airiness.

BYZANTINE ARCHITECTURE.

The ancient town of Byzantium, the modern Constantinople, was mostly in ruins when Constantine the Great
selected it for the new capital of the Roman Empire. He
rebuilt the old town and named it after himself, and in the
year A.D. 330 the inauguration of the new capital was celebrated. Later on, under Theodosius, the Roman Empire
was divided, and Constantinople became the capital of the
Eastern portion.

It was the great connecting-point between the countries
of the East and the West. The inhabitants of the new
city being mostly Greeks, the native artists and architects
employed by Constantine imparted a decided Grecian
character to the ornament and decoration, especially of the
churches and other buildings that were erected by this
emperor.

The occasion of the new political change and the rapid
spread of the Christian religion served to give a great
impetus to the building and lavish decoration of churches
and public edifices. Although the new architecture was
founded on the Roman originals, yet in the hands of the
Greeks both architecture and ornament assumed a new and
original character. From the time of the founding of Constantinople to the date of Justinian's reign (A.D. 527-565),
when the great church of Santa Sophia—holy wisdom—
was built, on the ruins of an older church that was said to
have been burnt down, we can guess that it must have
been a time of experiments and developments from the

basilica type of building to the well-defined domed style
of architecture known as the Byzantine.

The timber-roofed and vaulted style of structure now
gave place to the dome, which resulted also in a change
of the plan to the square form, instead of the rectangle.
During the two hundred years previous to the building of
Santa Sophia, the problem of dome construction, with
others of a difficult nature in building, had been successfully solved by the Greek architects of the Eastern Empire.
Justinian employed the Greeks, Anthemius of Thralles
and Isidorus of Miletus, as the architects of Santa Sophia,
and they succeeded in erecting a marvellous structure
that may justly be reckoned as one of the wonders of the
world.

Four vast piers, arranged on a square plan, support four
solid arches of masonry, semicircular in shape, and 100
feet span each. The four triangular spaces at the corners
and the spaces formed by the angles, the semicircular
arches and portions of the ring of the dome, are filled with
" pendentives," which may be described as continuations
of the dome. These pendentives partly support the dome,
and the other points of support are on the backs of the
great arches. The four pendentives meet in the circular
ring from which the dome springs. The dome is 46 feet
in height from the level of its base, and 107 feet in diameter, and is rather flattish in shape.

On the side of the dome, east and west, are two half-
domes, which crown apsidal walls. Other small apses are
domed over at lower levels, and vaulted aisles of two stories
run round the higher portions of the building, the whole
forming almost a cube-like shape.

After Constantinople was captured by the Turks (A.D.
1453), Santa Sophia was converted into a mosque and four
minarets, or Moslem towers, were added to its outer angles.
The interior of this church, besides the stupendous effect
of its unrivalled architectural construction, has its added
beauties and splendour in its inlaid marbles, its richly

carved cornices and arcades (Fig. 335), and its vaults and
domes glittering with gold mosaics of cherubim, and
dignified though gaunt and archaic figures. In the
capitals of the columns was used the sharply-edged and
undercut acanthus foliage, more in accordance with the
old Greek type than the Roman, but have a distinctly
Byzantine character of its own. Sacred signs, emblems,
and birds were often introduced into the capitals; the
general shape of the latter was a cubical form, the four

Fig. 335.—Cornice from Santa Sophia.

faces slanting inwards from above, this form giving a decided appearance of great supporting and sustaining power
(Figs. 336 and 338). Sometimes they were bossed out,
and often contained the elements of the Ionic and Corinthian orders (Figs. 336, 337, 339,. The wedge-shaped
portion on the top of the capital is an ugly but distinctive
feature of the Byzantine style (Fig. 338).

The splendour and magnificence of the decoration in
Byzantine churches is proverbial: the columns were often of

porphyry and serpentine marble, and the supports to the altar canopy (*baldacchino*), the screen (*iconostasis*) and the pulpit

Fig. 336.—Capital from Santa Sophia, showing the bossing-out of the ornament.

Fig. 337.—Capital from St. Demetrius at Salonica.

Fig. 338.—Capital from St. Demetrius.

(*ambo*) were often inlaid with gold, silver, and precious stones. The altar itself was a gorgeous piece of workmanship,

resplendent with gold and enamels, decorated with hanging lamps, vases, and candlesticks, all wrought in precious metal work, though the actual design and workmanship was rough and less refined than antique work.

The floor mosaics had patterns consisting of the cross,
the circle, and the cube, with interlacing lines, the ornamental forms here as elsewhere being of a symbolical

Fig. 339.—Byzantine Capital from Santa Sophia, showing the bossing-out of the
ornament.

character. Reliquaries, shrines, and chalices in gold, and
enamels, crosses, and other accessories of the altar, and
sculptured ivories of a devotional character, of Byzantine
workmanship, were made in great abundance. The larger
churches especially, such as Santa Sophia, and St. Mark's
at Venice, possessed great quantities of these treasures.
Sculpture was subordinate to painting as plastic art was
not encouraged, because of the dislike to images shown

by the early Christians, and so painting which led to the mosaic picture, which in its turn led to enamelling on metals, was favoured to a great extent by the Byzantine artists. Even flat bands with inscriptions and ornament were used instead of mouldings in relief.

The city of Ravenna being situated between Constantinople and Rome possessed some remarkable buildings, that do not belong exactly to the Eastern or Western type of architecture ; but on the other hand have strongly marked influences of each.

The most important is that of the Church of St. Vitale; it is octagonal in plan, and is like Santa Sophia in having a principal central dome, half-domes, and vaulted aisles. It is resplendent in elaborate decoration and carvings. The cathedral of St. Mark's at Venice is so well known from illustrations and photographs that it requires very little description. It was built in the years A.D. 977 — 1071, and its plans are said to have been drawn by Greek architects at Constantinople. Originally it possessed

Fig. 340.—St. Nicholas at Moscow.

all the features of a genuine Byzantine edifice, but has been altered externally, and in some places internally in both Gothic and Renaissance periods. The Byzantine domes have had bulbous coverings placed over them in later times. St. Mark's like Santa Sophia is square in plan, but has five principal domes, one in the centre, and one at each angle or end of the Greek cross plan. The aisles, with their series of low-level dome roofs, make the whole

building nearly square. The surrounding countries of
Bulgaria, Servia, Roumania, Armenia, and Russia, which
embraced the Christian religion of the Greek Church, possess examples of Byzantine architecture. The Russian
type in its later developments has distinctive characteristics of its own, particularly in the use and shape of the
dome. Russian churches consist usually of a storied
tower on which is placed five small domes of a bulbous
shape; these are built on the tops of elongated drums.
The bulbous tops of the domes grow into points, on which
are placed tall crosses. These and other fantastic elements are derived from the timber edifices of Persia and
other Asiatic countries (Fig. 340).

CHAPTER XVIII.

SARACENIC ARCHITECTURE AND ORNAMENT.

THE architecture of the Saracens in its most perfect examples has a thoroughly distinctive style of its own, and their ornament in its pure form is unlike the ornament of any style that has hitherto existed.

The originality of the latter arose from the experimenting in ornamental patterns that should have no likeness to plants, animals, or other natural forms.

This prohibition of the use of objects from nature in their ornament was one of the articles of the Moslem religion; but to get any pleasing variety in ornament and leave out all natural reminiscences in the designs is out of human power, so consequently we have, even in Saracenic ornament, natural forms put through a geometrical process of draughtsmanship. Saracenic ornament in what is sometimes called Arabian has leaf and bud-like forms interlaced with strap-work, which is often very beautiful and is known under the name of "Arabesque" (Figs. 341, 342).

The Saracens were originally composed of Arab herdsmen, nomadic wanderers of the desert, carriers or merchants, and dwellers in villages, who cultivated the land around them. The earliest building of any importance that can be called Saracenic is the "Kaaba" or Moslem temple at Mecca, which contained the sacred brownish-black stone placed by Mahomet in the south-east angle of this square temple. This black stone is supposed to be a meteorolite, hemispherical in shape, and about 6 by 8

inches in the widest dimension. Some hundreds of stone
images or "gods" used to be worshipped at Mecca by
the Mohammedans in their early days, or in what they call
their "days of ignorance," but these were destroyed by
the prophet's orders. Mohammed himself was a fanatic
that could neither read nor write; he made up the Korân
from many sources, such as the Bible, the Apocryphal

Fig. 341.—Arabesque Ornament from the Wekâla of Kâit Bey. (L.-P.)

gospels, the Talmud, and possibly a good many original
passages of his own, which he says he received from the
mouth of the angel Gabriel in visions. The Mohammedan
creed contains its essence in the words:—"There is no
God, but God, and Mohammed is his Prophet." This
text is found very frequently as a decorative legend on the
walls of the mosques and on painted tiles. At first
Mohammed's new religion was not favourably received,

for, after converting his near relations and a few other
followers, he had to fly from Mecca to Medina, to escape
assassination.

The "Hegira," or flight of Mohammed, took place A.D.
622. He compiled more of his Korán at Medina, and

Fig. 342.—Rosette in Mosque of Suyurghatmi-h; Seventeenth Century. (L.-P.)

altered parts of it, especially as regards the punishment of
idolaters, which naturally included his late persecutors.

The punishment was to be of an eternal nature in the
next world, and extirpation in this, unless they embraced
Islâmism. Mohammed very soon began to make his
power felt; he made a few marauding expeditions throughout the country, and gained many converts, especially

when they became convinced that Islâm was to conquer
the whole world by the sword. His army, however, was
nearly annihilated by the Byzantine emperor, Heraclius,
in a battle at Muta, but he recovered himself, and marched
on to Mecca, where he put to the sword all those that did
not embrace his religion, and destroyed all the remaining
idols in the city. He allowed his army all the plunder
they could get, after he had a tithe to himself, but it is said
that he led a very abstemious life, dressed poorly, and
resided with his wives in the shabbiest type of dwellings.
He died in A.D. 632, or ten years after the Hegira, from
which event is dated the Mohammedan era. After his
death many of the converts became backsliders, but his
successor, Abu-Bekr, and more especially the renowned
Omar—the second caliph—brought the Saracens to a great
power. They were very warlike, and capable of enduring
great hardships, and as they had everything to gain and
nothing to lose, they made war their sole trade, and carried their successful arms to India, Persia, Mesopotamia,
Syria, Palestine, and Egypt.

The islands of the Mediterranean, the northern coast of
Africa, Spain, and the south-east of France, were by them
also invaded, ravaged, and partly conquered.

In the youthful days of Saracenic power, as early as the
second caliphate, Persia and Asia Minor had been plun-
dered and pillaged of their costly and valuable objects in
silver, gold, embroidered carpets, and silken goods. The
wealth of the Moslem conquerors was now considerable,
and was accumulating fast; the sight of so much that was
fine and striking in the arts and architecture of the countries they had conquered, in the eyes of these people—who
were no better than barbarians or banditti—began to have
a more civilising effect on them. Add to this the influence
of the Byzantine architecture, especially at Constantinople,
with the Saracens, whose religion was in some respects
not unlike the Christian, especially as in both cases there
was the stern prohibition of idols or graven images; and

Fig. 343.--Alhambra Diaper, Superposed Ornament.

so it was quite natural that the Moslem mosque should be
built and decorated on the main lines of the Byzantine
Christian church. The dome and the niche (*mehrab*) came

from the Byzantine ; the minarets—which are not strictly essential in Moslem architecture—probably from the Perseopolitan columns. The Moslem dome, however, may have had its origin in the domed palaces of Persia, of the Achæmedian dynasty.   Saracenic ornament is mostly,

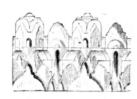

Fig. 344.—Stalactite Vaulting.

however, derived from the geometric Byzantine with a strong dash of Indian forms in its mixture. The super-posing in their ornament of different planes (Fig. 343), the class of ornament known as "mnemonic" (Figs, 362, 363), and the stalactite decoration of vaults and domes (Fig. 344)—all these three classes deserve the credit of being distinctly Saracenic, although some say that the stalactite ornament was known in Persia before the days of Mahomet.

Among the earliest mosques we may mention that of Omar at Jerusalem, which was supposed to be a small wooden mosque, now destroyed. Ferguson says it was the Mosque of El Aksah.

The Mosque of 'Amr at Old Cairo was built A.D. 641 by Amru-Ibn-al-Aās, the general and governor who conquered Egypt, A.H. 21 (after the Hegira). It has been frequently restored and enlarged. The columns which support the arcaded arches are classical in character, the arches are slightly horseshoe in the curve, and are tied together. The building is nearly square in plan (Figs. 345, 346).

The mosque of Ibn-Tūlūn (Son of Tūlūn) in Old Cairo was built by Ahmad-ibn-Tūlūn, founder of the house of the Tūlūn governors of Egypt, A.H. 263-5. This mosque and that of 'Amr are what are known as "cloistered" mosques. The plan of the latter (Fig. 346) gives a general idea of a cloistered mosque. The essential requirements of a mosque are very few and simple. Mahomet's mosque at Medina was a small square brick-built structure, with a

Fig. 345.—East Colonnade of the Mosque of 'Amr. (L.P.)

wooden roof plastered over : the chief thing required was
retirement from the public for meditation and prayer.

It was not essential that all the rectangular or square
court that forms the mosque should be covered with a roof,
provided there was sufficient shelter for the number of
worshippers, which was generally small at a time, and if

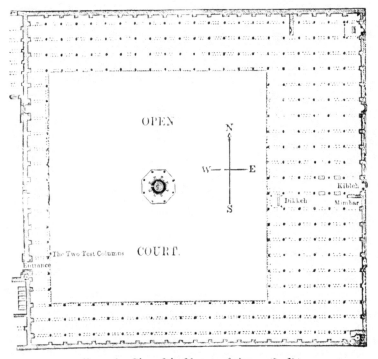

OPEN

N
W—+—E
S

Kibleh

Dikkeh   Mimbar

The Two Test Columns   COURT.

Entrance

Fig. 346.—Plan of the Mosque of 'Amr.   (L.-P.)

a larger space were required, a portion or all of the open
court could be roofed in. What we would call the east
end of a church corresponded to that part of a mosque
where the *kibla*, or line of direction, would be indicated—
towards Mecca—there the *mihrab* or niche would be fixed.
Close to the mihrab is the *mimbar*, or pulpit, for the
sermon, and in close vicinity the *dikka* or tribune, a raised

platform, from which the imām intones the prayers and reads passages from the Korān. The minaret is a later addition, but is seen on every mosque; it is used by the Muezzin, who ascends to its galleries and calls the faithful to prayer five times a day (Fig. 347). A fountain is necessary for the lawful ablutions before prayer.

The dome is not a necessary feature to a mosque; it only occurs over the tomb of some sultan or other dignitary, and may be used as a chapel, but only when it covers a tomb. The majority of mosques, however, have a dome, either as a principal feature, or attached to some part of the building. Cairo is particularly rich in domed mausoleum structures (Fig. 348).

The domes or cupolas in Moslem buildings generally swell up beyond the semicircle, and are raised con-

Fig. 347.—Minaret of the Mosque of Kaloum at Cairo.

siderably by having their lower parts straight-sided or cylindrical; this part is sometimes pierced with a row of small windows, and is recessed back on a pyramid-like story, with a square or polygonal base, which in its turn rests on the top of a square embattled tower. The dome is usually built of brick, the courses projecting roughly one over the other, diminishing towards the top, and thickly plastered over

Fig. 348.—Mausoleum at Cairo.

inside and out to get an even surface; sometimes the mortar is thicker than the bricks in Saracen buildings.

Fig. 349. – Mosque of Kaït Bey, Cairo.   (L.-P.)

Wooden frames are often used in the construction of
domes which support the plaster work.   Some domes are

built with slabs of stones on which a geometric pattern is carved on the outside (Figs. 348, 349) ; these are generally of a late period, as the tomb mosque of Kāit Bey, built about A.D. 1468 (Fig. 349). The oldest mosque in Cairo is that of Ibn Tūlūn (Fig. 350). It is a cloistered mosque, is built in a massive style, and has a high plain wall around it; it covers about four hundred square feet of ground. In the centre of the inner courtyard is a square stone building surmounted by a dome, one of the earliest carried on stalactites. This building is a century later than the cloisters, and is built over a well or fountain.

The great court is surrounded by arcades of pointed arches, that have a slight tendency to turn inwards at the base, and are built as piers of plastered brick ; it is said to be the first mosque built on piers, instead of the usual round columns.

The Saracens did not make columns themselves, but took them from the ruins of Roman buildings, or even from existing Christian churches, and as often as not used the capitals turned upside down as bases.

The Saracens have a form of capital of Moorish design which harmonizes with their architecture ; it has a slightly tapering, smooth, long neck, a heavy projecting head, and is well covered with characteristic foliated work (Fig. 351).

In the mosque of Ibn-Tūlūn there are only two columns ; these are placed at the niche or mihrab. Three sides of this mosque have two rows of arches, and the fourth—the side towards Mecca—which is the *līwān* or sanctuary, has five. The architect of this mosque was a Coptic Christian, who received £5,000 and a costly dress of honour as his fee. The total cost of the building was £60,000 (*Lane-Poole*). Around the arches and the windows, which were placed high up between the arches, are bands of palmated ornament. These borders, according to Mr. Stanley Lane-Poole, are the earliest examples of geometrical design and scroll-work that afterwards became so characteristic of Saracenic ornament.

They were made in plaster or stucco-work by hand, while the plaster was wet, and not cast in moulds, which was the case of later Moorish plaster ornament.

Fig. 350.—Arcades in the Mosque of Ibn-Túlún. (L.-P.)

The arcades were roofed over with sycamore planks resting on heavy beams, and the whole structure was crowned with crenellations or embattlements. One of the back walls of the arcades is pierced with grilles of stone, of beautiful tracery design.

The Arabian or Saracen arches are of three kinds—the Ogee, the Horseshoe, and the Pointed (Fig. 352, *a*, *b*, *c*).

A peculiar arrangement of cusped inter-arching, combined with the horseshoe arch, is seen in the *maksura*, or space in front of the mihrab, of the mosque of Cordova, built A.D. 786 (Fig. 353).

This arrangement of cusping, though characteristically Moorish, is anything but beautiful. The Mosque of Cordova was begun by the Caliph Abd-al-Rahman in the year before he died, and was continued by his son Hisham, and his

Fig. 351.—Moorish Capital.

grandson El-Hakim. It is one of the great congregational mosques, and occupied a space of ground 580 feet by 435 feet.

The minaret is often a feature of great beauty, and is preeminently distinctive of Saracenic mosque architecture; it may be called the belfry of the mosque. Sometimes

Fig. 352.—Arches : *a*, ogee; *b*, horseshoe; *c*, pointed.

it is engaged to the main building, and sometimes starts from the roof of the mosque. The base plan is generally polygonal, and the upper stories above the main gallery are often circular; the top is crowned with a pear-shaped cupola. That of the mosque of Sultan Hasan is one of the highest, being about 330 feet in height. One of the most ornate and beautiful is the minaret that adorns the mosque of Kāit Bey, at Cairo (see Fig. 349). From the roof of the mosque it starts on a solid square base, and develops into an octagon story, which is pierced with window openings, and has an elaborate cornice gallery, consisting of a pierced balustrade, supported by stalactite brackets. The next upper division is cylindrical, decorated with geometrical interlaced ornament; another story is above this,

Fig. 353.—Cusped inter-arching. Mosque of Cordova.

crowned with a cupola, on the top of which is placed a pear-shaped ball, ending in a finial. Wooden bracket-like forms project out of this, from which lamps are suspended at festivals. The minaret and dome are covered with elaborate carvings.

The *mimbars* or pulpits are singular in construction, and are usually well covered with decoration (Fig. 354).

The remains of domestic architecture are not very

Fig. 354.—Pulpit of the Sultan Kait Bey: Fifteenth Century.   (L.-P.)

plentiful—at least, of any examples of the best period of
the Saracen style. The main idea in the design of the

Fig. 355.—A Street in Cairo. (L.-P.)

houses was to have them built so that people outside
should see as little as possible of the inmates or inside,
and that the women especially should see as little of street

life as possible ; so the first row of the windows was placed high up, and all the windows were thickly latticed, so that little could be seen from the inside and nothing from the outside (Fig. 355). An interesting and picturesque feature was the *meshrebiyas*, or drinking-places, so called because they were little projecting shaded structures of lattice-

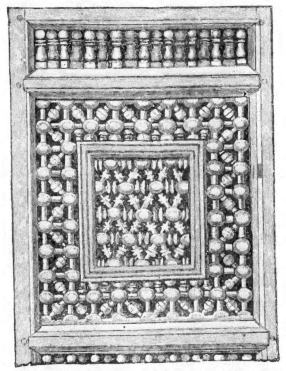

Fig. 356.—Lattice-work. S.K.M. (L.-P.)

work, supported on brackets, that contained the water in vessels and other drinks ; the currents of air that rushed through the lattice-work served to keep the drinking water cool.

The meshrebiyas are often very beautiful with their varied patterns of elaborate lattice-work, which is pecu-

liarly Arabian in design. It is composed of many pieces
of turned and carved pieces that are ingeniously fitted into
each other to form the pattern (Figs. 356-7-8). In the

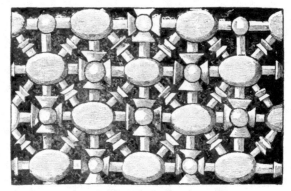

Fig. 357.—Lattice-work, S.K.M. (L.-P.)

museum at Kensington many examples of these lattice
patterns may be seen, and also some of the meshrebiyas.

In the illustration of a " Street in Cairo " (Fig. 355), two

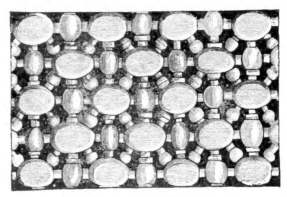

Fig. 358.—Lattice-work, S.K.M. (L.-P.)

of these meshrebiyas project on brackets from a house
front.

A richer style of the lattice-work decoration was used

in open panels and balustrades of the pulpits, where the triangles and hexagons that form part of the design are carved on the surface, and inlaid back and front with ivory or ebony.

The houses in Cairo of the purest Saracen style have the best part of the carvings and decoration in the inside ; they are generally two or three stories in height, but were much higher in the fourteenth and fifteenth centuries. The lower parts are built of stone, and the upper stories of brick and wood, plastered white.

The lower story has the stones coloured in alternate courses of red ochre and white limewash. The doorways are sometimes decorated by having peculiar voussoirs and interlaced ornament (Fig. 359).

There is an illustration of a shop-front in M. Bourgoin's "Eléments de l'Art Arabe" which is an exquisite example of Saracen work of good proportion and design in its doors and windows. Saracenic ornament, as it appears in plaster, stone, wood, and mosaic decoration, of the mosques, pulpits, and wekālas or khans, deserves special notice on account of its extreme originality of design and treatment, inasmuch as, whatever may be its true origin, we must certainly admit that there is a marked difference between it and the ornament of any other historic style.

The mosques built anterior to that of Suyurghatmish (A.D. 1356) were decorated in plaster. The rosette (Fig. 342) shows a transitional piece of work of great beauty, that looks like a copy in stone of low-relief plaster-work, and has every sign of a Byzantine-like origin, seen more especially in the leaf-like markings and general treatment of the six large central flowers ; the interlacing and other details are also Byzantine. It is quite likely that this example was designed by a Christian Coptic artist, as, indeed, nearly all the Saracen art in Egypt of this period was designed by Coptic Egyptians. Compare with this the illuminated Korān of the Sultan Sha' Ban, of a year or two later (A.D. 1368). All the floral work in this is

distinctly Persian in character, without any reminiscence
of Byzantine, but shows rather a Chinese or Indian influence (Fig. 360). It is probably copied from a Persian
embroidery.

Another example of Saracenic ornament is the stone

Fig. 359.—Doorway of a Private House. (L.-P.)

sculptured decoration from the portal of the mosque of
Sultan Hasan, in Cairo (A.D. 1358), (Fig. 361). From
being carved in stone the ornament is much stiffer than the
two previous examples, but it is more thoroughly Sara-

cenic or Arabian than either of them; the large flower-
like forms in elevation are evidently developments of the

Fig. 360.—Illuminated Korān of the Sultan Sha' Ban; Fourteenth
Century. (L.-P.)

Assyrian form of the lotus, and have here almost the form
of the fleur-de-lis. This type of design was successfully

Fig. 304.—Ornament from the Portal of Sultan Hasan.

developed in the Moresque diapers of the Alhambra, where the conventional leaves and flower forms were mixed with Saracenic inscriptions, and were redeemed from their aridity by the almost sensuous character of the colouring, which has a combination of red, blue, white, and gold, and further by the superimposed planes of the ornamental

Fig. 362.—Kufic Writing, from the Alhambra.

composition (see Fig. 343). It may be noticed that some of the leaf-work in these diapers have a feather-like decoration, which gives richness and variety to the ornament: these markings are evidently derived from the parallel veining of Byzantine acanthus leaf-work. The larger strap-work running through is interlaced in the form

Fig. 363.—Arabian Cursive Writing, from the Alhambra.

of pointed and horseshoe arches, which makes the ornament in appropriate harmony with the Moorish architecture, while the flat treatment of the whole is distinctively characteristic of all Saracenic ornament.

Two examples of Mnemonic ornament are given at Figs. 362 and 363. The former is a Kufic inscription arranged so as to form a band ornament. This is in the angular and older form of writing. The latter is an example of the cursive Arabian hand which was more generally adopted, and is termed the Vaskhy : it is more round and flowing than the Kufic. The typical feather ornament forms a background to most of these inscriptions.

Some of the finest specimens of purely Saracenic ornament are found on the singularly ornate mimbars or pulpits (Figs. 354 and 364). The simplicity of their straight-lined silhouettes is in restrained contrast to the extreme elaboration of their carved surfaces. The stone pulpit from the mosque of Barkuk is early fifteenth century work. It is made of solid stone slabs, with doorway, staircase, and canopy raised on small pillars and surmounted by the usual pear-shaped cupola. The stone slabs are elaborately carved with geometrical patterns, arabesques, and inscriptions, and are said to be the finest examples of stone carving in Cairo. Another pulpit Fig. 354 of the fifteenth century, made by order of the Sultan Kāit Bey, is built in wood ; it is now in the South Kensington Museum, and bears the name of this Mamlūk Sultan, who was the ruler of Egypt at the end of that century. The folding doors and the niche of this pulpit are decorated with stalactite ornament; the cupola is copper; the carving is most elaborate, and is also inlaid with ebony and ivory. Some of the carved panels from the building known as the wekāla or khan of Kāit Bey, show Saracenic ornament in its purest form—both the geometrical variety and arabesques. This Sultan and his artists have shown the most refined taste of all the great Saracen builders. The wekāla or khan is a rectangular building with an open court in the centre, and consists of numerous chambers that were occupied by merchants for a short season when they came to buy and sell in Cairo, and was, in fact, a sort of Eastern hotel.

The stabling was placed behind on the ground floor, and

Fig. 364.—Stone Pulpit in Mosque of Barkuk ; Fifteenth Century.

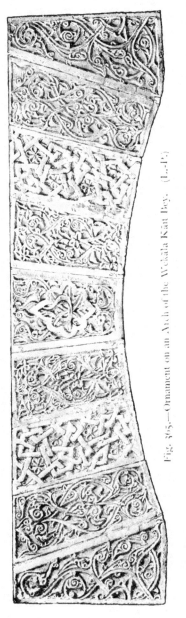

Fig. 365.—Ornament on an Arch of the Wekāla Kāit Bey.   (L.-P.)

the exterior consisted of a row of small shops. The wekāla of Kāit Bey had thirteen of these shops on one exterior, and between the seventh and eighth was placed a splendid arched gateway. It is a pointed arch of eight feet in width, the edge of which is decorated with three tiers of stalactites that are carved on the sides of the archway, and has a fine band of carved scroll-work running round the face of the archway and spandrels. One of the most beautiful examples of alternating interlacing and arabesque ornament is that which forms an arch over a horizontal panel of carved ornament. This arch is shown at Fig. 365. A fine characteristic piece of carved ornament from the same building is the subject of the illustration Fig. 341.

Figure and animal representation, though prohibited by the Moslem religion, was in many cases practised by the Saracen sculptors; for instance, in the Baptistery of St. Louis is a large copper bowl inlaid with silver figures (Mōsil work) made at Mōsil in the thirteenth century.

These figure and animal designs are from Mesopotamian
sources, as may easily be seen in the examples given—
from the Marīstan of Kalaun (Figs. 366 and 367), where
on the last a centaur is shooting an arrow at a unicorn,
balanced by a similar animal on the opposite side; and on
the other example is a peacock in the centre, with figures
of men on either side having drinking vessels and musical
instruments, an evident representation of a concert and
dances.

The scroll borders around this panel, and the execution
of the work, are in the Saracenic manner, but the motives
of the designs are Persian. Other similar carvings in
which animals figure and birds are introduced are to be
seen in the same building, and are of late thirteenth century work. These illustrations are taken from Mr. Stanley
Lane-Poole's "Saracenic Art in Egypt," after "Prisse
d'Avennes," to which the student is referred for an exhaus-
tive account of the Saracen art in Egypt. We extract
the following summary of this art from the above author,
who quotes from Franz Pasha, the architect to the Government of the Khedive. " While bestowing their full meed
of praise on the wonderfully rich ornamentation and other
details of Arabian architecture, one cannot help feeling
that the style fails to give entire æsthetic satisfaction; want
of symmetry of plan, poverty of articulation, insufficiency
of plastic decoration, and an incongruous mingling of wood
and stone are the imperfections which strike most Northern
critics. The architects, in fact, bestowed the whole of their
attention on the decoration of surfaces; and down to the
present day the Arabian artists have always displayed far
greater ability in designing the most complicated ornament and geometrical figures on plane surfaces than in the
treatment and proportioning of masses. Although we
occasionally see difficulties of construction well overcome
. . . . these instances seem rather to be successful experiments than the result of scientific workmanship. The real
excellence of the Arabian architects lay in their skill

Figs. 366, 367.—Carved Panels from the Maristan of Kalaun (after Prisse d'Avennes); Late Thirteenth Century. (1.-P.)

in masking abrupt angles by the use of stalactites, or brackets," &c.

This architect is right, generally speaking, in his admirable remarks, but we think, although it is admitted that Saracenic architecture lacks the cohesion and unity of parts that is the chief beauty in Greek and best examples of the Gothic, that in some instances, in the mosques and more particularly in the wekālas and in domestic architecture, the Saracen architects have proved themselves masters in the creation of architectural works second to none in point of beauty, while in their architectural application of ornament to the decoration of the various surfaces and other features of their buildings they are unrivalled. They have not only invented a new style of ornament, but in their correct application of it they have scarcely ever been equalled.

The decoration of surfaces, which is the chief glory of all Saracenic art and architecture, was the first and last lesson they learnt from their Persian masters in art, for Persian art, like the manners and customs of the people, has all its beauty and politeness on the surface.

CHAPTER XIX.

ROMANESQUE ARCHITECTURE AND ORNAMENT.

ROMANESQUE is the name given to the architectural style developed by the Western barbarians who overran the Roman Empire, after their partial civilisation, when they had learned the art of building. The style arose chiefly from the copying of Roman buildings and their remains, with some added features of Byzantine buildings.

Out of this Romanesque, in its turn, there sprang another style which was founded on the Romanesque and on the architecture of the Saracens. Towards the end of the eleventh century the new masters of the Roman Empire, in the course of their military expeditions to Asia Minor, Syria, and Palestine, were brought in contact with the Saracens and their architecture, and in coming back to Europe they brought with them new ideas of building, such as the pointed arch of the Saracens, which feature together with new forms of ornament were added by them to the prevalent Romanesque style, the mixture producing an entirely new style, which has been curiously named after the early Northern barbarians—the Gothic.

The subsequent Crusades against the Mohammedans had the effect, among others, of extending the knowledge of mathematics and geometry among the Crusaders, sciences in which the Saracens excelled; and in coming home again to the West, they applied their geometrical knowledge to the development of Gothic architecture to such an extent that, towards the end of the fourteenth century, this architecture could show examples of the most lofty and daring constructions in stone that were marvels in the science of building. Some Gothic buildings present with their fretted pinnacles, spires, flying buttresses, intersecting and pierced work, in flamboyant tracery, daring vaulting, and inter-penetrating mouldings, a worked-out solution of some intricate mathematical problem. In its complicated phases Gothic construction is more scientific than artistic, how-ever much one may admire the grouping or design of the Gothic pile as a picturesque conception.

Returning to the Romanesque style, we find that in the sixth century Theodoric the Ostrogoth had, in the erec-tions of churches, palaces, and of his tomb in Ravenna—his capital—sown the first seeds of the future develop-ments of the German Romanesque, and in some degree of the later German Gothic style. In producing these works his ambition was to emulate the grandeur of Imperial Rome. The Longobards, the successors of the Ostro-goths, continued this building activity through the Middle Ages, and have left to us monuments of their genius in the early and rude Duomo Vecchio of Brescia, and amongst many others of their noblest works were Sant' Ambrogio at Milan, and San Zeno at Verona.

Prior to the Carlovingian era, the Germanic people began to cultivate the fine arts in a tentative manner. This was brought about by the contact of German chiefs and warriors with Italian pomp and splendour, which also bred in them a love for personal adornment, that strongly marked the nobles and warriors of this period.

Charlemagne was crowned Emperor of Germany at Rome, on Christmas Day in the year A.D. 800. The dream and ambition of this great German Prince was to establish a mighty Christian Empire in the West of Europe that should rival pagan Rome itself, not only in military power, but in a widespread culture of literature, science, and artistic excellence.

These were the days of Chivalry, of the Crusaders ; the days when men were rich in high and lofty ideals ; when those knightly mystics, Wolfram von Eschenbach and Vogelweide, sang of the Parsival and the Quest of the Holy Graal, of songs of love and chivalry, of deliverance from wrongs, and of many stirring and tuneful themes.

Though Charlemagne never learned to read or write, he thoroughly appreciated the value of learning. He gathered together learned men, architects, and artists, and established a school of religious music. He built many churches, palaces, and bridges, and collected many statues from Rome and elsewhere for the adornment of his great church at Aix-la-Chapelle ; he organized and encouraged the professions and trades of his towns and cities.

The great tomb-church at Aix-la-Chapelle—or Aachen —was built by Charlemagne, and became the prototype of all subsequent churches erected in the Romanesque style in Germany.

It was in the region bordering on the Rhine that the great church building activity was developed in Germany. The cities of the powerful bishoprics rivalled each other in pomp and splendour, as we see in such buildings as the Doms of Spiers, Mayence, and Cologne, and in the Romanesque churches of Swabia, Franconia, Westphalia, and Lower Saxony. The Romanesque style is also found in the churches or Doms of Bamberg, Brunswick, and Osnabruck ; the Godehardi and Michael's churches at Hildesheim, the carving in which excels that in the churches of the Rhineland.

The distinctive characteristics of the German Romanesque are the great octagonal dome-like towers that arise from the crossing of the nave and transept, and the flanking towers at each end that are sometimes united to the central tower by an outside western gallery or façade. A fine modern church, built in the Romanesque style, is that of the Cathedral of Fourvière, on the hill overlooking the city of Lyons in France.

Some German Romanesque churches have a western as well as an eastern apse, and the church known as the

Apostelkirche in Cologne has the transept, both of which features are disturbing elements in any church where the chief attention should be directed to the culminating point

Fig. 368.—Round Arch Frieze.

Fig. 369.—Intersecting Blind Arcade

where the choir, reredos, or altar are usually found—in the apse or chancel, and at the eastern end only.

The church architecture of the West—the Romanesque

Fig. 370.—Rose Window.

followed closely the requirements of the Western ritual, while the churches which observed the Eastern ritual kept to the Greek or Byzantine models.

Romanesque churches of the tenth century are distin-

guished by the basilica plan, the apsidal east end, round-
headed arches, and single or double-light windows. The
walls have generally a decoration, consisting of a series
of flat pilasters—reminiscences of classic architecture—
and the roofs in many cases were vaulted. Arcaded decoration, with or without small columnar supports (Figs. 368
and 369) and rose windows Fig. 370) are features of the

Fig. 371.—Porch of the Heilsbronn Monastery, near Nüremberg.

Romanesque. Some of the round-headed doorways are
especially rich in character, and have often five or six
recessed columns (Fig. 371) that carry richly moulded
heads, and carved capitals of quaint animal and bird decoration (Fig. 372).

The shafts of the columns are usually plain, though in
some instances, for the sake of contrast, they are twisted

or imbricated, and the bases are copies of the classic orders (Fig. 373). Above the lintel and under the round arch mouldings is the lunette or tympanum; this space

Fig. 372.—Capital from Wartburg.

Fig. 373.—Romanesque Shaft and Base.

often has rich decoration of figures and ornament; sometimes it is divided into two spaces, when the entrance doorway is divided by a central pillar.

Fig. 374.—Roof Cornice of Church at Alstadt-Rottweil.

Fig. 375.—Later Romanesque Ornament.

The details and motives of Romanesque decoration are derived from classic ornament—mostly Roman—and are, as a rule, debased forms of the latter.

The cable or rope torus-ornament, the scale or imbricated work, the chevron or zigzag, bead and reel, scroll,
billet, checkers, and diapers, were all extensively used in
the Romanesque, many of which have been retained in
the later forms of Gothic ornament. Figs. 374, 375, and
376 are examples of the above ornaments.

The tower was a feature of later Romanesque work,

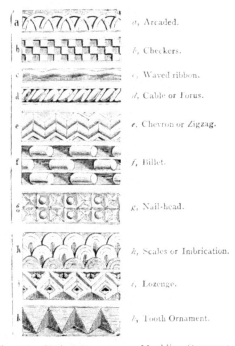

a, Arcaded.

b, Checkers.

c, Waved ribbon.

d, Cable or Torus.

e, Chevron or Zigzag.

f, Billet.

g, Nail-head.

h, Scales or Imbrication.

i, Lozenge.

k, Tooth Ornament.

Fig. 376.—Various Romanesque Moulding Ornaments.

which marked the broad difference between the latter
and Byzantine architecture ; these towers had their stories
decorated with semicircular arches on corbels or on small
pillars (Fig. 377).

The corbels usually consisted of masks or grotesque
figures, animals, dragons, or twisted snakes. These forms
of decoration were also used in the capitals and cornices,

both in the Romanesque transitional and Gothic periods. Grotesque forms were used very much as sculptural decora- tion in the Lombardic Gothic architecture. In Scandinavia and in Ireland this kind of ornament assumed the forms of snakes, serpents, and interlacings developed from them. (See Fig. 65, 69, 70.) The capitals were at first rude copies of the Roman Corinthian order (Fig. 309), deve- loped later—after the character of the Byzantine cubical forms—to a solid cubic shape, called in the Norman

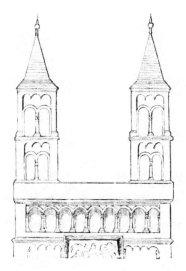

Fig. 377.—Towers and Round-arched Frieze, Abbey of Komberg.

style of Romanesque in England, the " cushion-headed " capital.

Window-openings were usually small, and the grouping of two or more lights under one arcaded head occurs in Byzantine, Romanesque, and Gothic buildings. The light came usually from the clerestory, but sometimes smaller circular windows were introduced into the end gables, which subsequently were developed into windows of greater importance and intricacy of design in the great Gothic chancels and in western lights.

Romanesque architecture, and especially its decorative ornamentation, was never quite free from Byzantine or

Fig. 378.—Capital from Palace of Barbarossa, Gelnhausen.

Saracenic influences. It was of itself an incongruous mixture, out of which, when the pointed arch of the Saracens was adopted, and the ornamental features modified to conform with it, the new ogival or Gothic style arose.

Fig. 379.—Capital from St. Cross, Winchester.

In every part of Europe in which the Romanesque took root, there may be noticed so many distinct varieties. The style in Rome and Central Italy naturally followed, as we have seen, the antique Roman forms. In the cathedral of Pisa the capitals are Corinthian, and there is a greater display here of mosaics and coloured marbles, both on the exterior and in the interior, than in most Romanesque buildings.

The style in Lombardy and Upper Italy is, on the other hand, different to that of Central Italy, as it there inherited the German traditions. The columns had in their capitals leafage of a different character to that of the classic orders, and had birds and animals carved amongst it, and the bases of the columns rested on animals. Doorways were square-headed, and had also a circular arch, over which was a pedimented canopy (Fig. 380). One of the finest examples of Lombardic Romanesque is the St. Zeno Church at Verona, which has a doorway of this description. The Church of Monreale in Sicily (A.D. 1174), and the Cathedral of Palermo, exhibit a mixture in which Byzantine and Saracenic influences are well defined; this was owing to the successive powers that were at different periods masters of that country.

Fig. 380.—Porch of St. Zeno at Verona.

The Normans at a later date made changes in the architecture of Sicily, and Norman architecture was developed to a great extent in this place.

It was in Sicily that Norman architecture first developed the characteristic zigzag feature that is seen so much in the Norman portals and window-heads in England (Figs. 381 and 382).

The pointed arch of the Saracens was added to the Norman Romanesque in Sicily. The Cathedral of Cefalu (1132), and the palace of La Ziza at Palermo, are examples. Nowhere else was the Romanesque of so mixed a character. The illustration from Palermo (Fig. 383) clearly shows the pointed Saracenic arch, used after the manner of the Romanesque round arching, while some other portions of

Fig. 381.—Norman Doorway, Sempringham Church, Lincolnshire. (G.)

the details are distinctly Byzantine. In the south of
France Romanesque architecture is far more ornate than
that of the Norman style in Normandy, or other parts of the
North; in fact, the latter style in France has its ornament
confined to purely linear decoration; but the churches that
were built at the end of the eleventh and beginning of the
twelfth centuries, which represent Norman architecture in

Fig. 382.—Berkeley Castle, Gloucestershire.   Fig. 383.—Pointed Arcading
                                                 from the Cathedral of Palermo.

its purest phases, were noble edifices, plain and solidly
built, of which the church of St. Etienne is a good example.
Its arcades rest on piers, it has a vaulted nave and
aisles, and has a fine transept. The gable of the nave is
flanked by two western towers, the western front is built in
three stories, and has two ranges of five-light windows.
The Cathedrals of Bayeux and Evreux may be mentioned
as two other fine examples of Norman architecture.

The Romanesque doorway (Fig. 384) from the South of
France illustrates the somewhat motley character of this
architecture in that part of the country.   Some churches
of this locality show the receding arches in the doors and
arcading, supported by engaged columns, which feature
was developed very much in the later Gothic.

The Romanesque style in England is seen in buildings
that were erected before the Norman Conquest.

The buildings of this period—the eleventh century—have
received the name of " Anglo-Saxon."   They are characterized by the round openings of
doors and windows, the latter being
sometimes triangular - headed.   The
tower of Earl's Barton, in Northamp-
tonshire, is an example of Anglo-
Saxon.   It has pilaster-like strips of
stone decorating and tying the
masonry together; small triangular
and circular stone-work connecting
the perpendicular strips — a reminiscence of arcading—gives a distinctive appearance of wood-framing to
the whole work, which is probably a
copy of the earlier timber construction.

Fig. 384.—Door of
St. Gabriel's, South of
France.

The Anglo-Saxon tower at Sompting, Sussex, and the
Saxon church at Bradford-on-Avon (A.D. 705), are also
examples of early work excuted in England prior to the
Norman Conquest (1066).

The work we understand as Norman in England was in
existence long before the Conqueror's time, and it is quite
likely that the subsequent English Gothic would have
developed just the same if the Normans had not invaded
England.

The English Romanesque, or Early Norman style, dates,
as near as possible, from Edward the Confessor's time
(1041-1065).   This king founded the great Abbey of Westminster, of which the Dormitory substructure walls and

vaulting still remain, but the rest of the original church has disappeared. On the Continent and in England, just after the year 1000, a great building period set in, as for many years prior to this date a corresponding period of an opposite kind, or a lethargy in the life of the Christian peoples, and consequently an inactivity in all building operations, was manifested, owing to the prophecy that the end of the world would come in the year 1000. When this was found to be a delusion, a building craze spread over Europe, and the eleventh, twelfth, and thirteenth centuries were the great building ages, when both Christian and Saracenic architecture advanced with leaps and bounds.

The Normans in England after the Conquest, no doubt, hastened the advancement of architecture; for the rule seems to have been that wherever they found a small or old church of the Anglo-Saxon type or period, they invariably pulled it down, re-dressed the stones, and built a much larger and better church on the same site, using up the old material when available, besides building many churches on new sites. The Normans were also much better builders than the Saxons, and at this time great numbers of Norman masons were brought over from France.

The strongholds, or castles, with their massive keeps, were built at this period by the new Norman barons, in order not only to have stately dwellings for themselves, but to protect their newly-acquired honours and possessions from their Saxon foemen. Remains of many of these strongholds, especially of the keeps, are still to be seen at Hedingham Castle at Rochester; Gundulph's Tower—the oldest—at Malling, Kent; Newcastle, Guildford, Colchester, Richmond, and Conisborough in Yorkshire, &c. One of the earliest is the great White Tower of London, in which is found the beautiful little Norman Chapel, one of the best and most perfect examples of Norman architecture in England. The Norman keeps, or towers, are uniform in design, having a square plan, with a square projecting turret at each angle, and a flat, thin buttress in the centre of the walls; windows were small, and were round or

Fig. 385.—The Landgrave's Room at the Wartburg.

square-headed. The doorways were round-headed, recessed, and were generally ornamented.

Portions of Canterbury Cathedral, as indeed, of almost all the principal English cathedrals, and many old churches, were built in the Norman period, which shows how extensively church building must have been carried on from the Conquest (1066) to the commencement of the reign of Richard I. (1189). The Norman and oldest parts

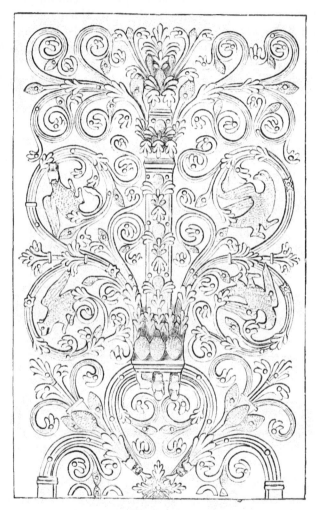

Fig. 386.—Romanesque Ornament, Iron Hinge from Notre-Dame, Paris.

of Canterbury Cathedral, built by Archbishop Lanfranc (1070-1089), are the towers forming the choir transepts.

Prior Ernulf, under St. Anselm, rebuilt much of Canterbury Cathedral (1130), and added richer elements to the ornamentation. The peculiar plain cushion, or cubic capital, found so much in England in Norman work, was meant to be carved or enriched afterwards, but often the want of funds, or haste and carelessness in after years, were the causes that left them plain, until it was too late, when the style had changed, and they were superseded by later developments. It is certain that they were not intended to remain so, for many have been left half-finished in the

Fig. 387.—Romanesque Panel from a Church at Bonn.

carving, and some plain ones are found to alternate with others of the same type, but richly carved, as at Canterbury and some other places. Sometimes the intention seems to have been to decorate them with painted ornament.

At Winchester and Rochester Cathedrals, St. Peter's Church, Northampton, the transepts of Exeter, Peterborough, and, above all, at Durham, the Norman style is seen both in its best earlier and later developments.

The ornaments are very few, the zigzag being the chief. The lozenge and billet are also used in the early work, but in the later, as in the rich doorways, such as that at Iffley, Oxfordshire (1160), grotesque masks, frets, interlacings, birds, dragons, fishes, and the quadruple form of the zigzag are added. The columns in some cases are twisted and banded, and Ionic volutes appear in the capitals. In some late Norman work the tympana are richly carved with figures and ornament. Many examples of Romanesque non-ecclesiastical buildings are still in existence in Germany, or have been skilfully restored as such, which give a tolerably good idea of the private dwellings of this period. The illustration (Fig. 385) is an example of the domestic Romanesque. It is the interior of the Landgrave's room at the Wartburg, Germany.

Examples of Romanesque ornament are given in the iron hinge from the Church of Nôtre Dame, Paris (Fig. 386), and the panel from Bonn (Fig. 387).

CHAPTER XX.

THE Gothic or " Pointed " style grew, as we have seen, out of the Romanesque. Churches were built in which the pointed arch was used side by side with the round arch of Romanesque. These were the buildings of the transitional period. In France, Germany, and in England some of the earlier Gothic buildings were purer in style than those of the later period. The work of the thirteenth century is more correct in artistic principles, more restrained, and less bewildering in the principles of construction than the work of any subsequent period. The true home of the Gothic style was in France, from which country it extended to Germany and England almost simultaneously. The Cathedral of Soissons in France may be mentioned as one of the transitional buildings (1212), though portions of it are of a still earlier date. It is noted for its early plate tracery and very ornate foliated capitals. The hall of the Hospital of St. John at Angers shows many features of the transitional style. Its vaulted roofs and arching are in the Gothic or Pointed style, and the windows are in the round-headed Romanesque. The hospital was built by Henry II., and completed A.D. 1184.

In England, portions of Canterbury Cathedral, the hall at Oakham Castle, Rutlandshire, and the Temple Church, London, may be given as examples of the transitional Romanesque or Norman to the Early English Gothic. In all the above examples, the square-moulded abacus with debased Corinthian foliage on the bell underneath may be seen, which indicates the transitional type of capital. The buildings of the transitional style may be distinguished from those of the earlier one by being much lighter in construction : the masons, having learned their trade better, found they could economise the material—

Fig. 388.—Cathedral of Notre-Dame, Paris.

which was a great thing in those days of rapid church building—by having more slender proportions, which led to the more refined and elegant style of the Early Gothic both in England and on the Continent.

The Church of Notre-Dame in Paris is a fine example of the Early French style (Fig. 388). The towers look unfinished, but they had at one time wooden spires. Chartres (1260), Rheims (1250), and Rouen 1280) are other typical examples of this period.

The period of the Early English style lasted from about A.D. 1190 to 1270, embracing the reigns of Richard I., John, and Henry III. This style is distinguished from the Norman transitional by the light and lofty pillars used singly or in groups and clusters, lancet windows, pointed arches, and by the additional use made of buttresses and pinnacles.

The slope or pitch of the roof is in harmony with the pointed arches and lancet windows, and also the pyramidal towers or spires. The greatest possible difference is thus exhibited between the Norman Romanesque and the Early English Gothic. Although the ground plan is hardly altered in the latter style, the general lightness and soaring vertical character of almost every detail, and the multiplication of buttresses and pinnacles, give to the Gothic erections of this period a triumphal look of mastery over the material that in the science of building was hitherto unknown.

The Early Pointed style in England is seen at its best in Lincoln, York, and Salisbury Cathedrals and in Westminster Abbey (Fig. 389).

The Cathedral of Cologne founded by Conrad von Hochstaden—that wonderful and huge pile of Gothic architecture—belongs partly to the thirteenth but more properly to the fourteenth century, having its foundations laid in 1248 and consecrated in 1327. It has been added to considerably even until modern days. It presents a slightly wearisome repetition of parts, especially in the buttresses, pinnacles, and other vertical forms of the exterior, that in a measure robs it of some part of the grandeur and sublimity which we should naturally expect in an edifice of its size and proportions. It is based partly on the design of the great Cathedral of Amiens in France. The very rich canopies and windows of geometrical tracery (Fig. 390) are later than the thirteenth century, and correspond closely to the Decorated period in England (1270 to 1380).

The interior of the Cologne Cathedral is strikingly illus-

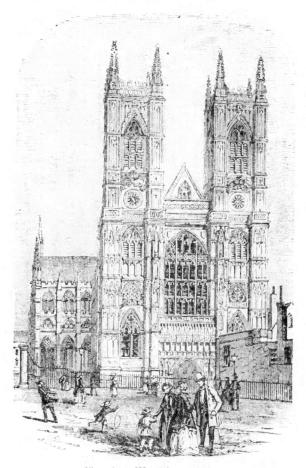

Fig. 389.—Westminster Abbey.

trative of the real spirit of the Gothic style. The consistent unity and simplicity of its stupendous and upward-soaring nave, and its still simpler choir—which has only as its ornamental features the stringcourse below the triforium and the carved capitals of the shafts—combine to produce in the spectator that feeling of reverence and deep respect, not only for the sacred associations of the building, but for the great master-spirits who conceived the design, and who were able to work out to such a degree of perfection

Fig. 390.—Window, Gable, and Parapet in Cologne Cathedral.

this great mathematical problem in stone.   This triumphal achievement of "stylistic orthodoxy" on German soil is as much, if not more so than any other Gothic building in Germany, indebted to French inspiration and French models.   There are also many other churches in Germany, in the country bordering on the Rhine—Strasburg Cathe-

dral for instance—that have strongly marked features of
the French ogival style.

The towers of St. Lawrence's at Nüremberg are somewhat Romanesque ; but the windows, door openings, buttresses, and pinnacles are in the Gothic style. The recessed
porch has a square-headed double doorway, richly
decorated (Fig. 391). The interior (Fig. 392) of this church
is extremely artistic in its general effect. The stonework

Fig. 391.—Porch of St. Lawrence, at Nüremberg.

is of that dark brown colour that is seen in so many
German churches ; the rich colour of the stained glass, the
pictures, and shields hung up round the piers and on the
walls, with their rich tones of gold and colours, the grace-
ful piers ending in the ribs and supporting the vaulting of
the ceilings, the carved rood-cross and pulpit, and above
all the great carved wood medallion of the Annunciation,
by Veit Stoss (1518), make up the richest of pictures,
which is a sample of what may be seen in many interiors
of German churches

Another interesting church in Nüremberg is that of St.
Sebaldus, more from its association with the name and
works of Adam Kraft, who carved the figure work on the
exterior, and Peter Vischer, whose celebrated work is the

Fig. 392.—Interior of St. Lawrence, at Nüremberg.

chief glory of this church—the Shrine of St. Sebaldus
(Fig. 393), one of the most important works of the fifteenth century—than from its merits as an architectural
work. The plan of this church is bad in having its nave
and aisles of equal width, which is at utter variance with

all ideas of good proportion and of the Gothic style. The shrine of St. Sebaldus is modelled and cast in bronze; Peter Vischer and his five sons laboured on it for twelve years before it was completed. It is Gothic entirely in

Fig. 393.—Shrine of St. Sebaldus, at Nüremberg.

construction, but most of the forms and details of the ornament and figure work are purely Italian; for at this time —the beginning of the sixteenth century—Germanic artists were fascinated and strongly influenced by the art that

flourished beyond the Alps.   A fine cast of this monument
is in the Kensington Museum.   The " Bride's Door" of St.
Sebaldus (Fig. 394) has an interesting canopy of German
tracery.

Art having gradually passed into the hands of the bour-
geois element, the principal cities in Germany, especially
those of the north, vied with each other in the erection of
town halls and civic buildings (Fig. 395).

Fig. 394.--The " Bride's Door " of St. Sebaldus, at Nüremberg.

In the Netherlands, in Brussels, Bruges, Antwerp, Lou-
vain, Nüremberg, Augsberg, and Marienberg, many quaint
edifices are still found of the fourteenth and fifteenth centuries, consisting often of brick glazed black and red, and
wide-jointed, or of stone throughout.   They have mostly
steep roofs, battlemented cornices, and stepped gables
They are decorated with little spires or pinnacles, and
have horizontal or pointed openings to doorways and
windows, richly decorated friezes and stringcourses, open

arcades under the first story, picturesques balconies, and corner turrets ending in corbels, which were often richly carved.

The Gothic style was introduced into Italy in the twelfth

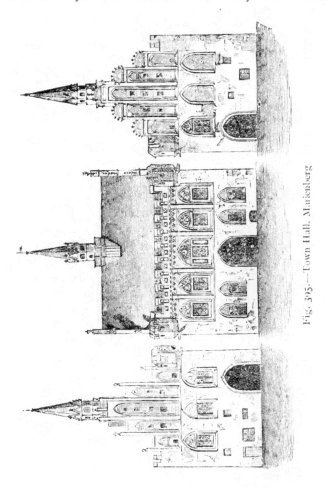

Fig. 395.—Town Hall, Marienberg

and thirteenth centuries, but it never took any great root in that country. In Rome there are no Gothic buildings of this period : there is one of the fifteenth century, the Church of Minerva, but is a bad example of the style.

On the other hand, there are some exceptionally fine
examples of Gothic canopies, of tombs and altars in several
churches in Italy. It is believed that they were copies of
French or English Gothic and were all the work of one
family of artists called the Cosmati. Mixed with these
Gothic forms in stonework they introduced bands and
panels of coloured mosaic, and also are credited with the

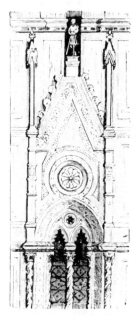

execution of much of the mosaic
beautiful pavement work known as
opus Alexandrinum. A particular
form of the Gothic style appears
in the north of Italy, and has been
called the "Lombardic" or the
"Pisan" style. This style of
Italian Gothic was never quite free
from classical influences. It is distinguished by having numerous
small columns employed to decorate exteriors and interiors.
Examples occur in the neighbourhood of Pisa, Lucca, and in places
bordering on the Rhine. The Lean-
ing Tower of Pisa (1174-1350) is an
example. Part of the Baptistery
(1278) and the earlier portion of
the Duomo or Cathedral of Pisa are
built in this style. Lombard Gothic
was therefore contemporary with
the Early English and French.

Fig. 396.—Window Gable,
from the Cathedral of
Florence.

In Florence a very beautiful mixture of the dome feature
with Gothic is seen in the Duomo or Cathedral, a well-
known and magnificent building. The window gable
(Fig. 396) gives a good idea of Italian Gothic. The
Cathedrals of Orvieto are other examples of Italian
churches in which Gothic forms are used. In all these
churches the façades are inlaid with coloured marbles of
elaborate panelling.

The Cathedral of Milan is the finest example of a church in the Gothic style in Italy, though it is by no means pure

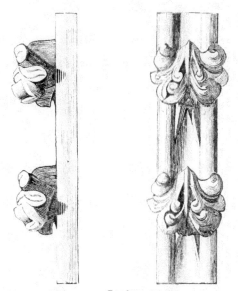

Fig. 397.— Crockets, Lincoln.

Fig. 398.—From the Temple Church.

Gothic. It is built of white marble and has some remarkably good stained-glass windows. The Palazzo Publico

at Florence and that of Siena are built in the Italian
Gothic style.

One of the most beautiful buildings in the world is the

Fig. 399.—Dog's Tooth or Nail-head Ornament, from Stone Church, Kent.

well-known Doges' Palace at Venice. The predominant
forms are Gothic, especially the lower arcading and the
pointed window openings. It rests on columns and arches

Fig. 400.—Spandrel, from Stone Church, Kent.

which compose the lower story, and has also the second
story arcaded, and pierced in its upper part with quatre-
foiled openings. Above this is a high rectangular story,

400A.—Priests' Entrance, Bishopstone Church, Wilts.

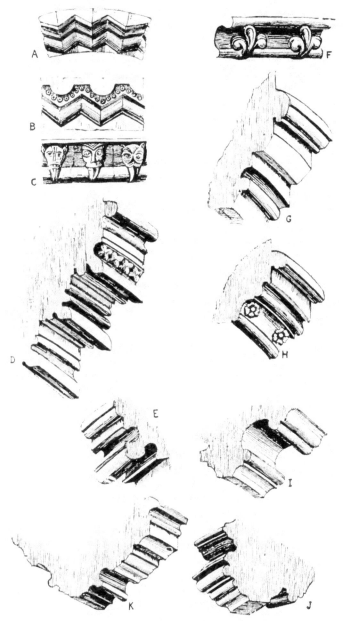

Fig. 401.— Norman and Gothic Mouldings.

a b c, Norman; *d e f*, Early English; *g h*, Decorated; *i j k*, Perpendicular.

Fig. 402.—Pedestal, Henry VII.'s Chapel.

built with lozenge-shaped slabs of pink marble, and pierced
with a row of large pointed windows, and has smaller
circular openings above these. A richly designed battle-
ment crowns the walls of the upper story. The caps of the
columns are beautifully carved, and sculptured figure

Fig. 403.—Place House, Cornwall.

subjects decorate the corners of the building. This palace
was a long time in building; before it was completed
the style had perceptibly changed, so in consequence
the portico in some parts belongs to the fourteenth and
some to the fifteenth century.

Throughout Venice the architecture with Gothic pretensions is mixed very much with fifteenth and sixteenth Venetian or Renaissance forms. The ogee arch was used very much, and the Decorated style of windows and doorways, arcadings, and balconies with Italian forms made a quaint mixture that gives a very pleasing appearance to some of the Venetian palaces.

Gothic architecture in England has been divided into

Fig. 404.—Flamboyant Panel. French, Fifteenth Century.

Fig. 405.—Flamboyant Panelling. French.

three styles : the Early English, which lasted from about A.D. 1189-1272, in the reigns of Richard I., John, and Henry III. ; the Decorated, A.D. 1272-1377, in the reigns of Edward I., II., and III. ; and the Perpendicular style, A.D. 1377-1547, from the time of Richard II. to Henry VIII. After this it became debased, and finally merged into the Tudor or English Renaissance, sometimes called the "Elizabethan." A still later mixture of English Gothic with Italian or Flemish Renaissance details was developed in the reign of James I., which has been called "Jacobean." The two latter styles never found much favour in ecclesiastical architecture, but were developed mostly in domestic and civic buildings, and used in the designs of pulpits, screens, and church furniture. A great quantity of carved oak and chestnut furniture was made in the Jacobean style.

The various styles of English Gothic have their transitional periods that extend and overlap them so much, that makes it extremely difficult in some buildings to determine which style they belong to ; the difficulty is usually got over by assigning them to their respective periods as the

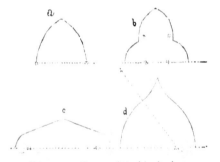

Fig. 400.—Forms of Gothic Arches.

a, Pointed ; b, Cusped ; c, Depressed ; d, Flamboyant.

beginning, middle, or end of a style. We have already noticed Early English, which is the best and purest form of the Gothic in England. In it we see the finest development of window tracery based on geometric lines. Mullions take the place of piers, windows have two or more lights, the beginnings of the flying buttress, pinnacles, crockets (Fig. 397), columns in clusters, round-headed capitals with or without the characteristic trefoil foliage (Fig. 398) known as Early English foliage (Fig. 398), which has been developed from the Romanesque. The ornament called "dog's tooth" is common to the early examples of this style, and is also a Romanesque decoration (Fig. 399).

The Decorated style is a rich and more ornate phase of the preceding style, and is further marked by the extensive use of the ogee arch in doorways and windows (see Fig. 400A), and by the greater profusion of sculptured foliage, flowers, and ornament in the decoration. The ball flower used in the hollow mouldings is characteristic of this style, as the tooth ornament is of the Early English.

The Perpendicular style, as its name denotes, is characterized by its long and narrowly divided windows and similar panellings. Instead of the flowing lines of tracery

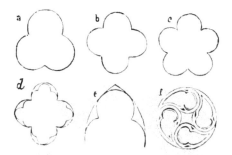

Fig. 407.— Forms of Gothic Tracery.

a, Trefoil ; *b,* Quartrefoil ; *c,* Cinque foil ; *d,* Cusped Quartrefoil ; *e,* Pointed and Cusped : *f,* Flamboyant.

in the windows, the mullions are of a straight lined and vertical character, and are divided at intervals by transoms, or horizontal divisions. The pedestal (Fig. 402) from Henry VII.'s Chapel is of Perpendicular panelling. The beautiful fan tracery seen in Henry VII.'s Chapel in Westminster Abbey and in Gloucester Cathedral is a variety of this panelling. The doorways in this style have pointed but depressed arches, and as a rule are enclosed with square-headed mouldings or labels. The spandrels formed by this arrangement are filled with tracery and shields. Towers and cornices have battlements, &c. (Fig. 403). A general squareness is given to all the ornaments,

and a more severe and dry character is the chief feature
of the Perpendicular decoration.

The Flamboyant Gothic style of the Continent is contemporaneous with the English Perpendicular. The panels
at Figs. 404 and 405 are very good examples of Flamboyant panel decoration. Forms of Gothic arches and
tracery are given at Figs. 406 and 407.

CHAPTER XXI.

RENAISSANCE ARCHITECTURE AND ORNAMENT.

MANY things tended to bring about the art of the Renaissance. The great impulse given to learning by the study of the writings of the Greek and Roman poets, lawyers, and philosophers, and the keen study of the rich legacy of art and architecture left by Greece and Rome, may be reckoned among the chief causes which led to the development during the fifteenth and sixteenth centuries of the Re-Birth or Renaissance both of literature and art.

Dante, and his successors Petrarch and Boccaccio, were called " Humanists," for the reason that they studied and advocated the knowledge that was needful to man in his progress and in relation to his life in this world, and did not confine themselves wholly to theology, which was the case with those who devoted themselves to learning in the Middle Ages. This led to a wider spread of knowledge among the people, which was greatly stimulated by the invention of printing. The rulers of the people also encouraged learning and promoted the arts to an extent unknown before. In Florence, especially, under the powerful and beneficent rule of the Medici family, art and literature received every attention, and made rapid progress in every department of cultured knowledge and skilful handicraft.

Great artists like Niccola Pisano, Brunellesco, Donatello, Giotto, Alberti, and others of the early period, whose individuality and great personality did more than anything else to bring about the epoch and the art of the Renaissance, studied with evident purpose the existing remains of the art of Ancient Rome. In this they only followed the movement of the day in every branch of art and learning: all classes in every walk of life were then directing their footsteps to Rome in the pursuit of knowledge. About the year 1414 the discovery was made in the Monastery of St. Gall of the celebrated codex of Vitruvius, a work wherein the learned writer had set forth the principles of Roman architecture of the Augustan era. This work was reprinted later at Rome, and was very much used by architects as a guide for the better understanding of the Roman temples and other buildings. As the Gothic style in France, Germany, and in England was approaching its climax, the art of the Renaissance in Italy was developing, and the period of decadence in the former was contemporaneous with the finest period of the latter— towards the end of the fifteenth century. The transition, or early beginnings of the Renaissance, has been called the Trecento (1300) style, which in its ornamental features is characterised by a free use of conventional foliage, mixed with Saracenic or with Byzantine ornament, interlacings, and scroll work; in sculpture and painting by a closer study of nature and of antique remains, with an endeavour to shake off the former stiff Byzantine traditions; and in architecture by the use of the round arch and a revival of some other features of the classic orders. Niccola Pisano, Arnolfo di Lapo, Orcagna, and Giotto were some of its exponents.

The next division is known as the Quattrocento (1400), which is more properly the early form of the Renaissance. To this period belong the real founders of the style: Filippo Brunellesco (1377-1446), Lorenzo Ghiberti (1381-1455), and Donatello (1386-1468); the former more particularly in architecture, and the latter two in sculpture. The ornament of the Quattrocento period—the fifteenth century—is distinguished by its prominence of elaborate natural forms in festoons, scroll work, and other compositions ; all the ornament was decoratively arranged more or less geometrically, but the details and actual working out were closely copied from nature. The bronze gates of the Baptistery of San Giovanni (1425-52) are the finest examples of the Quattrocento style, both as regards ornament and figure work. The modelled work in high relief of fruit, flowers, and foliage on these gates, and similar work on great medallions and altar-pieces of Luca della Robbia (1355-1430) is characteristic of this style. These natural forms, mixed with tracery ornamentation, acanthus foliage, treated in symmetrical arrangements, and occasionally cartouche or strap-work, were used in the Italian ornament of this period. The panel forms were usually Byzantine, but the rest of the ornament had no symbolic meaning. Besides Luca della Robbia, the name of Jacopo dell' Quercia (1374-1438), the Sienese sculptor, may be mentioned as one who executed some of the finest work in figure and ornament in the above style.

The Cinquecento style (1500) was the culminatory effort of the Renaissance. It is the art of Italy in the sixteenth century, and is entirely devoid of symbolism in its ornament. Although the difference is great in the matter of style between the classic ornament of the Greeks and that of the Italian Cinquecento, yet in their aim and expression they are identical, for in both there is the same striving to reach the highest possible æsthetic ideal, the same delight in the production of beautiful lines and forms for their own sakes, and a similar expression of appropriate fitness—the outcome of a correct conformity to architectural principles—pervades the ornament of both styles.

Returning to the art of the early Renaissance, we have to mention two great names, already referred to—Giotto in painting, and Niccola Pisano in sculpture, who may be justly called the harbingers of the new era of Italian art. The latter was the first to go to the antique for his inspiration and style in sculpture. It appears—according to

Vasari—that in Pisa there had been accumulated a great collection of antique sculpture—the spoils of war—and among them a sarcophagus, on which the "Hunt of Meleager and the Calydonian boar" was wrought with great skill, which was placed for ornament on the façade of the Cathedral: this and other antique remains in the city were studied to great advantage by Niccola, to the great improvement of his style. One fine work of his, executed in the spirit of the antique, was the pulpit for the Church of San Giovanni in Pisa, on which are great numbers of figures, representing the Universal Judgment. For the Cathedral of Siena he also executed a similar work with subjects from various passages in the life of Christ. On this pulpit he had the assistance of Arnolfo and Lapo, his pupils, and probably also that of his son Giovanni. These works proved the great turning-point in sculpture, from the archaic productions of the Middle Ages to an era of better things, although in execution they left much to be desired. Giotto was not only the great painter who first invested his works with poetry, feeling, and expression, but was also a skilful architect, as his fine Campanile, or bell-tower, in his native city of Florence bears witness. Dante and Petrarch were his friends, the former especially so; the portrait of Dante by Giotto still exists in the Chapel of the Podesta at Florence.

Brunellesco, as we learn from Vasari, was one of the most interesting of men, and one of the most capable artists of his time, a man of acute genius and ready resource. In the early Renaissance period architecture was studied by nearly all sculptors and painters, and many, as we have seen, were apprenticed in their youth as gold-smiths. Brunellesco was no exception to this rule, for we find that he was a clever goldsmith and worker in niello.

The greatest work of his life was the building of the cupola or dome of the Cathedral of Florence—he was the only architect of his day that was found able to do it. The Cathedral was the work of the Florentine architect,

Arnolfo di Lapo, the foundations of which were laid in the year 1298. Brunellesco also built the sacristy and dome on the Church of San Lorenzo, which was decorated with sculpture by Donatello, and was the architect of the Pitti Palace, besides many other works. He gained his knowledge of the construction of domes in Rome, more particularly from that of the Pantheon, having drawn from and made models of the domes of all that was worth copying of the ancient remains at Rome, in company with his friend Donatello, the sculptor.

The latter, with Brunellesco, Ghiberti, and a few other sculptors, competed with their designs for the work of making the celebrated bronze doors of the Baptistery of San Giovanni at Florence, when Ghiberti's design was adjudged the best, and of which Michelangelo at a later period said, when speaking of the gates, that they were "fit to be the gates of Paradise." Brunellesco's design was good, was more restrained in character, and was more consistent with correct architectural principles than Ghiberti's; but the latter's design was so fresh and so vigorous, that in spite of its being too picturesque for sculpture it won universal admiration.

The next great name in architecture is that of Leon Battista Alberti (1404-1472), who naturally follows Brunellesco. His most complete work is the Rucellai Palace at Florence; he built and restored many churches, tombs, and palaces; was a great mathematician, and very learned in Latin, in which language he wrote poems, plays, and treatises on painting and architecture.

The Rucellai Palace is a very fine work of the Renaissance. It has the three orders of architecture in its pilasters, with their entablatures. The lower story has a small square window placed high from the ground between every two pilasters, and has two square-headed doorways. Between each pair of pilasters in the upper stories are round-headed windows, which have each a double light divided by a small column. The style of building is called

" rusticated," like so many of the Italian palaces (Fig. 408). This is a roughened form of stonework, and was copied from Roman buildings, which, together with the heavy cornices and symmetrical repetition of windows, gave these palaces a heavy and imposing look. Another palace of the Rucellai type is the Cancelleria at Rome, which was built by Bramante (1444-1514), a native of Castel-Durante, in Urbino, who also built St. Peter's at Rome, and

who was the greatest architect of the Renaissance, of whom Michelangelo testified " that Bramante was equal to any architect who has appeared from the time of the ancients to our own, can by no means be denied." Michelangelo himself was the architect of the dome of St. Peter's, and his sublime works in sculpture and fresco adorn the interior.

The Cancelleria Palace is a masterpiece of elegance and good proportion. It has two imposing doorways, and the plainness of its lower story contrasts agreeably with the upper two, which have rows of roundheaded windows enclosed in flat or

Fig. 408.—Portion of the Strozzi Palace.

square-headed architraves, and are placed at agreeable distances above the entablatures of the lower stories. The two upper stories are divided alternately into wide and narrow divisions by pilasters, the windows being placed in the wide divisions. This building is a marked improvement in point of beauty on the Pitti and Rucellai palaces.

The Farnese Palace is another typical building of the Renaissance. The design of it is attributed to Antonio Picconi, who took the surname of San Gallo (148 ?-1546). It is built in three stories, without pilasters, with a widely projecting cornice, and has rather a monotonous look with its numerous windows of equal size. Michelangelo is said to have designed some of the windows and the cornice (Fig. 409), though some say that the architect Vignola was the designer of the cornice. The central doorway is "rusticated" and arched, and the angles of the building are of dressed stones.

The celebrated building known as the Certosa (Charter-house) of Pavia was begun by Borgognone in the year 1473, is an example of the most ornate phase of the Renaissance, and offers a widely-marked contrast to the almost bald simplicity of the palace just described (Fig. 410). As a whole, the façade of this building cannot be called a model of good architectural composition, but it is easier to criticise its faults in this respect than to suggest improvements. It contains, however, many striking elements of beauty, and is full of useful suggestions to the architect and decorative artist.

The plan and shell of Renaissance buildings were usually of the Romanesque or Gothic types; the dome, columns, and ornament generally were all borrowed from the Roman remains.

The column, round arch, and horizontal lintel or architrave feature were extensively used in the palaces and other buildings of Venice (Fig. 411), though the Renaissance style had a difficult task to make headway in Venice against the strong Byzantine and Gothic traditions that had hitherto prevailed.

Fig. 409.—Upper Story of the Farnese Palace, Rome. Designed partly by M. Angelo.

The general type of the Venetian palaces is a solid panelled wall and pier arrangement or rusticated lower story, which supports a central loggia, or arcaded second story, that has circular-headed windows and heavy cornices and balconies. The whole façade is richly decorated with engaged columns and pilasters.

The Cornaro, now the Mocenigo Palace, the Grimani
on the Grand Canal, now the Post Office, and the Spinelli
Palace, are said to have originally been built from the
designs of the great military architect, San Michele, of

Verona (1484-1588), to
whom the Signori of
Venice owed so much as
the designer of their fortifications.

Jacopo Sansovino, who
built the Library of San
Marco at Venice (Fig. 411);
Palladio (1518-1580), the
well-known writer on
architecture ; Scamozzi,
and the Lombardi family,
may be mentioned as
other celebrated architects
and ornamentists, who
executed many works in
Venice and in Verona,
Florence, Padua, Vicenza,
Rome and Milan, etc.,
during the sixteenth cen-
tury. It was the tendency
of the Renaissance period
to build palaces and
castles, and in the later
times municipal and pri-
vate dwellings, as learning
and the arts were getting
into the hands of the lay-

Fig. 410.—Portion of the Certosa of Pavia.

men, in contrast to the days of the Middle Ages, when the
clergy and monks were the architects and master-builders :
in those days hardly anything but churches had architectural pretensions ; but the case was different in the
Renaissance times, when the architects were not bound by

the strict canonical laws of *style*; hence we find a greater variety and wider range of ideas expressed in the art of the period, due in a great measure to the individuality of the artists, which has given to the art of the Renaissance a different character in every country, district, or city to which it had spread.

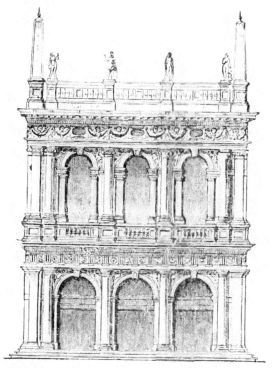

Fig. 411.—Library of San Marco, Venice. By Sansovino.

The greatest Venetian architect of the seventeenth century, Longhena, flourished (1602-82) when the Renaissance had entered into its Baroque phase or period of decadence. He built many churches and palaces in Venice and in some other cities of Italy, but his greatest work is the celebrated Church of the Salutation—"Santa Maria della Salute"—in Venice, a picturesque building that has been painted and photographed more frequently than any other church in the world. With its domes and bell-towers, and its great buttresses decorated with figures that support the drum of the dome, it presents a striking object of picturesque beauty. This church and the Pesaro and Rezzonico palaces are exceedingly rich and ornate, but are overloaded with figures and decorative details—the Pesaro Palace especially—which is very characteristic of the florid work of the seventeenth century. Their magnificence of style reflects the palmy days of Venetian grandeur, and contrasts strongly with the simpler and better architecture of the early Renaissance period.

The influence of the Italian Renaissance spread to France in the days of Louis XII., and Francis I., the monarch who did so much for French art. Afterwards, in the reign of Henry II. and Catherine de' Medici, who greatly favoured Italian art and artists, we find the Renaissance taking a deep root in France. Fra Giocondo was summoned to France from Italy by Louis XII., who reigned 1495 to 1515, and caused to be built the Château de Blois, and the Château de Gaillon in Normandy (1502-10) In these two buildings the native French Gothic received a grafting of the Italian forms. This was the case in France for a long time, as in that country the Gothic style was then in the full zenith of its Flamboyant period.

The Castle of Chambord is one of the finest examples, and a portion of the Château de Blois, by Viart, the architect of Francis I.

The early French Renaissance is quite different from the Italian, partly from the reasons we have stated, but it has a liveliness and exuberance that is full of inventive resource. The buildings are noted for their pointed roofs, and for their multitude of picturesque towers and pinnacles, and also rich carvings of a refined class of ornament.

The French Flamboyant Gothic and the Italian Decorative forms are happily blended in this style, to which the

name of "François Premier" (Ier) has been given. This
style was chiefly brought about by the employment of the
Italian sculptors and architects, Serlio, Vignola, Primaticcio, Il Rosso, Cellini, and others who had been invited
by Francis I. to build and decorate his châteaux and
palaces. Primaticcio was also entrusted with the task of
collecting a series of antique casts and copies of antiques
from Rome for the gardens of the palace at Fontainebleau.
This, no doubt, had the effect of helping to form the taste
for classic art among French artists. Owing to all the
above circumstances, French art began to show more of
the influence of the Italian style. The Roman orders were
henceforth invariably used, but still the new style was
modified in a great measure to suit the French taste.
What is known as the Henri Deux (Henry II.) style is
another French development of the Cinquecento, in which
there is a preponderance of strap-work, with figures, masks,
grotesques, cartouches of all kinds, and much of the conventional Saracenic ornament. The monogram of Henry
II. and the arms of Catherine de' Medici often appear in
this ornament, as seen in the decorations of the Château
d'Anet (1548) and on the Oiron or Henri Deux pottery.

Pierre Lescot (1510-1578) designed the western façade of
the Louvre, in Paris, and Jean Buillant designed the oldest
parts; these two architects and another, Philibert Delorme,
brought the Renaissance to such a head in France that it
became immediately the national style.

The great names in architectural sculpture of the early
French Renaissance were Jean Goujon and Paul Ponce,
who carved the principal figures of the façades of the
Louvre. Towards the early part of the seventeenth century
the architecture began to assume a more florid character,
under the hands of Lepautre and Du Cerceau. It became
richer, but less pure in style, an example of which is the
Apollo Gallery of the Louvre, designed by Lepautre. By
the time of the latter half of the seventeenth century the
desire for show and the expression of magnificence,

especially brought about by the "Grand Monarque,"
Louis XIV., assisted by the efforts of his architects,
Mansard, Perrault, Lemercier, and Blondel, who ministered
to the whims of the powerful King, speedily laid the foundations for the loose and unrestrained Baroque or Rococo
style which subsequently followed. The name of "Louis
Quatorze" has been given to the style developed in the
reign of this king. "Louis Quinze" and "Louis Seize"
are names of subsequent French styles, which will be
considered under the head of Renaissance Ornament.

The tame and spiritless palace of Versailles was designed
by François Mansard, who invented the Mansard roofs
which have been used together with this style for nearly
all the palatial buildings of Europe. The purity of the
Italian Renaissance was forgotten or ignored by the
nations of Europe, and the stiff and pompous buildings of
Louis XIV. were accepted as the patterns that all civiliza-
tion was eager to copy. Even old churches and mediæval
castles were transformed in some portions of their interiors
into Louis XIV. imitations. In Windsor Castle the great
ballroom has been vilely treated with the meaningless
incrustations of this period, by the way of decorations,
endeavouring, however, to make amends for its tasteless
poverty of invention by the arrogant display of its rich
covering of gold leaf.

In the late seventeenth and during the eighteenth
centuries, the Rococo or Baroque phase of the Renaissance was in vogue in Italy and France, and indeed
everywhere in Europe. The main characteristic of the
Baroque style is the undue prominence given to the
ornament and decoration, which arose from a gradual
forgetfulness of the Roman and Greek principles of construction, and a want of order in the arrangement of the
principal forms in the architecture. By degrees these
forms took a secondary position : columns supported
nothing or only a few mouldings, cornices and pediments
were broken, brackets and consoles were inverted, mould-

ings ended in scrolls, hanging curtains were represented on stone carving, also wreaths of roses; pediments and gables had weak outlines of carved forms, shells and rock-work (*rococo*) ending in weedy scrolls, which doubtless was a Chinese inspiration, grafted on the prevailing style; in fact, the utmost license and riot in decoration seemed to be allowed, as it aimlessly sprawled over architecture, furniture, and interiors, until art had almost evaporated from the decorative productions of the age.

In spite of this, however, something must be said in favour of the Rococo : at the least it was homogeneous in its way; some of the figure work that forms part of the ornament is very fine, the finish and perfection also of the carved, painted, and gilt surfaces, from a technical point of view, leave usually nothing to be desired. The curved and broken character of the ornament is excellent for show-ing the play of light and shade on the gilded surface, and the effect of some interiors is very rich and brilliant; but when decoration takes the place of construction, however well executed it may be, it becomes more of an incrustation than a requirement.

Lorenzo Bernini (1589-1680) and Francesco Borromini (1599-1667) were Italian architects who chiefly brought about the Rococo in Italy. They treated the classical forms with extra-ordinary freedom. The column espe-cially was degraded in its use. It some-times supported only a few mouldings, and at other times was carried through two or three stories, when its proper function is to represent one story. One kind of architectural style a little later than this period was called the "Jesuit

Fig. 412.—Portion of the Façade of St. Paul and St. Louis at Paris.

Style" (Fig. 412), in which churches of the Jesuit Order were built. On the vaulted ceilings of these churches a florid type of painting of sacred subjects was used as decoration.

In Spain the Renaissance, mixed with some Saracenic features, produced some very good work; the typical example of Spanish Renaissance is the Escurial, the great palace of the Spanish kings.

In Germany the Italian Renaissance made but a tardy advance, and was never thoroughly at home in that country. German Renaissance is far less refined than that of other countries which were influenced by the Italian style. It is chiefly in painting, furniture, book illustration, and in goldsmiths' work that it appears at its best, and not in architecture. This was owing to the art of Germany being at that time in the hands of the burghers when the advent of the Renaissance took place, and also that the mass of the people were more concerned in the study of ethics and philosophy than the arts. Another reason may be added, that the nation was unsettled, and occupied with the great religious upheaval of the Reformation. All these things proved to be sufficient to retard the advancement of the Renaissance in Germany for more than a hundred years. One of the best examples of the Renaissance we can point to in Germany is the Castle of Heidelberg, built by the Elector Otto Heinrich (1556-1559). The two façades of this castle, which are now in ruins, have engaged columns and pilasters; the windows have rather heavy-headed features, and are richly carved; statues are placed in the niches between the windows. The portico of the Town Hall at Cologne is another example, and the Cloth Hall at Brunswick is a very interesting specimen of German Renaissance. It is deficient in proportion, however, by the extreme horizontality of its eight series of low stories in the principal façade, but is otherwise very picturesque.

The German Renaissance towards the later periods was characterised by its elaborate carving of ornament, figures, and animals in wood and stone; armorial bearings, escutcheons, shields, and cartouches or ornamental labels were very common in German work, and in most other forms of Renaissance ornament in Europe, except in the purest form of the Italian Cinquecento, when highly decorative vase forms and labels took the place of the shield and cartouche work of the Quattrocento period.

The Renaissance in England made its earliest appearance in the reign of Henry VIII. John of Padua was an Italian architect employed by that king. Hampton Court Palace in its earlier portions, built by Cardinal Wolsey in 1515, is Gothic, but it has been considerably added to since, and partly rebuilt in the time of William III. in a kind of Renaissance.

In the reigns of Queen Elizabeth and James I., the Elizabethan or English Renaissance and the Jacobean respectively were predominant. The latter style was developed by Dutch architects working in England on the Elizabethan models, and is distinguished by shield work and carvings in high relief, in opposition to the lower relief cartouche and strap-work of the Elizabethan style.

The Elizabethan Renaissance is more like German work than the French, but, of course, has its native peculiarities, developed from its mixture with the Tudor Gothic of the time. This mixture is seen in many of the old halls and mansions built about this time in England Wollaton Hall is a fine example of the Elizabethan (Fig. 413), and Holland House, Kensington, is another fine mansion of the same style (Fig. 414).

These castellated buildings of the Elizabethan style, in red brick and stone dressings, are in singular and pleasant harmony with the grand parks and richly wooded English landscape with which they are usually surrounded.

Inigo Jones, in the early part of the seventeenth century, and Sir Christopher Wren, his successor, were the greatest names in architecture of the English Renaissance period. The former was a close follower of the Italian architect Palladio, and designed, usually, his buildings after the Roman models. The palace at Whitehall, the church and

piazza in Covent Garden, and Crewe Hall in Cheshire were
built from his designs.

The Cathedral of St. Paul's is too well known to need
description. It may be mentioned as the most important
example of the late Renaissance in England. It was
thirty-five years in building (1675-1710), and although

Fig. 413.—Elizabethan. North Entrance, Wollaton House.

some details and the ornament generally incline to the
Baroque, the building as a whole is one of the finest and
most impressive works ever produced in any country.
Wren built a great many churches in London during the
time that was occupied in the building of St. Paul's, St.
Stephen's, Walbrook, being one of his finest. Chelsea
Hospital, the Royal Exchange, together with some City

Halls and twenty-five churches, were built from his designs or under his directions.

The architecture of the present day in France leans mostly to Renaissance traditions.

In Germany, Greek and Roman styles find favour, but

Fig. 414.—The Ancient Parlour, Holland House.

Gothic and Renaissance, and sometimes Romanesque style of buildings are now erected.

In England about one hundred years ago there was a Greek revival, due in a great measure to the publication of Stuart and Revett's works in connection with their close

study of Grecian architectural remains. St. Pancras
Church, in London, is one of the outcomes of this revival.
Sir William Chambers was the architect of the beautiful
riverside building — Somerset House, on the Thames
Embankment (1725-1796); he also designed a great deal
of furniture and the State carriage. He published important works on architecture and furniture, which had
considerable influence on the design of the latter in
England. In the first half of this century a Gothic revival
took place, which was greatly brought about and assisted
by the writings and architectural work of A. W. Pugin.
The Houses of Parliament, built by Barry, are the finest
examples of the Gothic revival in England. They are
built in the Perpendicular or Tudor style. Sir Gilbert
Scott was a late exponent of the modern Gothic style
(1811-78), and was the architect of the Albert Memorial
in Kensington Gardens, St. Pancras Railway Station and
Hotel, London, besides building and restoring many
churches in the Gothic style.

The architecture of the present day in England tends to
the Renaissance, with a slight mixture of Gothic and much
that is original in the ornamental details, but Gothic is
still a favourite style for churches.

ORNAMENT OF THE RENAISSANCE.

The ornament of the Renaissance period was founded on
he Roman. Before describing the former it will be
necessary to say a few words concerning its prototype, the
Roman. More than anything else the great use of the
acanthus foliage characterizes the ornamental art of the
Romans. The treatment of the acanthus in Roman architecture has already been noticed in the first part of this
work. A fine boldness and freedom was everywhere
apparent in the Roman treatment of this foliage (Figs. 28
and 29).

Large scrolls of acanthus (see Fig. 319) in which

birds, reptiles, and insects are arranged to fill the unoc-
cupied spaces are used in pilasters, friezes, and panels.

Chimeras as whole or half figures with foliage endings,
griffins, and large vases well decorated, were used as
symmetrical arrangements in friezes.

The well-known acanthus scroll frieze from Trajan's
Forum is a very typical example of the soft-leaved acanthus.
The rosette of the scroll, as in nearly all classic ornament, is
made up from acanthus-leaves arranged in a radiating
manner, like a flower (Fig. 415).

Some of the ornament on the antique Roman bronze and

Fig. 415.—Rosette from Scroll, Forum of Trajan.

silver work is particularly beautiful and delicate, as may
be seen on the silver wine crater found at Hildesheim
in Hanover, which is one object of a collection found
at that place in the year 1869. These and the treasures
found at Pompeii and Herculaneum, together with the
wall paintings at the same places, give us a good idea of
Roman art in domestic decoration and the minor arts and
crafts.

The Pompeian objects, chiefly in bronze (Fig. 417) and
the wall paintings (Figs. 418-20) are as much Greek as
Roman in style, as they are chiefly the work of Greek
artists executed for the Romans.

The Baths of Titus and Diocietian and the palace of the
Cæsars on the Palatine Hill, Rome, were decorated with
grotesques similar to those of Pompeii, and were studied
to great advantage by Raphael and his pupils and assist-

Fig. 416.—Nest of Scroll. Roman Panel. Florence.

ants when decorating the Loggia of the Vatican. Thin
tendrils, festoons of fruit, animals, masks, all kinds of
grotesque forms and birds flying and playing in and out
of light scrolls, architectural constructions of a light and
fantastic character, and panels of landscapes formed the

subjects that were painted on the walls, which were often divided into friezes, panels, and dados. These decorations

Fig. 417.—Objects of Art handiwork, from Pompeii.

were executed in tempera colours of bright reds, greens, yellows, blues, and black. The antique grotesques, so called from being found on the walls of underground chambers, or "grottos," together with the figure subjects

Fig. 418.—The Goddess Demeter enthroned. Wall painting from Pompeii. (B.)

taken from Greek gems, furnished Raphael and his celebrated pupils Giovanni da Udine (1487-1561) and Perino

del Vaga (1500-47) with fanciful ideas for the decoration
of the Loggia of the Vatican, and the Villa Madama, at
Rome. These *grottesches* were painted in a kind of fresco
or tempera on a white ground with a fairly bright variety
of colouring. Some portions of the decorations were
executed in stucco relief made of a composition of lime and
marble dust, and were sometimes gilded. Giovanni da
Udine, or Ricamatore, as he is also called, was especially
celebrated at this stucco-work, and in the drawing of
animals and birds. He, and another celebrated artist,
Primaticco, assisted Raphael's great pupil Giulio Romano

Fig. 419 — Pan. Wall Painting at Herculaneum. (B.)

(1492-1546) in a similar kind of decoration at the ducal
palace of Mantua. The latter artist executed the principal
figure work at Mantua, and also at the Villa Madama.

There is no lack of good examples of Italian ornament,
especially in carved marble and wood, in the churches and
palaces of Italy and France.

The Museum at South Kensington is rich in casts and
in real examples of Italian ornament, has excellent copies
of the Raphael pilasters and other examples of painted
decorations. In addition to this the maiolica plates and
vases furnish good examples of painted decoration of the
Renaissance period.

It is only necessary here to illustrate and describe a few

examples of the style, as they appear in architectural
decoration, for under the heads of the various historic

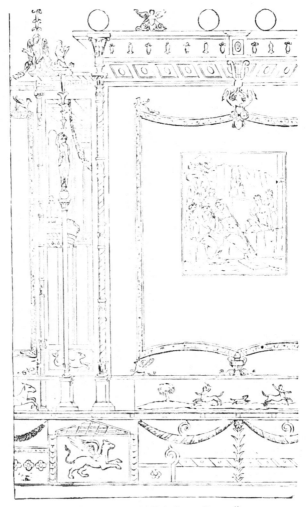

Fig. 420.—Mural Painting.   Pompeii.

industrial arts many examples of Renaissance ornament
will come under our notice in a succeeding volume.

Fig. 421.—Pilaster by
Donatello.

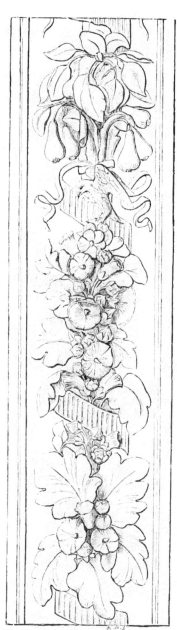

Fig. 422.—Ornament from Baptistery
Gates, Florence.

Belonging to the ornament of the fifteenth century, or as it is called the "Quattrocento" (1400), we have a beautiful little pilaster (Fig. 421), designed by Donatello (1386-1438). The portion of the ornament of the architecture from Ghiberti's bronze gates of the Baptistery of Florence (Fig. 422) shows the use of natural forms ornamentally arranged, which was one of the characteristics of the Quattrocento style; and the tabernacle (Fig. 423) shows the transition between the use of the natural forms and the more severe conventional ornament of the Cinquecento period. Luca della Robbia (1400-81) was one of the ablest masters of the Quattrocento, and Riccio, called Briosco, was also an artist of this period who was engaged on the decorative work of the ducal palace at Venice.

The Cinquecento (1500) is the name given to the style of the sixteenth century. So many brilliant names belong to this period that it becomes a difficulty to give in our space an adequate selection of this work. It was towards the end of the fifteenth century that many of the ancient monuments had been excavated ; and the Italian artists from Michelangelo and his great contemporaries down to the artists of lesser powers, followed the strong inclination of the times in their deep study of the antique, and sought more and more to invest their creations with the spirit of ancient art. The lingering traditions of Byzantine forms that were in some degree a part of the Quattrocento style were now entirely excluded from the purer art of the Cinquecento, and anything that had a precedent for existence in the antique was copied or imitated in a modified manner, and improved upon in point of delicacy in the treatment.

Though the arabesques of Raphael and his pupils in the Loggia of the Vatican (1515) have been severely criticised as being full of coarse absurdities and designed with questionable taste, still, taking them as a whole, they were a decided improvement on the grosser absurdities of the Pompeian school of grotesque decoration, and they

Fig. 423.—Tabernacle. End of Fifteenth Century. Italian. (P.)

are certainly distinguished by good drawing and clever execution. Doubtless the later achievements in painted decoration at the Villa Madama and the ducal palace of Mantua had less incongruities of design and were more refined than the Vatican pilasters, but they lack the freshness, the boldness, and virility of the latter. It is not always a good argument, for instance, to say—which has

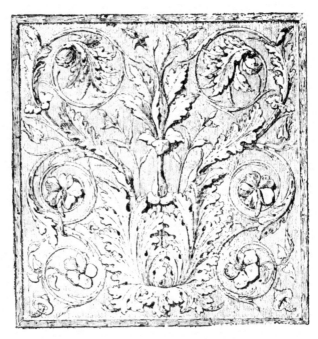

Fig. 424. - Cinquecento Floral Ornament.   Acanthus, Oak, Convolvulus, &c.

often been said of the decoration in question—that a thick stem should be used to support heavy masses, for it can be said with equal truth that a thick stem may be painted to look like a weak vegetable flabby stalk—like that of a cabbage—and so have really a weaker appearance than one painted to represent the fibrous stem of a woody tree; and besides, if a thin stem supporting a heavy mass is vigor-

ously drawn, it will look strong enough, and be useful also
in giving the necessary amount of contrast that is wanted
in decoration. Such a thing may be quite admissible in
painted ornament that would be out of place in sculptured
work or in architectural forms.

The Cinquecento artists were better craftsmen than the
Romans. The design and delicacy of finish on some of
the sculptured ornament of
the sixteenth century have
never been excelled in any
period of the world's art
history. It is strange that
many of our would-be
teachers in design of the
present day are not in sym-
pathy with it; perhaps
however, it is not to be
wondered at, for they may
have tried, and found how
difficult it really is to get
within measurable distance
of its excellence. It is
cheap and plausible to say
that a style is dead with
the people who created it;
but this is not what the
artists of the sixteenth cen-

Fig. 425.—Venetian Panel. Sixteenth
Century.

tury said, and we know what they produced out of a dead
style. By all means let us have originality, if it is good
art, but let us have the good art first.

In the Cinquecento ornament we find that a greater
variety of plants, animals, and designed objects, such as
vases, candelabra, and armour, were made use of than is
generally found in antique ornament. The acanthus, vine,
oak, and poppy foliage have all been simplified to a
general type of acanthoid leafage (Fig. 425). Such animals
as the lion, goat, and the dolphin fish form occur fre-

A. M. SPARKLING. DEL.

Fig. 426.— Cinquecento; from the Martinengo
Tomb, Brescia.

Fig. 427.— Candelabra and Vase Panel.

quently, sometimes almost naturally, but more often with foliated endings (Figs. 425 and 426). Some compositions are made up entirely with well-chosen vase and candelabra forms (Fig. 427).

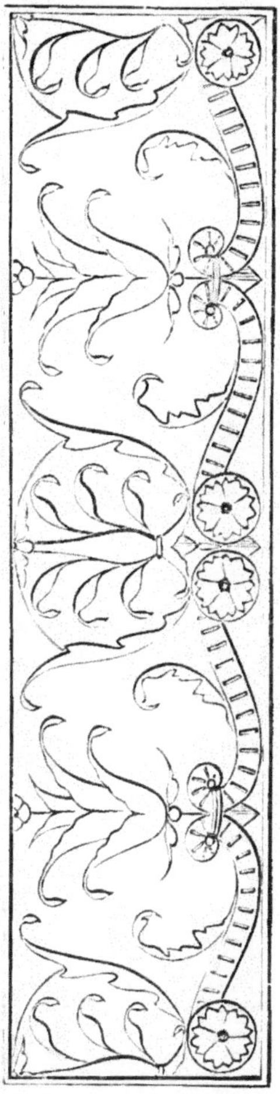

In the Cinquecento, the Greek guilloche pattern with rosettes is used, and an Italian rendering of the anthemion, and also of the Greek honeysuckle band pattern (Fig. 428).

The Lombardi family of Venice were celebrated as sculptors in ornament. Pietro the elder (1481) was the architect of Dante's tomb in San Francesco at Ravenna, but his greatest work was the Church of Santa Maria de' Miracoli at Venice, in which he was assisted by his sons Tullio and Antonio in the sculptured decorations. Tullio was the most gifted as a sculptor, and his ornament is the best of the Cinquecento period at Venice (Fig 429).

Martino Lombardo was the architect of the Scuda di San Marco at Venice, in the decorations of which he was aided by Tullio. Some of the best specimens of the ornament of this period are to be found on the Martinengo tomb, in the Church of the Corpo di Cristo (1530). The ornament bears a strong resemblance to the Lombardi, but the sculptor is not known (Fig. 426).

The ceilings from Serlio's book of architecture, and from

Fig. 428.—From a Marble Fountain in the Louvre. (1508.)

Fig. 429. - Panel from Santa Maria de' Miracoli, Brescia.   By Tullio
Lombardo.   (1500.)

Fig. 430.—Panel from the Façade of Santa Maria de' Miracoli, Brescia.   (1530.)

San Spirito, by Sansovino, are good examples of the Renaissance panelling and decorative filling (Figs. 431 and 432.

One of the purest examples of the Cinquecento in France is the ornament found on the pilasters of the monument erected to Louis XII. at St. Denis, Paris Fig. 433. The

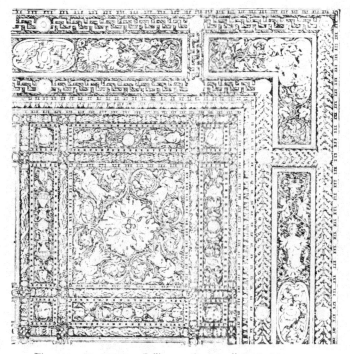

Fig. 431.—Renaissance Ceiling. From Serlio's *Architecture.*)

sculptors are said to have been Jean Just and François Gentil. The figure work on this monument was executed by Trebatti, a Florentine sculptor. Another phase of the Renaissance in France is the Henry Deux style. It is illustrated in the carved door-panels from the Château d'Anet (Figs. 434 and 435) '1548), where the tracery, inter-laced work, and shields are combined to form the features of this ornament. The initial letter H of the king and

the crescent arms of Diana of Poitiers are seen very often
on the shields.

Jean Goujon and Jean Cousin were employed on the
decoration of this castle.

An extremely rich example of French carved wood is

Fig. 432.—Ceiling Decoration, from San Spirito, Florence.   By Sansovino.

the panel from the Château Gaillon, in Normandy (1515)
(Fig. 436).

The above examples, and the chimney-piece panel by
Germain Pilon (1560) (Fig. 437), another sculptor employed by Catherine de' Medici, are a few of the best
specimens of the Cinquecento period in France.

Fig. 433.—Pilasters, from the Monument to Louis XII., St. Denis, Paris.

Fig. 434.—Carved Panel, Henry II. style, from
the Château d'Anet.

Fig. 435.—Carved Panel, Henry II. style, from
the Château d'Anet.

Fig. 436.—Carved Wood;
Château Gaillon. (1505.)

Elizabethan ornament, or that of the Renaissance in England, is characterized by a preponderance of strap-work, and has animals, masks, rosettes, half-lion or half-human terminals, debased class of mouldings, and very little foliage. The example given—the panelling from the Old Guard Chamber, Westminster (1600), exhibits a strong influence of Saracenic tracery that was prevalent in much of the later furniture and textiles of the Renaissance (Fig. 438).

Shield-work was not so prominent in the pure Elizabethan as in the Jacobean (James I.) style; the carved stone

Fig. 437.—Panel from Chimneypiece; Louvre. By Germain Pilon.

escutcheon-like work from Crewe Hall, Cheshire, attributed to Inigo Jones (Fig. 439), shows the beginning of the Jacobean shield-work. This style is best seen in the carved-wood furniture of the period, and both it and the Elizabethan are generally speaking offshoots of the Flemish and German phases of the Renaissance. Elizabethan ornament is of great variety, the panelling and other arrangements are sometimes composed purely of strap-work of a rectangular flat perforated appearance, sometimes seen in the doorways and chimney fronts, as at Hardwick Hall, Haddon Hall, Speke and Crewe Halls. Another kind is of a more curved variety, with figures and

Fig. 438.—Elizabethan Panelling, from the Old Guard Chamber, Westminster.

animals, as seen in the illustration from an old house at Exeter now in Kensington Museum (Fig. 440); another kind is carved in rectangular or curved and notched frames of cartouche work with the smaller spaces and little panels carved in imitation of jewels with oval or lozenge-shaped

Fig. 439.—Doorway, Crewe Hall. Inigo Jones.

Fig. 440.—Elizabethan Carved Ornament, from an old house at Exeter. (1590.)

facets. Columns of Ionic or Corinthian orders, and classic mouldings, dentils, and the egg and tongue were frequently used. The ceilings were often panelled and moulded,

Fig. 441.—Example of Dietterlin's Architecture; German, Sixteenth Century.

inclining in this respect more to the Gothic than classic. A bizarre kind of Renaissance architectural feature was prevalent in Holland and in some parts of Germany, which seems to have been the model for much of the "bolt and lock" style of some Elizabethan gateways. The architect Dietterlin, of Strassburg (1550-1599), was an extraordinary exponent of this twisted and bolted form of fantastic architecture, which had become only too fashionable at this period. The illustration (Fig. 441) shows an example of what might be called a mild specimen of the style of Dietterlin. The popularity of the Dietterlin craze was owing to the circulation of several volumes he had published of his impossible designs, some of which designs were evidently adapted by the Elizabethan architects, but in a much more reticent spirit.

LONDON: PRINTED BY WILLIAM CLOWES AND SONS, LIMITED, DUKE STREET, STAMFORD STREET, S.E., AND GREAT WINDMILL STREET, W.

ART PUBLICATIONS.

BROOME—Brush-work for Schools. By Florence Broome. With forty-eight Designs in Colour. Small 4to. New Edition. 5s. net.

BULLMORE—Memory Drawing of Plant Form and Design. By W. R. Bullmore. In Two Parts, each consisting of six Artistically Printed Plates in Portfolio. Price 1s. net each Part; postage 2d.

BULLMORE—Copies in Silhouette for Brush-Drawing. By W. R. Bullmore. Part I. Natural Forms. Part II. Simple Patterns. Books, 6d. each net; postage extra.

BULLMORE—Senior Brush-Drawing Cards. By W. R. Bullmore. Part I. Natural Forms. Part II. Simple Patterns. Each consisting of twelve Cards. 1s. 3d. net each; postage 2d.

This work contains the same examples as the author's "Copies in Silhouette," Parts I and II, but printed on stout cards instead of in book form.

DAWSON—Elementary Design. By Charles Frederick Dawson. With numerous Illustrations. Second Edition. Demy 8vo. 2s. net.

DOUGLAS—A System of Brush-drawing. By R. Smeaton Douglas and Ada Hill Walker. Oblong 4to. 3s. net.

FURNISS—How to draw in Pen and Ink. By Harry Furniss. With numerous Illustrations. Demy 8vo. 3s. 6d. net.

HARBUTT—Harbutt's Plastic Method, and the use of Plasticine in the Arts of Writing, Drawing, and Modelling in Educational Work. By William Harbutt. With fifty-six Illustrations. Crown 4to. 4s.

HARBUTT—Plastic Methods for Plastic Minds : A Teacher's Handbook of easy Lessons in Modelling in Plasticine for Infants and Young Children. By Mrs. Harbutt. With thirty-four Illustrations. A New and Revised Edition. Small 4to. 1s. net.

HARPER—A Practical Handbook of Drawing, for modern methods of Reproduction, with many Illustrations showing comparative results. By Charles G. Harper. New Edition, Revised and added to. Demy 8vo. 7s. 6d.

HATTON—The Craftsman's Plant-Book : or Figures of Plants selected from the Old Herbals. With numerous Illustrations in colour and black and white. Arranged with Notes and additional Drawings, and an Essay on the Use of Plants in Decorative Design. By Richard G. Hatton, Hon. A.R.C.A. (Lond.). Demy 8vo. [In the press.

HATTON—Perspective for Art Students, Artists and Draughtsmen. By R. G. Hatton. With 208 Illustrations. Large Crown 8vo. 5s.

HATTON—Design. An Exposition of the Principles and Practice of Decoration. By R. G. Hatton. With 177 Illustrations. Demy 8vo. 5s. net.

HATTON—Figure-Drawing. A new work for Artists and Students. By Richard G. Hatton. With nearly 400 Diagrams. Demy 8vo. 7s. 6d net.

HATTON—Figure Composition. A companion to "Figure-Drawing." By Richard G. Hatton. With numerous Illustrations. Demy 8vo. 7s. 6d. net.

JACKSON—Wood-Carving as an Aid to the Study of Elementary Art. By F. G. Jackson. With numerous Illustrations. Demy 8vo. 3s. net.

JACKSON—Metal Work : Chasing and Repoussé for Home Art Workers. By Frank G. Jackson. With numerous Illustrations and Diagrams. Demy 8vo. 3s. net.

JACKSON—Decorative Design. An Elementary Text-book of Principles and Practice. By Frank G. Jackson. Fully Illustrated. Third Edition. Large Crown 8vo. 7s. 6d.

LONDON: CHAPMAN & HALL, Ltd.

ART PUBLICATIONS—*continued.*

JACKSON—**The Theory and Practice of Design.** An Advanced Text-book on Decorative Art. By FRANK G. JACKSON. With 700 Illustrations. Large Crown 8vo. 9s.

JACKSON—**The A B C of Drawing and Design.** By FRANK G. JACKSON. Crown 4to. In two parts, with numerous Illustrations. 2s. 6d. each net.

These Illustrations, with additional exercises, have also been prepared on stout cards.

To correspond with Part I. { Set I. 30 cards, 2s. net.
{ ,, II. 50 ,, 2s. ,,
To correspond with Part II. { ,, III. 30 ,, 2s. ,,
{ ,, IV. 24 ,, 2s. ,,
{ ,, V. 12 ,, 1s. ,,

LANTERI—**Modelling.** A Guide for Teachers and Students. By E. LANTERI, Professor of Sculpture at the Royal College of Art, South Kensington.

VOLUME I.—With a Portrait Drawing of the Author by Professor A. Legros and forty-two full-page Plates and other Illustrations and Diagrams. E. ONSLOW FORD, R.A., contributes a Preface. Crown 4to. 162 pages. 15s. net.

VOLUME II.—With numerous Illustrations and a Preface by Sir W. B. RICHMOND, R.A. Crown 4to. 15s. net.

LINDSAY—**Geometrical Drawing.** By C. T. LINDSAY. With numerous Illustrations. Demy 8vo. 6s. net.

LUNN—**Pottery.** A Practical Handbook for Art Teachers and Students. By R. LUNN, Teacher at the Royal College of Art, South Kensington. Demy 8vo. 5s. net.

MANN—**The Art of Shading.** A Complete and Graduated Guide to the Principles and Practice of Drawing in Light and Shade. By WILLIAM MANN. With forty Illustrations. Demy 8vo. 3s. net.

MIDGLEY and LILLEY—**Studies in Plant Form and Design.** By W. MIDGLEY and A. E. V. LILLEY. With numerous Illustrations. Tenth Thousand. Revised and Enlarged. Demy 8vo. 6s.

MIDGLEY—**The Life and Leaf Set of Drawing and Design Cards.** By W. MIDGLEY, A.R.C.A. London. 4to. 2s. net.

MUYBRIDGE—**The Human Figure in Motion.** An Electro-Photographic Investigation of Consecutive Phases of Muscular Actions. By EADWARD MUYBRIDGE. Illustrated with numerous full-page Photo-Mezzotint Engravings reproduced from the Original Negatives. Oblong. 20s. net.

MUYBRIDGE—**Animals in Motion.** An Electro-Photographic Investigation of Consecutive Phases of Progressive Movements. By EADWARD MUYBRIDGE. Ninety-five full-page Photo-Mezzotint Engravings, reproduced from the Original Negatives, and more than 1,000 Half-tone Figures of Horses, Dogs, Elephants, Lions, and other Animals, while engaged in walking, galloping, leaping, or some other act of motion, and of Birds while flying. Oblong. 20s. net.

POYNTER—**Ten Lectures on Art.** By E. J. POYNTER, R.A. Fourth Edition. Large Crown 8vo. 9s.

RHEAD—**Studies in Plant Form and Natural Objects.** By GEORGE WOLLISCROFT RHEAD, R.E. Set 1.—PLANT FORMS. Set 2.—NATURAL OBJECTS. Per Set, 6s. net. Each contains six Outline and six Tinted subjects.

RHEAD—**Memory Drawing of Plant Form, and Blackboard Drawing.** Twelve Cards of Plant Form to meet the above Syllabuses, drawn from Nature by G. W. RHEAD, R.E. Price 2s. 6d. net. Size, 10 in. × 7 in.

SEEMAN (O.)—**The Mythology of Greece and Rome,** with Special Reference to its Use in Art. Edited by G. H. BIANCHI. Sixty-four Illustrations. New Edition. Crown 8vo. 5s.

STATHAM—**Modern Architecture.** A Book for Architects and the Public. By H. H. STATHAM. With numerous Illustrations of Contemporary Buildings. Large Crown 8vo. 10s. 6d.

STATHAM —Architecture for General Readers. A Short Treatise on the Principles and Motives of Architectural Design. By H. H. STATHAM. With 250 Illustrations drawn by the Author. Third Edition, Revised. Large Crown 8vo. 12s.

TAYLOR—Elementary Art Teaching. An Educational and Technical Guide for Teachers and Learners. By E. R. TAYLOR. With over 600 Diagrams and Illustrations. Second Edition. Large Crown 8vo. 6s.

TEBBS—The New Lace Embroidery (Punto Tagliato). By LOUISA A. TEBBS. With thirty-four Illustrations. New Edition. 4to. 5s. net.

TEBBS —The Art of Bobbin Lace. A Practical Text-book of Workmanship. Illustrated with original designs in Italian, point de Flandre, Bruges Guipure, Duchesse, Honiton, " Raised " Honiton, Appliqué, and Bruxelles. Also how to clean and repair valuable lace, etc. By LOUISA A. TEBBS. 4to. 5s. net.

VINYCOMB—Fictitious and Symbolic Creatures in Art. With Special References to their Use in British Heraldry. By JOHN VINYCOMB. With numerous Illustrations. Demy 8vo. 10s. 6d. net.

WARD and AITCHISON—The Principles of Ornament. By J. WARD. Ed. by GEORGE AITCHISON, A.R.A. Fully Illustrated. Large Crown 8vo. 7s. 6d.

WARD—Colour Harmony and Contrast. For the use of Art Students, Designers, and Decorators. By JAMES WARD. With sixteen Coloured Illustrations and several Half-tone Pictures. 10s. 6d. net.

WARD—Floral Studies for Decorative Design. By JAMES WARD. In Portfolio. 20s. net.

WARD—Progressive Design for Students. By JAMES WARD. With forty-two full-page Plates, comprising upwards of 1,700 Drawings. 8vo. 5s. net.

WARD—Historic Ornament. A Treatise on Decorative Art and Architectural Ornament. By JAMES WARD.

VOLUME I.—Prehistoric Art ; Ancient Art and Architecture ; Eastern, Early Christian, Byzantine, Saracenic, Romanesque, Gothic, and Renaissance Architecture and Ornament. With 436 Illustrations. Second Edition. Demy 8vo. 7s. 6d.

VOLUME II.—Pottery, Enamels, Ivories, Metal Work, Furniture, Textile Fabrics, Mosaics, Glass, and Book Decoration. With 317 Illustrations. Demy 8vo. 7s. 6d.

WARD— Fresco Painting : its Art and Technique. With special reference to the Buono and Spirit Fresco Methods. By JAMES WARD. With four Plates in Colour and thirty-one Half-tone Illustrations of Italian and other Fresco Paintings. Royal 8vo. 10s. 6d. net.

WORNUM—The Analysis of Ornament—The Characteristics of Styles. By R. N. WORNUM. New Edition. Fully Illustrated. Royal 8vo. 8s.

PLANTS AND ANIMALS AS FOUNDATIONS FOR DESIGNS IN FORM AND COLOUR.

VERNEUIL--The Animal in Decoration. By M. P. VERNEUIL. Introduction by EUGENE GRASSET.

This magnificent work consists of Ten Parts, each containing six Coloured Plates, treating of the use of certain animal forms in decorative design. Sixty Plates. In Ten Parts, each containing six Plates, 8s. net per part.

GRASSET—Plants and Their Application to Ornament. Edited by EUGENE GRASSET. First Series.

This magnificent work contains seventy-two Coloured Plates. In Twelve Parts, 8s. net per part.

GRASSET—Plants and Their Application to Ornament. Edited by EUGENE GRASSET. Second Series.

This magnificent work contains seventy-two Coloured Plates. In Twelve Parts, 8s. net per part.

LONDON: CHAPMAN & HALL, LTD.

Lightning Source UK Ltd.
Milton Keynes UK
UKHW041514210420
362053UK00004B/908